THE SOPHISTICATED TRAVELLER

· THE SOPHISTICATED TRAVELLER ·

ENCHANTING PLACES AND HOW TO FIND THEM

EDITED BY

A. M. ROSENTHAL & ARTHUR GELB

IN ASSOCIATION WITH

MICHAEL J. LEAHY, NORA KERR

AND THE TRAVEL STAFF OF

THE NEW YORK TIMES

EBURY PRESS ☙ LONDON

Published in 1986 by Ebury Press
Division of The National Magazine Company Ltd
Colquhoun House 27-37 Broadwick Street
London W1V 1FR

ISBN 0 85223 528 3 (hardback)
0 85223 563 1 (paperback)

Illustrations by Joe Ciardiello
Cover illustration by Michael Doret

Computerset in Great Britain by ECM Ltd, London

Printed and bound in Great Britain
by Butler & Tanner Ltd, Frome

CONTENTS

PUBLISHER'S NOTE

The Sophisticated Traveller Series was originally written, edited and compiled for an American audience and in view of the fact that it is the outstanding quality of the writing that readers will most appreciate, factual information (including prices) remains as in the original American edition. When prices are given they should be taken as a general guide, since inflation and fluctuations in the exchange rates can have a significant effect on costs.

INTRODUCTION

The special lucid sunshine on an autumn day in Stockholm. An American sees it and is transfixed with wonderment. 'Oh, yes, of course,' the Swedes say, and are quite calm about the discovery.

An Englishwoman wanders the streets in a New England seaport. She thinks of Nathaniel Hawthorne at his dreary ledgers. She wonders, did he, too, imagine that he scented on the breeze the exotic aromas of the faraway Spice Islands?

An American walks into a Ladakh temple, meets a monk, stares incredulously at his zippered Eisenhower jacket. The monk lifts a huge horn, and the temple is filled with a high mourning keen.

Discovery, new worlds – new thoughts and impressions – that is what travel is all about or it is nothing but motion.

Sometimes it is the discovery of the totally unexpected – the realization that a girl moving along the banks of a canal in Kashmir walks so delicately and with such rhythm that she is not really walking, but dancing.

Sometimes it is the shock of seeing the totally familiar among the exotic – is that really a *zipper* on the monk's jacket?

This is a book of discovery by a group of very sophisticated travellers indeed – famous writers, journalists, specialists. All are tied together by the bond of the truly knowing – that discovery in travel is everywhere. It is in a simple peasant dish as well as an elegant banquet. It is in a small grey stone in a temple courtyard in Japan, as well as in the Cathedral at Chartres.

It is a book of new places to see and old places seen freshly. It is a book of discovery and travel, which is to say the same thing.

A.M.R & A.G.

FROM THE
ENGLISH CHANNEL
TO THE ADRIATIC

LANDFALLS IN HISTORY

Hammond Innes

Some travellers collect country houses; others ecclesiastical buildings, gardens, restaurants. I seem to collect fortresses. And since I have spent quite a slice of my life at sea, mostly with my wife and sailing our own boat, many of these have been sea fortresses on the shores of Europe, vast landmarks that have produced in me a sense of excitement.

It is difficult to explain what this means to those who are not sailors. You come across the sea – the Channel, the Mediterranean, even an inland sea like the Marmara – and there is the land. But where is the shelter you are seeking?

For many hours perhaps you have been voyaging on the wind, navigating by the speed at which your sails have driven you through the water, by how the wind and tide and breaking seas have moved you, and you are searching, searching through the glasses, hoping to God you have got it right, that the port you have been aiming for will emerge over the bows.

Then, suddenly, there it is, that huge medieval fortress described as 'conspic' in the pilot book, standing there solid and reassuring. Then I feel like Cook or Magellan or those distant Vikings who first sighted Vinland, the sense of discovery as strong as if I had crossed an ocean. I have made it, and there to prove it is the fort guarding the entrance to the port.

And the forts themselves, all so different: some isolated on a rock, water all round, others high above town or port, still others on headlands formidably guarding harbour or river entrance. And different in architecture, of course – particularly in architecture, for a fortress is like a battleship, its fabric and design constantly adjusted to the firepower of the age in which it was built.

Single-towered forts are the simplest: the Martello towers, for instance, erected, like the concrete emplacements of World War II, around the southeastern shores of England against the threat of invasion during the Napoleonic Wars. One of them, the **Wish Tower** at **Eastbourne** on England's south coast, was the first fort of which I was ever really conscious, for I played there as a very small child. It is about forty feet high, with something of a moat that now contains conveniences.

All these Martello towers are roughly the same, and most of them remain intact, landmarks on bleak shores of beach or on small cliffs. They mounted two or three guns, and their design was based on a similar tower at Cape Mortella in Corsica (hence the name), which had been singularly effective in withstanding a British sea attack in 1794.

The defensive half-circle formed by the Martello towers was almost a repetition of the forts of the Saxon shore erected by the Romans against the barbarians of eastern Europe more than ten centuries ago. The Normans used several of these same sites – the sturdy bulk of **Pevensey Castle** is perhaps the most impressive example. But when you look at that castle now, against the flat background of Pevensey marshes, you have to remember that at the time of the Norman Conquest those marshes were an open tidal haven that reached inland almost to the low hills where Harold, last of the Saxon kings, died and where the village of Battle now stands.

But the castle that really bowled me over as a child was **Tintagel**, on Cornwall's Atlantic coast. It still has something of the same effect on me today, though I have never approached it from the sea, only from the land. Perhaps that is the way it should be approached, for the whole essence of the place is the narrow, crumbling neck of land that connects the outer mainland ward with the inner fortress on its spectacular rock headland, and the only way to storm it in King Arthur's day was that dreadful little passageway of land that looks as though it could be defended single-handed.

When I first saw it, I was a schoolboy invited to take part in an Arthurian pageant, train fare and tented accommodation provided, and all I knew about it was that it was the castle of the Pendragons, the birthplace of Arthur. (Dragon, incidentally, means war leader, and I like to think that Arthur was the last of the Comes Littorii Saxonii, the Counts, or war leaders, of the Saxon Shore; the title and military organization were maintained after the Romans left.) It must have been a miserable August, for I remember nothing of the pageant, only the greyness, the black gleam of wet granite, the rain, the wind and the cloud mist – and that castle, its gaunt stone ruins gleaming black and desolate in the rain, the white of the surf, the boom of the big, curling breakers, the noise of the wind and the spray tossed high.

It was so in keeping with the legend – the Round Table, Arthur, Sir Lancelot and Sir Galahad, Camelot, Merlin and the dreadful Mordred. I can see it still, the end of chivalry, my imagination reeling with fine deeds, and all of it mixed up with another legendary king, Mark of

Cornwall, and the deaths of Tristram and the Irish princess Isolde.

Was Arthur really conceived on that wild headland, to the roar of the wind and the thunder of the Atlantic in the cove below where Merlin sat, waiting in a cave? Geoffrey of Monmouth, writing his history of Britain in 1165, says he was. Never mind. Let us not look too closely at a legend so enthralling. For myself, I returned several times to lie on the wind-scoured greensward above those ruins, seeing the occasional sail pass and dreaming dreams. As well as the castle, I think I discovered myself on those granite cliffs.

I have never seen the tower on Cape Mortella, but sailing down the west coast of Corsica, we once came upon a Pisan tower standing like a barrel on a hill; it was described very aptly in the pilot book as 'a round tower of great diameter in the middle.'

The defensive principle is the same for any single keep, but most of them are square, like the Saracen tower on Isola Giglio off Italy's west coast. I saw it first from a naval ship and was so excited by its position and its design that I went back there later, and later still used it as the setting for a book.

Saracen towers are built with the entrance on the second floor so that to storm one requires scaling ladders and men demented enough to risk a bloody end. You can see this same simple yet effective design throughout the Arab world. The British pickets in the Khyber and Malakand passes, erected so many centuries later, adopted exactly the same primitive defence technique.

There is a castle at **Orford**, near my home in East Anglia, that has nothing left of it now but the keep standing tall on its hill and looking out across the Ore estuary to the North Sea. It is the first castle in England for which the building costs have been preserved in the Exchequer rolls: The price, complete with all innovations, £1,400, a bargain for the builder, Henry II, for it gave him control over Hugh Bigod of Thetford, Earl of Norfolk and until then virtual ruler of East Anglia.

Constructed in 1165, it was the first keep built with three towers projecting from the walls to enable archers to pour down enfilading fire on any assault. It was strategically placed to control the great haven ports of Dunwich, Orford and Goseford, but Dunwich is now almost entirely under the waves, and Goseford, at the mouth of the Deben, has vanished completely. Only Orford remains as a small boat harbour, and in the little village, right opposite the excellent Kings Head Inn, is a very East Coast seafood eatery, the Butley-Orford Oysterage.

Prior to Orford the fashion in Norman keeps was square or rectangular. At the great Cinque Port castle at **Dover**, on the chalk hills overlooking the strait, the keep is a single rectangle, and yet it was built by the same king a decade after Orford.

Dover, like Pevensey and **Burgh Castle** (Gariannonum) overlooking the Broadland marshes of Norfolk, is part of that Saxon shore defence, and now that so many of the great inland tidal waters have become land, the rivers constricted between artificial banks, it is the Strait of Dover that poses the major invasion threat. Thus Dover's castle has additional fortifications and underground batteries dating back to the Napoleonic period, and it is from one of these that the coast guards now monitor the traffic in the busiest stretch of water in the world.

There are four or five fortresses that have been great landmarks for me in my sailing. First was **Marstrand** on the Swedish coast. We had sailed straight from England's East Coast, through the Kattegat, past the Paternoster light on its iron framework, and after four days at sea, before I even saw the Swedish coast, there it was, standing up out of the sea like a stranded hulk. I described it at the time as looking more like Fort Churchill's monstrous grain elevator seen from twenty miles out in Hudson's Bay than a castle. But inside, it was grim indeed, the bedboards of quite recent convict occupation still on display.

And then, after exploring the inner leads among ice-scoured skerries, we went on to Denmark, sailing into Copenhagen, past the **Tre Kroner** that stands guarding the fairway, past the crane that hoisted the masts onto the Danish fighting ships and seeing the copper spars all green against a blue sky. So much of it the same as when Nelson ignored his admiral's order, putting his telescope to his blind eye, and began that great naval battle. Such an ancient exciting waterfront, guarded by the Tre Kroner and other forts (and Hamlet's Elsinore so disappointing by comparison).

Two great fortresses were our stepping stones into the Mediterranean, both of them very much a part of our history, yet I'd never seen either of them until I sailed my boat into their harbours.

The first was **Gibraltar**. Seeing the Rock come up out of the sea is something I shall never forget. It was very difficult to visualize it as honeycombed with galleries and bristling with hidden armaments. We lay the night against a high stone wall, a levanter blowing outside and a series of thunderstorms hammering the dark outline of the Rock with bolts of lightning that sizzled and banged as they struck.

Gibraltar never shows its teeth to the world, but **Malta** does. At the end of a long voyage we sailed past Fort St. Elmo and into Grand Harbour, and I have never sailed into such a fabulously fortified place – stone everywhere, all of it the colour of honey in the sunshine. St. Elmo, St. Angelo, Birgu, Senglea – if you know the history of it you can almost smell the great siege of 1565. But it is the stone of Malta I always remember, the beautiful mellow warmth of it, and that it is soft when cut from the rock but becomes hard when exposed to the air.

Before they came to Malta, the Knights of St. John were in **Rhodes** for more than two centuries, turning themselves from crusaders on land to religious corsairs at sea. The impact of the island is quite as overwhelming as Malta – Mandraki harbour, two miles of very broad city walls, a moat cut in solid rock and, of course, the Street of the Knights.

I dined out by the harbour entrance once, looking across to my boat, which was moored where the Colossus once stood, the walled city beyond and the castle brilliant with lighting for a *son et lumière*, and little lanterned fishing boats being towed past in line like ducklings. A world of sea chivalry living on in the vast defences they built against the Moslems.

Halicarnassus, too. Now called **Bodrum**, it is on the Turkish coast, and standing over the blue sweep of the harbour are the high towers of the Knights' 'tongues,' or nationality groups. They built their castle out of stone taken from another wonder of the ancient world, the tomb of Mausolus. From the top you can see the submerged pattern of the inner harbour that held the castle guard ship.

Away from the islands, on the north shore of the Mediterranean, the fortresses are more often of Venetian origin. The one I remember most vividly I saw only once in a still dawn, the brown stone bright in the sunrise. This was **Methone**, which rises out of the sea in the south-western corner of the Peloponnesus, its three-tiered tower like one of those boxes within a box. It was on the pilgrim route to the Holy Land, but perhaps I remember it so well because of the magic of that sunrise, and the quiet.

The Venetian-Turkish fort that dominates the port of **Pylos** is a nasty place with a nasty little garden surrounded by death cells; scratchings of World War II prisoners mark the dark stone walls. But in the northwest corner of Pylos Bay is a battlemented medieval fortress built on the defensive site where a handful of Athenians beat back the Spartans in 425 BC. And, to go back even further, a few miles away is the palace stronghold of Nestor, the king to whom Tele-machus, son of Odysseus, turned for news of his father after the behaviour of his mother's suitors had become insupportable. Ithaca, you must remember, is little more than a day's sail to the north.

So much of legend and history lies in the mainland and islands of Greece – the roots, in fact, of our own civilization and democratic forms of government – that each Aegean voyage has been a process of discovery that never palled. And of its many fortresses, one of the most spectacular is **Palamidi**. It towers high above Nauplia, and you climb to it by a staircase of 857 steps.

But it is the little Venetian gem of a fort at its foot on the island of

Nisis Burji that steals the show. It has its own tiny harbour, and we ate there alone and in moonlight, waves lapping at the castle stones, Palamidi high above and in silhouette; an evening of pure magic. And not far away, another, older stronghold, all rock and tragedy – **Mycenae**, where King Agamemnon and his Queen Clytemnestra are supposed to lie in sunken graves.

Twice I have sailed with fortresses designed by Vauban as my objective. In about 1678 this siege specialist began the task of ringing France with a string of fortresses that represent the ultimate in castle building. Some of them are on islands: **St. Marcouf**, for instance, in the Baie de la Seine, near where the Allies landed in World War II.

It came at us out of a sun-glow of mist after a night sail through dense fog – lonely, mysterious, deserted. Landing there from our dinghy, we were met, not by a caretaker, but by thousands of sea gulls incubating eggs, feeding their young and prepared to dive-bomb any intruder.

The other Vauban fortress was in the Bay of Biscay and had very different occupants. It was on **Île de Ré**, and, sailing in just before dawn, all we saw of it was the crouched bulk of the massive redoubts. Dead tired, we moored under the walls and dived for our bunks, so that it was early evening before we went ashore.

Vauban, like the Venetians, built his island fortresses with little harbours of their own, and this was what I had come to see. A gate in an iron railing led in the right direction. A notice on it said *INTER-DIT*. Almost immediately we were into a passageway between high walls.

'Listen!' My wife had stopped. 'I thought I heard footsteps.' The click of metal against metal, the echo of what might be voices murmuring. The passageway had a sudden eerie feel to it. But then it opened out to a view of the sea, the wall of the castle above and the moon just risen. And there it was, the castle harbour I had come to see, with towers at the ends of the encircling jetties and everything pale silver in the moonlight.

Somebody coughed offstage. (It really was like a stage set, a pavé ramp leading up from the horseshoe of the harbour and the massive castle walls behind us, with an arched entrance and wooden doors.)

'Listen!' A friend crewing for us had his back to the sea. 'Somebody whispering.' He went to the great doors, and as he peered forward to read a notice, there in the gap between roadway and door appeared a pair of disembodied boots caught in the sudden glare of arc lights.

We went back rather more quickly than we had come. And next morning, sailing out in the daylight and seeing the watch towers, gaunt against the skyline, the click of bolts, the whispers and the footfalls were explained. The castle of Île de Ré was a prison.

But what prison we did not realize until later, at Île d'Aix. This is another Vauban island stronghold, the castle where Napoleon was imprisoned before he was taken to St. Helena. Here a Frenchman explained that it was to Île de Ré that the convicts of Devil's Island had been moved when France's dreaded penal settlement in French Guiana was finally closed.

After Vauban, fortresses began to go deeper underground. From the Lines of Torres Vedras in the Peninsular War to the Maginot Line was a logical progression, as stone gave place to concrete. The last of these line fortifications was the Atlantic Wall, with its gun embrasure views of the sea, and those labyrinthine island fortresses the Germans built in Norway.

But the discovery of these opens the imagination to wars that are far too recent. Better the ruins of old struggles, where imagination, reaching back into legend, can roam more freely.

FORTIFIED ISLAND

Britain has more than its share of fortresses by the sea. What follows is a selection of traditional hotels and inns that might serve as bases for travellers who wish to explore Tintagel, Orford, Eastbourne and the Saxon shore defences by land.

TINTAGEL

The Mill House Inn, Trebarwith, Tintagel, Cornwall PL34 oHD (telephone: Camelford 770200), the winner of the Automobile Association Inn of the Year award for 1985, is installed in a converted mill. Rates, which include English breakfast, are about $25 a person.

    Trebrea Lodge, Trenale, Cornwall PL34 oHR (Camelford 770410), looks out from a building dating to 1315 across fields to the sea. Dinner, bed and breakfast are about $25 a person. Closed from the beginning of November to the beginning of March.

    Willapark Manor Hotel, Bossiney, Cornwall PL34 oBA (Camelford 770782), is a country-house hotel set among 11 acres of woodland and gardens with panoramic view of sea and cliffs. About $25 a person for dinner, bed and breakfast.

ORFORD

The Kings Head, Front Street, Orford IP12 2LF (Orford 271), is a thirteenth century inn once used by smugglers. (It is also the only known hostelry where brewers' drays have to enter the adjacent churchyard to lower beer into the cellars.) The dining room specializes in local seafood, and dinner for two is about $35. Double rooms are about $20; closed in January.

    Butley-Orford Oysterage, Market Hill, Orford IP12 2LH (Orford 277), offers a seafood platter, priced at about $5, that consists of smoked salmon, smoked mackerel with mustard sauce, prawns and cockles with mayonnaise, smoked eel and horseradish, and two kinds of oysters. Famous for oysters from their own beds and wild Irish salmon. Reservations strongly recommended. Closed in January and February.

WOODBRIDGE
Seckford Hall, Woodbridge, Suffolk IP13 6NU (Woodbridge 5678), is a partly Tudor country house, furnished with antiques and set among gardens and wooded grounds. The restaurant specializes in lobster taken from its own tank, broiled with butter sauce. Double rooms are about $60; rooms with a four-poster are a few dollars more.

 Melton Grange Hotel, Woodbridge, Suffolk IP12 1EX (Woodbridge 4147), is a country mansion set in its own park and woods on the outskirts of Woodbridge. Double rooms are about $55, including breakfast.

EASTBOURNE
Grand Hotel, King Edward's Parade, Eastbourne, Sussex BN21 4EQ (Eastbourne 22611), has attractive traditional public rooms, a garden and an outdoor swimming pool. Double rooms with balconies overlooking the sea are about $110, including breakfast; suites are about $190.

BATTLE
Netherfield Place Hotel, Netherfield, Battle, East Sussex TN3 3PP (4455), is a Sussex mansion that has been converted into a luxury hotel. Double rooms with four-poster or king-size bed are about $90, including breakfast.

LEWES
Shelleys Hotel, High Street, Lewes, East Sussex BN7 1XS (Brighton 472361), is a clad-in-vines house, part of which dates from 1526. Double rooms are about $85, including breakfast.

DOVER
White Cliffs Hotel, Sea Front, Dover CT17 9BW (Dover 203633), is an old, established seafront hotel, recently renovated. Double rooms with sea view are about $60, including breakfast.

GREAT YARMOUTH
Carlton Hotel, Marine Parade South, Great Yarmouth, Norfolk NR30 3JE (Great Yarmouth 55234), is a traditional Victorian seafront hotel. Double rooms with sea view are about $60, including breakfast.

AFLOAT IN FRANCE

A. Alvarez

The Hotel-Barge *Papillon* was at Narbonne when I joined her, and getting there was, decidedly, not half the fun. It meant flying from London to Paris, changing planes and flying on to Montpellier, where I was to be met. But at Heathrow the baggage handlers staged one of their flash stoppages, so the plane took off late, leaving me only twenty-five minutes to make the connection at Charles de Gaulle Airport. Another passenger and I sprinted through the caterpillar entrails of Terminal 1, scattering the duty-free shoppers in the arcade; we commandeered a bus to drive us to Terminal 2 and made the connection just as the gates were closing. But at Montpellier my luggage was nowhere to be found; nor was it on the next flight, four irritable hours later. There was a driver and a blue bus with *Péniche-Hôtel Papillon* painted on its sides waiting for me, but during the hour's drive to Narbonne, as P. G. Wodehouse put it, 'the general chitchat was pretty much down and out.'

The *Papillon* was moored in the marketplace in the centre of town – or rather, in the canal twenty feet below the level of the marketplace – a great dark shape with faint yellow light coming through the curtains of the saloon amidships. The town was already asleep, and not a sound came from the barge. Then the hatch doors opened, and the troubles of the journey vanished like a conjurer's egg. Dinner had already begun, and the candlelight glowed on a polished oak table, cut crystal glasses, painted plates, linen napkins in silver rings and, in the centre, a bowl of red and purple flowers.

I was welcomed with relief and fed tenderly, as though I were a survivor of a disaster: a warm salad with bacon and chicken livers, lamb with garlic and herbs, a chocolate-and-orange mousse, a selection of local cheeses and two good Burgundys to wash it down, one white, one red. By the time I waddled out to telephone the airport at midnight, the world was so transformed that I was not surprised to hear that my bag had shown up. It had arrived at Montpellier and was to be delivered the next morning. It arrived, in fact, just before 7 am. I woke long enough to hear the taxi driver bring it aboard, then drifted back to sleep.

When I woke again all I could see through the porthole was a line of plane trees over a stone balustrade. Up there, above the canal, the market was in full swing, but the noise seemed to be coming from far off, muted by water and the drop. That sense of distance and calm is, I discovered, typical of barge life. My stateroom was long and thin, with pale blue wallpaper and curtains and a flowered Victorian handbasin between the two beds. The cupboards and drawers were pale oak; the portholes and lamps were brass. There was a bowl of flowers at the head of the bed and more flowers in a little holder between the portholes. At the end of the room was a glittering bathroom with greyish-white tiles and a heated towel rack; one wall curved sharply to the shape of the hull; the tub was deep and coffin shaped. In a drawer by the bed was a hair dryer and a converter for electrical attachments. Every detail had been thought about, every potential emergency provided for.

The other two staterooms are equally luxurious; one had twin beds, the other a grand double bed, its sheets and pillowcases trimmed with broderie anglaise. The *Papillon* is owned by two New York business-men, Richard Cohen and Richard Benioff, whose respective wives, Ann and Mary, were partners for twenty years in their own interior decorating firm. They closed their business when Ann Robertson married Dick Cohen a few years ago but joined forces again to transform the battered old hulk their husbands had bought in Holland into what they proudly call a state-of-the-art barge, creating the comfort and calm of a luxury hotel within the confines of a canal vessel.

The oak-panelled saloon, upholstered in muted orange, has large curtained windows, a sofa, an armchair, a brass reading light, an old oak dining table and chairs, a bookcase full of paperbacks and a hi-fi system; the drinks cupboard is lit from the inside to show off its glass doors inset with panels of painted butterflies. Each member of the crew has his own cabin aft – unusual in a canal barge. The galley is spacious and equipped with everything a top-class chef might need. There is also a freezer, a washing machine and a garage amidships for the bus. Stacked neatly over the stern are a half-dozen bicycles for passengers who want to work off their energy or their meals.

There was a crew of four, three of them English, all of them young, friendly and expert. Leigh Wootton, the captain and the oldest, was educated at Pangbourne, a naval school where, he said, 'they prepare you for any career, as long as it's boating.' Although he was only twenty-four, he had had seven years' experience on barges and owns one himself at Auxerre. Frederic, the first mate, was a harassed-looking Frenchman with a witty, rather squashed face, a wild shock of hair and a sweet smile. Between canal journeys, he was studying speech therapy. Jane, the cook, who trained at the Cordon Bleu School in London, was a tall blonde with lively brown eyes and a delicate face. She had just celebrated her twenty-first birthday but cooked like someone with twice that many years' experience. The housekeeper, Sally, was a Norfolk farmer's daughter, one year older than Jane; she also trained at the Cordon Bleu School and spent a year cooking for Lord Rothschild's family in Cambridge.

The first day began at the leisurely pace at which it was to continue. While Jane and Sally were buying fresh meat and vegetables – before breakfast one of them had gone to the baker for warm croissants and bread – the Cohens and I wandered around Narbonne, peering at the thirteenth century fortified archbishops' palace – now a museum and civic centre – and the extraordinary unfinished cathedral, absurdly high and about as long as a small chapel. The great arch where the nave was to have begun was bricked off centuries ago and hung with massed organ pipes. But the organ was silent that morning; the only sound was the forlorn chirping of a bird hidden somewhere far up in the fan vaulting of the roof.

Back at the barge there was a flurry of activity while the bus was craned aboard. Having once been a commercial vessel, *Papillon* has its own crane, but the bus is a tricky cargo to handle: hooks on the wheels, pads to protect the paintwork, an elaborate pulley system to guide the thing across the cabin roof into its niche on board. The vessel tilts heavily as the crane takes the weight of the bus. Down in the galley something slides and falls; a piercing Engish voice says, 'Oh, damn.' Then the barge slowly rights itself. A crowd had gathered to watch on the footbridge over the canal, although a group of tramps on the towpath, with their dogs and bottles of wine, blankly ignore us.

The canal leaves the centre of Narbonne by passing under the Pont des Marchands, which is not a bridge at all but an ancient house spanning the river. The *Papillon* slides under the arch with less than an inch to spare. Two birds crash out in panic, and we have a closeup view of the ancient timbers and stones of the underside of the building. There are long, deep scars in the stonework made over the centuries by barges less skilfully piloted than ours. Beyond is a weir and a lock into which we nose delicately. The *Papillon* is so long that the lock gates will barely close without touching its stern. The lock keeper spins the wheels that control the sluices, and there is a mild banging as the water floods in. We rise solemnly and with great dignity until we are level with the traffic buzzing past on either side. Then the forward gates are opened, and we move slowly forward down the canal, leaving behind us the road, the traffic and the outskirts of Narbonne. And that, in effect, is the last we see of the twentieth century for the next forty-eight hours.

There are two reasons for this sense of timelessness. First, the Canal du Midi is a masterpiece of seventeenth century engineering that has been kept up, modified and, in places, modernized but not basically altered since it was opened in 1681. The olive-shaped locks, the stone lock keepers' houses and noble flights of steps are still beautifully in place, still more or less as designed by Pierre-Paul Riquet, the tax collector turned engineer who conceived the idea of a 150-mile waterway from Bordeaux on the Atlantic to Sète on the Mediterranean. Second, although European canals are still used commercially, most land transport is now by road or rail, and the modern landscape has organized itself accordingly. It is the traveller by car who gets the public image, the face that the house or town wishes to present to the world. Meanwhile, the canals have been forgotten, and you move on them through the countryside as though through a deep, secret artery, with a resident's view of the houses and villages you pass, the view from the back garden, private and unprepared. Perhaps that was what it was like to travel by horseback in the days before the automobile. Certainly on a barge there is an overwhelming sense of having gone back a century or more in time to a more intimate and peaceable world.

The forward deck of the *Papillon*, where the guests spend most of the day, has comfortable chairs and low tables and is bordered on three sides by window boxes of flowers and plants. Sitting there in the sunlight, with a view across the vineyards to a village church or a château, white and turreted against distant woods, is like being in a gently moving garden. As the day warms up, bees congregate around the flowers, butterflies float haphazardly by, dragonflies shimmer and dart. Around noon a tantalizing smell of cooking begins to drift up from the galley. The part-owners, Dick and Ann Cohen, are spending a few days on board en route to Sicily for a week's holiday. Ann passes the morning weeding the flower boxes, arranging and rearranging the deck furniture. 'Once a decorator, always a decorator,' she says, by way of apology. 'Save yourself, honey,' her husband answers. 'Sicily needs a lot of work.'

Dick Cohen is not the sort of man you would expect to be addicted to barging. He is an exceptionally fit sixty-year-old, an insurance broker who lives a characteristically driven New York life and has difficulty in winding down; back at home he ploughs endlessly up and down his swimming pool every day after work or walks for miles at a pace that would defeat most joggers. Yet on the first canal trip he took – on Leigh Wootton's barge in Burgundy – he fell helplessly in love with the pastime and decided to buy a barge for himself.

As we move slowly through the sunny, indolent morning, I begin to understand why. The secret is enforced relaxation; you do not hurry because it is impossible to hurry. The *Papillon* is ninety-six feet long, weighs eighty tons and once under way generates considerable momentum. So each curve of the canal has to be set up for carefully in advance and negotiated with caution. And there are a lot of curves on the Canal du Midi because Riquet, to save the expense and trouble of locks, designed it to follow as much as possible the contours of the gently rolling landscape. The barge and the canal dictate their own leisurely pace, and once on board, passengers find there is nothing to do except relax. Lunch is served as we go: a quiche of courgettes (zucchini) and lardons, topped with a cheese soufflé; cold meats, salad, cheeses, fruit, white wine, coffee. Through the big windows of the saloon we watch the trees go past while we eat. The sunlight, reflected from the water, dapples the ceiling. Rushes sigh in our wake.

Later, to work off the meal, I cycled for an hour along the towpath. I saw a single car on a back road way off across the vineyards, a man and his son fishing on the opposite bank, another man walking his dog, a lock keeper's house with a dramatic display of flowers framed in old tractor tyres painted yellow. The towpaths are lined with precisely spaced trees – sycamores, poplars, umbrella pines – planted originally to shade the horses that used to pull the barges. In high summer the canal is probably the one consistently shady place in the whole Midi.

I stopped at a lock to watch the *Papillon* approach. From a distance it seems as big as a cruise liner within the confines of the canal. Its hull is black above the waterline, then dark green, then pale green; its superstructure is pale green, white and red. On either side of the bow is a silver anchor and the name painted in white on a red background; above is a little red door into what was once the forepeak, then the bank of flowers along the forward deck. It is all so big and colourful that village dogs bark at its approach.

We moored that evening in the middle of nowhere. There was mist in the air; a bridge made a perfect circle in the glassy water; the lights from our saloon spread vaguely toward the opposite bank. But the air was cool, and it was good to be below with the candlelight and the wine and another splendid meal. Good, too, to wake to utter silence, with sunlight filtering through the plane trees, the deck wet with dew and the heavy smell of damp earth mingling with the smell of coffee. Good, finally, to know that today would be exactly like yesterday: a sedate journey through deepest countryside – out of time, out of place.

Barging, on a first-class vessel, combines the pleasures of a gently nomadic life, the comfort and cooking of a luxury hotel and the privacy of your own home. It seems to me an irresistible formula for a successful holiday. All day we chugged quietly along under the long cathedral arch of sycamores, charting our progress by the avenues of trees ahead and behind. At the tiny village of Poilhes workers were rebuilding the bridge, and the scaffolding beneath it was so low that Leigh and Frederic had to dismantle the protruding steering wheel in order to slide the barge through. Apart from that, nothing disturbed the calm. As the evening light thickened, we entered the Souterrain de Malpas, the oldest canal tunnel in the world (Riquet's engineers banged it through a hillside in six days after having been told it was impossible). Birds flittered in and out of the honeycombed rock at its entrance. The blast of our horn, warning other traffic of our approach, sounded like the end of the world.

That night we moored just short of Béziers, above another of Riquet's marvels, *les ecluses de Fontserannes*, a sequence of seven locks, like a great, wet, mechanical staircase. We started down them at seven o'clock the next morning, squeezing delicately into each with only inches to spare. The lock keeper, watching us with beady eye, was a smartly dressed woman in her thirties, with a child and a mongrel; a Gauloise was plastered to the corner of her mouth. At the bottom was a circular pool with the exit at 90 degrees to the locks. Frederic walked in front of the *Papillon* heaving on a rope, as though walking an enormous, obstinate dog. Beyond was an avenue of cypresses, then a noble nineteenth century aqueduct over the River Orb. We moved across it slowly, a couple of hundred feet in the air, to make an appropriately majestic triumphal entry into Béziers, where the real world, alas, was waiting.

ROYAL MEANDER ALONG THE LOIRE

John Vinocur

In 1669 Molière introduced his play *Monsieur de Pourceaugnac* at a command performance at Chambord castle. The guidebooks tell of a bored Louis XIV, of royal fidgets and of a King who never smiled. Midway through opening night, Jean Baptiste Lully, who had written music for the play and was also acting in it, sensed gathering disaster and jumped off the stage onto a harpsichord, smashing it to bits. Big yuks from the King, a triumphant play, and a major precedent for Harpo Marx and Mel Brooks.

The guidebooks, squeeze-boxes of history, record that Louis didn't get back to Chambord very often; by the early 1700s, they say, the Loire Valley, after centuries of glory, was in decline: no more mock naval battles between the sandbars, no more buffets of pigs' snouts and sweetmeats, no more peregrinations by barge from château to château. The stonework chipped, the pennants faded, tourists came. Someone named Arthur Young, who wrote *Travels in France* in 1792, reported that the valley's roads were good. Henry James, who was through about a hundred years later, found Chambord, its 440 abandoned rooms, its intricateness, oddly touching. In *A Little Tour in France* he described hearing the château talking 'with a muffled but audible voice, of the vanished monarchy, which had been so strong, so splendid, but today has become a sort of fantastic vision . . .'

A century after James's visit, history along the Loire flows even more quietly: It can not only be reported that during a recent four-day tour of the river's banks there were no known assaults on harpsichords, but that the châteaux' muffled voices have become exquisitely drowsy. If you listen, there is not much more than the sound of slow, regular breathing. The Loire has become a distillation of languor, the river usually a molasses-paced affair and the life around it geared down to an elegant shuffle. The river actually runs from east to west across the middle of France, but I think of its valley as being located in a psychic Deep South of slow movement, of subconscious understanding that anything that was ever going to happen on this full, green part of the earth happened very long ago. Driving under canopies of plane and willow trees along the Indre, one of the Loire's tributaries, from Montbazon to Azay-le-Rideau, we came across a nuclear laboratory, tucked into the woodland but surrounded by barbed wire fences and floodlights. So untroubled, so unplugged from time does the valley seem that this sentinel grimness came as a shock. Here? My God, we said. In a minute or two, we had driven past. A curve in the road and we were meandering again, the only rhythm the region really allows. There were châteaux ahead. 'As thick as gas stations,' a friend said.

We drove south from Paris, the three of us, and I think we had the right approach to the Loire in mind: no approach. We had no checklist of castles, just rooms reserved in places far enough apart to require a little daily driving through the countryside. We would see Chenonceaux, of course, which stands on six piers across the Cher River, asymmetrical, a less-is-more masterpiece of proportion; and we would see Chambord, a more-is-more extravaganza, mass and abundance, the French Renaissance in full dress; to miss them, three-star monuments of French genius, would have been plain dumb.

As everyone insists on saying, **Chambord** is most striking at first view. If you come through the forest that surrounds it, first contact is fairy-tale stuff – a clearing, and all of a sudden the wonder and power of Francis I's castle: eight round towers and so many pinnacles, gables, turrets, cupolas and chimneys that you lose count. It is an enormous place, unabashedly royal, rising straight out of the ground. Up close, there is so much detail, so much caprice on so much stone, that the senses overload. **Chenonceaux** is easier to absorb because, by modern standards, it looks habitable, its gallery stretching out, ranch-house style, across the Cher. Chambord has an ingenious staircase inside, but not too much else, which made me wonder whether Francis's hunting guests were given floor plans to deal with the place's immensity. Chenonceaux, on the other hand, is much more finely decorated, with paintings, and tapestries and marble statuary that Catherine de Médici brought up from Florence. Push your imagination a bit as you go down the long gallery, its chequered black-and-white marble floor suspended above the river, and you think you're walking on water.

But we wanted to ramble, and the best day we spent was an easy one that began at Chaumont-sur-Loire, just south of Blois, and ended down the river, at a restored mansion in Montbazon.

The **Château de Chaumont** is a bit of an oddity because – unlike Chambord, Chenonceaux, Azay-le-Rideau or Chinon – it actually stands alongside the Loire. High on a bluff over the river, with its thick turrets, Chaumont has something of a medieval look. The particularly nice thing about Chaumont is the long, uphill walk to the park that surrounds the castle itself, leaving buses and souvenir vendors below and out of mind. The day we were there, the high grass in the acres of rolling fields around the castle had been half mown, and a rich odour arose from the rippling sheets of green. If you stand in front of the castle, you can look in any direction and find nothing that disturbs the unity of meadow and forest; inside Chaumont's courtyard, your back turned to the park, you overlook miles of river and valley, farmland quilted yellow, green and brown. Mme. de Staël spent some time in exile in the castle and after moving out wrote of the 'monotony of solitude.' That is the long, enforced view; for a morning hour in the pale sunshine, solitude still ruled at Chaumont, but it was joyous.

We ambled south. Looked at places where the Loire had flooded (submerging tennis courts and vegetable gardens, but affecting not a whit of the valley's imperturbability); bought a post card in Amboise; dropped off our bags in Montbazon, slipped into **Saché** for lunch. The village is barely a paragraph in the guidebooks, and that's fine. Balzac liked it and worked in the small château there – a very liveable-looking place that now houses a small Balzac museum. Alexander Calder, the sculptor from New Jersey whose mobiles mocked everything that is grave and self-important in art, had a studio there too. I met him before his death in 1976, and he told me a story that caught his view of the world: 'We once went over to Picasso's joint, where he made pottery, in Vallauris. He was in back working on plates. He had kind of an upraised crosshatching on them and bullfight drawings. I said, "Ahh, that's so the meat doesn't slide off, huh?" He didn't say anything, but he had a red face.'

I thought about that, keeping the meat on the plate as we ate in an extremely good restaurant, the Auberge du XII Siècle, just off the village square. It's a lucky little village: a black-and-red Calder stabile sitting in front of the town hall, a fine place to eat, a handsome château. The Loire Valley's ease with being itself, which Calder loved, seems to permeate Saché. Nothing much to do. Grace. Comfort.

Saché is just up the Cher from **Azay-le-Rideau**, with the château that Balzac described as a diamond. It is a hands-down marvel, human-sized, circumscribable, particularly interesting in that there is nothing exhausting in its scale. It is smaller than Chenonceaux, but integrates water, woodland and stone in the same way. A central alleyway bordered by chestnut trees leads through a park to the château, and from a distance you can see its reflection playing against the surface of the river. The château is creamy white, and its roof slate-grey. Against the trees and dark water, it is a delicate, refined composition.

To tell the truth, I find Azay a little perfect, perhaps a bit overbred and maybe a little short on craziness, or excess. But it is also faintly modern in a way that tells just a bit about the people who built the

Loire castles and then lived in them: There are initials everywhere, carved into the woodwork and chiselled into the stone, not by sixteenth century hooligans, but by the original owners, who seem to have been very keen to put their mark on things. This monogram habit gets carried further: The château brims with bas-reliefs of salamanders, Francis I's 'I-walk-through-fire' symbol. In the Middle Ages salamanders were believed to be something like asbestos – able to resist and put out fire. Seen in the sooty light of a spring day, the stone salamander above a fireplace looked strangely like the crocodile on a Lacoste shirt. But I promise: the château at Azay-le-Rideau doesn't wrench the definition of the word exquisite.

We saw some real Lacoste shirts at our next stop, the **Château d'Artigny** in Montbazon, the hotel where we spent the night. Built between 1912 and 1930 by the Coty family (the perfume people), it stares out over the valley of the Indre, but the building itself reminded me of Newport mansions. After looking at the châteaux, staying at the Château d'Artigny gives you a bit of the feeling of living in castlelike spaces: a great staircase, an immense central hall and a lovely park. Best by far was a big country-club-sized bar with an extraordinary choice of Calvados, marcs, rums, Cognacs, Armagnacs, fruit eaux-de-vies. After dinner, we sat on a deep green couch and sampled three Cognacs dating from times before the hotel was built. Before going to bed, I went for a walk. The hotel, white by day, seemed awash in a pinkish, apricot light, magical against the black valley and the pin dots of white in the black sky.

When I got back to my room, I read. The Loire, the book said, inspired painters and poets, contained staggering and challenging historical wealth and could not be grasped without a systematic plan. It seemed an admonition of a sort, an accusatory finger leaping off the page and waggling at me, saying I had done all this grandeur a small injustice in not providing a little more rigour in our approach to it. But I felt no shame. The Loire Valley, taken ad hoc, bit by unorganized bit, is soft and calm and beautiful.

A HERITAGE OF PAMPERING

Patricia Wells

I like to think of the Loire Valley as France's well-bred region. Everything here – the architecture, the food, the scenery, even the character of the people – has a well-mannered, self-assured quality. The Loire has little in common with the rusticity and remoteness of the Pyrenees in the southwest, the folkloric playfulness of Alsace, the heady aromas and fierce sunshine of Provence. It's a region that makes you feel secure, even a bit pampered.

Châteaux abound, for visiting, for exploring, for spending the night. Lazy rivers and single-lane bridges, pocket-size villages with little farmers' markets, add a pleasant aura of romance and minor adventure.

The food here has a soft, rounded quality: delicate mushrooms cultivated in mammoth caves near the town of Saumur; rosy-fleshed salmon plucked from the roving Loire River; pure, pure white asparagus that grows swaddled in darkness in fine, sandy soil, pushing through the earth through the night, coming to life just as the world is beginning to awaken; fresh goat cheese with that elusive character. Even the wines, like Vouvray, Savennières, Sancerre, are mild, gentle, golden and blend naturally into the landscape of the meal.

One spot that typifies the Loire's careful breeding is the proud and elegant **Château d'Artigny**, in the town of Montbazon. As you take the long, shaded drive up to the château, arriving just as the sun begins to think about setting, you realize that if places like this didn't exist in reality, they'd exist in the mind of any romantic soul who has ever dreamed about the Loire.

Even if you don't spend the night at the Château d'Artigny, reserve a table in the round, central dining room (one of several) and hope that the skies will be clear and sparkling. One evening I sat and watched a handsome, middle-aged French couple at table. They were both dressed in pink – she in a simple, bright rose sheath, he in a pale pink shirt with a button-down collar. By chance, I glanced over just as they clinked glasses holding raspberry-coloured cocktails. At that very moment, the sunset burst through the arched windows, spreading a haze of orange and rose. There was no need to listen in on the couple's conversation – their joy, and sense of celebration, radiated from the table.

The Château d'Artigny experience is a very special one: the setting, service and accommodations could scarcely be improved upon, and the food is, as the French say, 'correct.' The chef has imagination and wit. Now that ravioli has become the culinary cliché of the 1980s, he has come up with an understated, amusing appetizer: a single ravioli filled with caviar swimming in a delicate sauce, surrounded by chunks of langoustine and sole. As a main course, he offers an old-fashioned *épigramme d'agneau* – nuggets of lamb and two tiny lamb chops, breaded and fried, paired with lamb sweetbreads and lamb's tongue. It's a complex dish that seems right in these surroundings, the proper food to serve in a grand château set in the midst of a sixty-five-acre park.

The château is worth a visit if only for its wine list, a thick, impressive tome that includes not only a range of Bordeaux spanning the last forty years, but also just about every wine you'll find in the region. A white to sample is Gaston Huet's dry 1982 Vouvray, a wine with plenty of finesse, a perfect aperitif that you can drink into the meal.

A modest but charming contrast to the grandeur of d'Artigny is **La Taillandière**, the home of William and Ginette Hausser, just outside the village of Villandry. It is a *ferme-auberge* (the French equivalent of the British bed-and-breakfast), one of many in the region. Besides being much less expensive than a hotel, a *ferme-auberge* is far more personal, allowing you to meet the French and experience a bit of the local life and architecture first-hand.

The impeccable Hausser house has been carefully restored; thick stone walls, huge fireplaces, even a working bread oven, have been preserved. Guests may rent their own private cottage on the grounds or, for shorter stays, take one of the two comfortable bedrooms decorated with sturdy French antiques. And for breakfast, instead of those foil-wrapped packets of commercially made jam, you'll get fresh plum and strawberry conserves from Mme. Hausser's own gardens. As you leave, be sure to stop and sample the goat cheese from the farm just around the corner.

Another homey establishment, albeit a castle, is the fifteenth century **Château des Réaux** in Bourgueil, which is owned by Florence and Jean-Luc Goupil de Bouillé. There the family dog romps around the grounds with his favourite toys while the châtelaine hops in her car after breakfast to drive the children off to school. Guests may even take dinner with the family in the huge, tastefully decorated dining room, overlooking a moat and a lush expanse of lawn. They should hope that when breakfast time comes, Mme. Goupil de Bouillé will have some of her honey-flavoured pear preserves on hand.

Days for touring are also days for visiting local markets, and among the nicest in the area are the Valençay market on Tuesday, the Saumur market on Saturday, the Romorantin market on Wednesday and Saturday, the Chinon market on Thursday. The local markets offer a little bit of everything: clothing stalls and bric-a-brac on one side, live rabbits and chickens on another. Farmers come to sell their home-made goat cheese, hand-picked strawberries and tomatoes; fishmongers offer fresh fish from the Loire; and in the autumn and winter months, there are wild mushrooms, game and home-made wild boar pâtés.

In the region's restaurants, Loire Valley salmon remains one of the greatest delicacies. Among the best places for sampling it is **Jeanne de Laval**, an old-fashioned family *auberge* in the village of Les Rosiers. Dining there, you'll swear that time stopped somewhere in the 1950s, that nouvelle cuisine had never been invented. The cosy restaurant is well worn but far from shabby. Eager, bright-faced waitresses scurry about, and the voice of the chef, Michel Augereau, booms from the adjacent kitchen. In the warmer months, guests begin their meals on the rear terrace overlooking a slightly overgrown but enchanting rose garden. They can sample the local wines as they examine the menu.

The offerings could not be more traditional. The Loire Valley salmon is available from mid-February until the end of June. In spring, there are fat white asparagus with hollandaise and perchlike Loire River sandre with *beurre blanc*. Autumn and winter months bring roast pheasant and partridge and wild hare stews.

Between meals, visits to vineyards and mushroom caves are in order. Across the river from Les Rosiers, outside the town of St.-Hilaire-St.-Florent, is Louis Bouchard's **Musée du Champignon**, where you can wander at will through expansive underground caves, passing beds of *champignons de Paris* at various stages of development. At the end of the tour, visitors can purchase fresh, dried and preserved mushrooms, as well as local wines.

A bit farther west along the Loire, in the tiny village of Epiré, travellers will find one of the region's more charming little wine cellars, hidden in the cool basement of the former village church. The Savennières wine made there is called **Château d'Epiré**, and visitors will be greeted by Robert Daguen, who has been cellar master for thirty-seven years. For anyone who is used to vast, air-conditioned wine cellars full of spotless, modern, stainless-steel vats, Château d'Epiré will come as a real surprise.

Here the wine, made only from the Chenin Blanc grapes that grow on the property's twenty-three acres, is aged in old oak barrels, and each tiny plot of the vineyard gets its own private cask. When customers come to buy the wine, Monsieur Daguen, dressed in classic blue overalls and high rubber boots, will urge them to sip samples from half a dozen different casks and select the wine that catches their fancy. In the end, I, like so many others, drove off with more cases than I'd intended to buy, but with a certain contentment. Months later, as I sipped this handsome, handmade wine, I'd be able to remember the cuckoo that sang as the cellar master filled my glass – and rest assured that a tiny corner of gentle old France would be waiting for me next time I headed back to the Loire.

ROYAL PROGRESSIONS

Château d'Artigny, 37250 Montbazon; telephone: 47 26 24 24. Closed December and first two weeks in January. About $45 a person, including wine and service.

La Taillandière, Fèrme-Auberge Hausser, 37510 Joué les Tours; 47 50 08 31. Rooms about $20 a couple, including breakfast.

Château des Réaux, 37140 Bourgueil; 47 95 14 40. Rooms about $45 a couple, including breakfast.

Jeanne de Laval, 49350 Les Rosiers; 41 51 80 17. Closed last week in November through third week in December. About $35 a person, including wine and service.

Musée du Champignon, Caves Louis Bouchard, St.-Hilaire-St.-Florent, 49400 Saumur; 41 50 31 55. On the left bank of the Loire, on D751, about two miles west of Saumur. Open daily from March 15 to November 15, from 10 am to noon and 2 to 4 pm.

Château d'Epiré. To be certain that the cellar master will be there to greet you, call ahead for an appointment: 41 77 10 57.

THE TREASURE OF LANGUEDOC

MacDonald Harris

One of my favourite places in France is a town that for a long time I thought nobody else knew about. When my wife and son and I first went there, it was early in the season, and the town and the hotel were almost deserted. I was so charmed by the place that I eventually used it as the setting of a novel. When the book came out, one friend after another told me, 'I thought I was the only one who knew about Conques!'

Conques, in the Department of Aveyron, is a small town about three hours' drive north of Toulouse. It has only about four hundred inhabitants, and until recently it was not visited much. That is, not since the Middle Ages. Then it teemed with travellers on foot and horseback who stopped to pass the night there, and its attractions were celebrated throughout Europe.

Conques lies on the medieval pilgrimage route from Flanders and northern France to the shrine of Santiago de Compostela in Spain, and it was a favourite stopping place for pilgrims. This is the key to the mystery that at first puzzles, why there is such a large church in such a small town. The name of the town, in fact, comes from the Spanish word *concha*, in reference to the scallop shells the pilgrims brought back from the sea as evidence of their visit to the shrine.

Pilgrimages were the only medieval form of tourism. The most famous one was that to Compostela, near La Coruña in the western-most part of Spain. It attracted not only the genuinely devout and those seeking remission of some sin, but others simply setting out for a good time, mountebanks and pedlars and some with even more dubious motives, thievery or fraud – one can get a notion from the *Canterbury Tales*. The custom was at its height from the eleventh to the thirteenth centuries. It was then that the church at Conques flourished.

There was a small and humble monastery on this site, hidden away in the remote hills of the Languedoc, from the earliest Middle Ages. When it began to prosper, later, it was because of a shrewd piece of religious business. Sainte-Foy was a Christian maiden who lived in the nearby town of Agen in the fourth century. When she was martyred around AD 303 by the Roman governor, her relics were preserved and venerated by the faithful. In the ninth century the monks of Conques became so devoted to Sainte-Foy that they sent one of their number to Agen in the guise of a pilgrim. He stayed in the monastery there for ten years, until he finally had an opportunity to steal the relics. He brought them back to Conques, where they have been ever since.

Over the centuries, scores of monasteries along the track to Compostela gradually developed into hostels for pilgrims. If there were precious relics in a monastery church, this was an attraction to the devout. So Conques flourished. The present Romanesque church was begun in the eleventh century and completed in the twelfth. At its height, hundreds of pilgrims stopped to spend the night and to venerate the relics – which by this time included numerous others in addition to those of Sainte-Foy. The monks prospered. The finest goldsmiths of Europe were engaged to fashion odd and priceless containers for the sacred objects. The attraction of Conques today is the same as it was in the Middle Ages – the relics, and the reliquaries that have been made to hold them.

The church itself is a surprisingly large and beautiful structure for so remote a part of the world. The reason, of course, is that the church was there before the town, which grew up gradually to serve the needs of the church and the monastery. Its best-known feature, and the one that attracts art historians, is the tympanum of the west façade. This elaborately carved semicircle is of a different stone from the rest of the structure, and more sophisticated and complex than anything else in the church. Its subject is the Last Judgement, a theme dear to the Middle Ages, which enjoyed seeing the good rewarded and the wicked punished – especially the latter.

Some figures are curious. At the entrance to Hell the biblical monster Leviathan, his mouth open wide, swallows the damned, who are pushed in by a devil with a heavy club. A knight in chain mail is being prodded by demons with pitchforks on a delicate part of his anatomy – his only sin, in fact, was that he was an ambitious neighbour of the abbey who disputed with the monks over some land. Near him are some poachers who hunted in the woods of the abbey. They are being roasted on spits, and the rabbit they hoped to catch is helping with the job. The adulterers are bound and nude while devils debate their punishment. One sinner, caught in a net by an energetic devil with a paunch, is Etienne, Bishop of Clermont and governor of the abbey in the tenth century, who conspired with two nephews to loot the treasure of the church.

Inside, the church seems immense, but it is rather stark and bare. The only embellishments are on the capitals of the columns that support the vault. There are 212 of these, all different – at least so the guidebook tells you, although we did not shinny up all of them to verify this. They are elaborately decorated with palm leaves, acanthus leaves, tracery, birds, griffins, monsters and sacred scenes. One portrays the entire Last Supper, a difficult feat on a small block of stone with four sides. Another depicts the arrest of Sainte-Foy, with the Proconsul Dacien handing the sword to the executioner. On the same capital – medieval art is often sequential like a comic strip – the saint is dragged away by a soldier, with an angel behind her to give her encouragement.

The iron grille-work enclosing the chancel is also celebrated. According to legend, it was hammered from the bonds of Crusaders, felons and other prisoners liberated through miracles of Sainte-Foy. This would have taken a great many chains and shackles, and in addition the iron has been identified as of a later period. Like so many other legends, this one is charming but apocryphal.

The grille was erected around the chancel to protect the relics from thieves. But the relics are no longer in the church. Since 1955 they have been on display in the strongroom of the former sacristy – all that remains of the medieval monastery. The collection is called the Tresor, and it is a treasure indeed, in two senses – the reliquaries, most of them in gold and other precious metals, are also priceless for their historical and artistic importance.

Upon entering the small, rather long and narrow room, one is struck with a sudden impression of gold from all sides. At the centre, dominating the room, is an odd and somewhat stubby golden figure in its own glass case, the *Majesté d'Or de Sainte-Foy*. A majesty, so called, is a statue in precious metal designed as a reliquary to hold relics of a saint. There were numbers of them in the Middle Ages, but the Majesty of Sainte-Foy is the only one preserved. It is said to be the first example of free-standing figurative sculpture after the decline of Rome.

The figure, about three feet high, is made of solid gold sheets on a wooden matrix. There is a good deal of mystery about the origins of the statue. The head is older than the rest of it and too large for the torso; it is probably that of a Roman emperor. The seated figure is sumptuously decorated with jewels and precious stones. Some cameos and intaglios are Hellenistic; others date from the Roman period. The medieval gems are cruder, but some of them are of outstanding size. The hollow head is said to contain part of the skull of Sainte-Foy. A 1954 examination conducted under the auspices of the National Agency for Museums verified that some of the fragments are from the cranium of a female child or young girl. The expression on the face of the statue is curious and somewhat unsettling. It might be called a

Mona Lisa smile, except that the saint is not smiling. She is simply knowing and mysterious, faintly amused.

There are a score or so of other sacred and precious objects on display in the room. The so-called A of Charlemagne is a triangular reliquary of heavy gold encrusted like the Majesty with gems. According to legend, Charlemagne distributed to each of the abbeys in his realm a golden letter of the alphabet, reserving the first for Sainte-Foy as a sign of his preference. In actual fact the object dates from at least two centuries after the Carolingian period. The Reliquary of Pépin is a jewelled coffer with an intricate representation of the Crucifixion in gold repoussé on the front. The roof-shaped cover suggests that it was intended to symbolize the House of God. Perhaps most curious of all is the Arm of St. George, a golden reliquary in the form of a forearm and hand with two fingers raised in blessing. It is said to contain the humerus of the very arm that slew the dragon – and the golden effigy is that of a right arm. In spite of its gruesome qualities for the modern mind, this object is oddly and movingly beautiful. The Tresor is open only in the afternoon and, like many French museums, is closed on Monday.

The first time we visited Conques, I had not been in the strongroom for ten minutes before the idea of a novel suggested itself to me, and my palms began to sweat. The sheer monetary value of the objects in the room was incalculable. In spite of its heavy walls and its locks, the place seemed a set-up for some improbably cinematic bandits with automatic weapons and a helicopter. There was no one in charge except an aged and genial Norbertine Father, who seemed anxious to engage in conversation. He was surely an octogenarian at least.

I began asking him what you might call Thieves' Questions. I explained to him first that I was a writer. 'How many gendarmes are there in town, Father?'

'Four, and a brigadier.'

'But they could call for reinforcements?'

'Oh, yes, from Rodez' – a town about half an hour away.

'You could cut the telephone lines,' I suggested.

'But the gendarmes have a radio.'

'Perhaps you could *plastiquer* their antenna.' He agreed that was a good idea.

'I imagine one could land a helicopter here?'

'Of course. Be sure, my son,' he added, 'to send me a copy of the book when you've written it.'

'I'm not sure that what I write is suitable for a monk.'

'Ah,' he told me placidly, 'we're more au courant than you may imagine, these days.'

And so I wrote *The Treasure of Sainte-Foy*. Needless to say, my bandits did not succeed in their sacrilegious caper, although I did kill off the friendly old monk in the course of my imaginary crime. When we returned to Conques two years later, in fact, he was gone and a younger monk had taken his place.

IF YOU GO
Where to Stay
There is only one hotel in Conques, but it is a good one. It is called the **Sainte-Foy** and it is rated 'Comfortable' by the Michelin guide. It is really more than that. The dining room, which is open for dinner only, is excellent, featuring Languedoc specialities and wines (Gaillac, Corbières). The average bill is about $12 a person.

For one dinner, one of us began with *cepes à la bordelaise,* the enormous mushrooms of the Midi, as large as apples, sliced in a marinade of garlic and rosemary, and the others with the local trout poached in white wine – this is simple country fare, not Cordon Bleu cookery. Next came quail, broiled with thin strips of country-cured ham, another speciality of the region. We finished with Cabecou, the local goat cheese, which some people may find a little strong. For wine we had little choice; we were strongly urged to try a Gaillac and we did. The light red was quite suitable with the game.

In addition to the dining room, the hotel has a small garden where you may take your breakfast, weather permitting. The hotel's 20 rooms are all sizes and shapes, and at least one, Room 9, which is up a long set of stairs, has a window that opens directly on the façade of the church. Room rates at this writing, with the dollar very high against the franc, range from about $10 to about $30; breakfast is another $3 or so.

It is impossible not to enjoy a night here, if you do not mind the adventure of leaving your car in a kind of dungeon cut into the solid limestone cliff under the hotel; it is only two cars wide but three cars deep, so that you are likely to be called from your dinner, or even your slumbers, to move your car so that somebody else can get out. After the first time, we left our key at the desk, and the boy moved it.

Getting There
Conques is not very accessible; you cannot get there by train, and it is too far out of the way for organized bus tours. The only way to reach it is by car. The best way to approach it, I think, is the way we did the first time – from the small country road (Departmentale 232) winding over the plateau of the Rouergue to the west, which comes out suddenly onto an escarpment with a breathtaking view of Conques in the Valley of the Dourdou below. On this road, scarcely wider than an American sidewalk, you cross the river on a narrow fourteenth century stone bridge made for oxcarts, not for cars.

A more conventional approach, from Paris and the north, brings you through Limoges and Aurillac and then by various secondary roads (you will need Michelin map No. 76) through the hills to Conques. From the south the route is a little more direct – from Toulouse through Montauban to Rodez, and then up the Valley of the Dourdou on Departmentale 601.

Side Trips

This part of the Languedoc is rich in Romanesque churches, most of them dating from the tenth and eleventh centuries. **St.-Pierre de Bessuejouls,** near Espalion, half an hour's drive from Conques, has some remarkable decorative sculptures in an eleventh century square belltower. The church of **Perse,** also near Espalion, has interesting stonework, including a tympanum, dedicated to the Pentecost, that is almost as curious as that of Conques.

In the village of **Castelnau-Pegayrolles,** farther south near Millau, there are two eleventh century Romanesque churches. One of them, **St.-Michel,** has some unusual decorations in a nonrepresentational filigree pattern, perhaps showing a Moorish influence. **St.-Pierre de Nant,** about a quarter of an hour's drive south of Millau, has some extraordinary and grotesque capitals surmounting the double columns supporting the nave. All these churches can be visited in a single afternoon, if you are in a hurry. Finally, at **Villefranche-de-Rouergue,** half an hour's drive west of rodez, there is a fine Carthusian monastery with a Gothic cloister.

— MacD. H.

THE GRAND, CONVIVIAL
PLAZA-ATHÉNÉE

Phyllis Lee Levin

In Paris, there are hotels that are cosy, contemporary, grand – and then there is the Plaza-Athénée, a silky blend of all those qualities. Even from a distance, as you inch off the great, clotted Champs-Élysées and turn right at the Rond Point, the Plaza, as Parisians call it, looks especially inviting. Number 25 on the broad, worldly and comparatively serene Avenue Montaigne, the hotel's classic façade is dressed with half-hoop awnings that glow like welcoming lanterns, their intense orange warming the pewter grey Paris sky. With the Eiffel Tower looming just across the Seine, the improbable beauty of the setting almost seems studied, its harmony too contrived.

Once the car and the luggage have been whisked away, you pass by snippets of garden, under a ruffled glass canopy and through the revolving door. The Plaza's lobby is regal, with the grace of a palace ballroom, but the Plaza's guests are amazingly diverse in what they wear at court. And this, precisely, is what is so singular about the Plaza, the essence of the hotel: this gilded atmosphere of prismatic crystal, princely furniture, murals, palms, ruby gladioli and coral roses, a habitat for such guests as that blonde woman, for instance, in her sable jacket, black leather pants and silver loafers, that man in blue velour jogging suit, that quintet thickly draped in Middle Eastern white.

A mahogany booth, where keys and mail are handed out and requests to the concierge are registered, runs the length of one side of the room. The registration desk is literally a desk, ornamented with ormolu and placed at an angle in the far corner. It is presided over by an official in severe navy blue, who, after checking their passports and reservations, escorts guests to their rooms. (His polite English is fluent enough to dampen all efforts to speak broken French.) As you leave the lobby for the inner central hall, the radiant dining room, the Régence (Michelin awards it one star), is straight ahead; turning left, a corridor of glass vitrines, shining with the wares of famous jewellers, leads to a well-stocked news-stand and a small lift.

On a recent visit, my husband and I were shown to Room 122, at which we arrived reams of carpeted halls later. The minuscule entrance was furnished with a small refrigerator, stocked with Champagne, among other necessities; beyond it, the general soothing loveliness of the bedroom was immediately apparent. Brass-handled French windows led to a narrow, iron-railed balcony that overlooked the seven-storey courtyard, its walls joyous with vines, orange awnings and window boxes of scarlet geraniums. Below, the terrace was planted with palms, firs, impatiens by the tub full. Mirrored and trellised, with two small, vividly blue pools, it opens off the dining room. In high summer, meals are served there at tables shaded by more orange canvas.

Our room was panelled with pale beige cut velvet, its woodwork painted in two shades of creamy white. The upholstery was another beige, the quilted bedspread another white, the carpet a dark amber. Some awed pinching led us to decide that the peach-coloured curtains were, indeed, made of pure silk taffeta worthy of a ballgown. The closets were built-in armoires, connected by a small desk in the centre. The quality and beauty of the furnishings seemed to imply an unwritten pact of civility between guests and host.

A check of the desk revealed stationery, information that one-day cleaning and laundry services were available (roughly $15 for cleaning a suit, $4 for washing an evening shirt) and that room service (offering everything from hamburgers to *foie de veau aux raisins*) operated around the clock. The bathroom was sparkling, leaf-patterned and all tiled; a request to a maid produced the bubble bath and shower cap with which it should have been supplied.

A little after lunchtime, we were seated in the Régence, waiting for some sherry, admiring the restaurant's rosy dignity, its Porthault linens, the perfection of its flowers. The eighteen-inch-high menu offered beluga caviar, *escalope de loup aux épinards*, or even grilled T-bone *à l'américaine*. When we requested salads, however, we were informed, most apologetically, that light meals were served just down the hall in the Relais.

The Relais is all Art Deco, all blond tones, maize linens, touches of claret. There was a wait, since it was Friday and, like every weekday, the designers, their models and clients were lunching and, not incidentally, wearing the latest thing in boots, diamonds and leather jackets. (It may be the greatest fashion show in Paris.) Seated at last, my husband had a clear soup and I had a small green salad.

But if one can take only one meal at the Plaza, then unequivocally it should be tea, served in the high, wide, columned and cushioned corridor called the Galerie des Gobelins. This repast epitomizes the spirit of the hotel, the expert blending of all privileged worlds. Somehow, this is never clearer than when, at the nod of the ambassadorial headwaiter to his uniformed steward, a tea cart is rolled soundlessly among the clustered Louis XIV-style chairs and settees, from the silver-haired man in starched collar and navy blue pinstripes to the burly one flashing gold medallions from his open-throat shirt and the narrow brunette in sequined T-shirt and blue jeans tugging three poodles.

And finally, when a tall woman in raincoat and grey Garbo fedora rushes by, as does a bellboy with a three-foot vase of those six-foot ruby gladioli, and the discreet pianist meanders into 'Cheek to Cheek,' it is possible to wonder if time hasn't stopped, or even reversed. One might think of taking bets now on whether, in seconds, Fred Astaire, on holiday in Paris, will come bounding in after Ginger Rogers.

The Plaza-Athénée is the sum of two pre-World War I establishments whose French soul seems even more intensely visible since its purchase by the English group Trust House Forte in 1968. The original 160-room Hôtel Athénée, which opened in 1867, was sold and merged in 1911 with the Société de l'Hôtel Plaza. Eight years later the hotel was enlarged to the designs of the architect Jules Lefevre, whose embellishments include the courtyard, the Régence restaurant and the elaborate suites that have housed, among others, the kings of Spain, Jordan and Denmark.

Though the hotel has more than two hundred rooms, including forty-four suites, it is operated more like a club whose management is willing to cater to the cultivated eccentricities of its members. The Plaza's files record which clients like or don't like flowers, prefer blue or green, bring their own linens (or silks), hang their own paintings. The King of Spain requires a direct, private line to his closest deputy at home; one woman sends her maid a few hours ahead of her arrival to unpack. Another, who likes at least six pots of azaleas in her room, requires that an upright piano be put in place of one of the beds. Still another arrives with thirty suitcases; extra shoe cabinets are mandatory. Baby sitters and dog walkers are readily provided.

The royal suite, consisting of a living room and two bedrooms, is in every way a palace apartment away from the palace. Painted in antiqued white with gold, furnished with a mix of period pieces and the finest fabrics Paris can muster (which are very fine indeed), the basic suite can be expanded into a duplex or, on rare occasions, to all thirty rooms on a single floor. (The basic suite is about $1,000 a day.)

The 8th Arrondissement, where the Plaza stands, can be a surprise to the visitor who usually stays in one of the hotels near the Opéra or the Place Vendôme. The neighbourhood is both residential and commercial, opulent but also friendly. For high-fashion window shopping, little beats Avenue Montaigne with, just for a beginning, Guy Laroche to one side of the Plaza, Ungaro across the way,

Valentino and Hanae Mori to the right. (Serious shoppers who cannot afford serious prices, however, can walk around the corner to the vicinity of the Rue Boccador, where there are small shops with affordable, or at least semi-affordable, treasures.)

But one of the unsung virtues of the Plaza has nothing to do with fashion and everything to do with music, theatre and dance. At 13 Avenue Montaigne, the Champs-Élysées Theatre, far smaller than Carnegie Hall (but not as comfortable), schedules recitals by such soloists as Jessye Norman and Marilyn Horne, performances by the French National Orchestra and a varied repertory of operas. On concert night, the Plaza's guest might order a substantial tea or even a room-service club sandwich, reserving a table at the Relais for after theatre, when half the audience tumbles in for a light or ample supper.

The last spot to explore before bedtime (it closes at 1.30 am) is the Bar Anglaise – red and green leather with a plaid carpet – tucked away in a corner past the hairdresser and the stock-market ticker. Here you can sip Calvados and listen to such old favourites as 'Bye Bye Blackbird,' sung in Italian and French.

Bedtime in Room 122 meant drawn shutters, drawn curtains, bed turned down and a towel placed on the rug, on either side of the bed, presumably to protect our bare feet from lint (it couldn't be dirt) from the carpet. The quiet was almost startling.

But even at the Plaza, not everything was perfect. When I called the next morning to order continental breakfasts and a copy of *The International Herald-Tribune*, I was told there would be a wait, and that it was impossible to predict its length because the hotel was so crowded that all the room service tables were in use. Also, the newspaper required a separate call to the news-stand.

But though it seemed like hours, the wait was a matter of possibly fifteen minutes. With the arrival of the table, set with cornflower blue china and brimming with brioches, croissants, rolls, jams, hot chocolate and a rose, and with the next doorbell's announcement of the newspaper, serenity was restored. It was not ruffled even when it came time to pay the bill at the end of the night's stay. Our room and service charges were $190; meals and snacks brought it up to $254.70.

IN WALES, A BOOKWORM'S HOLIDAY

Israel Shenker

The welcome mat was out for me at St. Deiniol's, as long as I was not deliberately working to undermine the Anglican religion. It seemed so little to ask. I dismissed every subversive impulse and applied for admission.

St. Deiniol's is probably the world's only residential library, and William E. Gladstone (1809–1898) founded it and set the rules. Having served the nation four times as Prime Minister, he was used to getting his way – and getting out of the way when Disraeli had more votes.

Year after year, Gladstone spent about six months at Hawarden (pronounced HAR-den) Castle, seven miles from Chester, just across the Welsh border. There he raised a large family, felled hundreds of trees for relaxation, and spent the toiling hours in his library-study known as the temple of peace.

Near the end of his life he founded the temple's annexe at St. Deiniol's, setting it up near the castle in a ramshackle structure and endowing it with £30,000 and 30,000 books. At age eighty he trundled many of the volumes over in a wheelbarrow, helped to shelve them, and was chagrined to find that 3 per cent of his purchased books were duplicates.

'The tin tabernacle' is how Peter Jagger, the Anglican minister who serves as warden (boss) and chief librarian of St. Deiniol's, describes the old place. Gladstone believed in spending money on books, not buildings, but after his death a stately sandstone building was erected as a gift to the nation and to those admitted to St. Deiniol's.

There is room for forty-six guests in single-, twin- and double-bedded rooms, each with desk as well as hot and cold running water – not quite as austere as monks' cells, but hardly the stuff of Helmsley, Hilton or Hyatt. On the other hand, do they have a stately oak library with about 130,000 books (great oaks from 30,000 little acorns grown), including 50,000 from the Victorian era, a thorough representation of English literature down to the close of the nineteenth century, a huge collection on theology from the seventeenth century onward? Can any of them boast of having the Gladstone family papers – a quarter of a million items – and even the 107 volumes of notes on some 5,130 English churches by Sir Stephen Glynne, Gladstone's brother-in-law? Do they have 38 volumes of Gladstone speeches, or books with Gladstone's annotations? And what about the pamphlet collection – about 40,000 separate loads of invective – including the one by Gladstone on the Vatican and civil allegiance that sold over 150,000 copies and earned him £2,000? Pope Pius IX himself helped with sales, by calling Gladstone 'a viper attacking the barque of St. Peter.'

'So you wish to undertake some research?' the library brochure asks. 'Are you writing a book? Would you like to catch up on your reading? Must you get away to prepare for an examination [or] need free access to a wide-ranging library?' I dismissed all such suggestions. All I wanted to do was satisfy my curiosity about a place that would not rent me an austere lodging before receiving a testimonial from 'a person holding public office, e.g., a university or college appointment, a clergyman, doctor or an already established Reader at St. Deiniol's.'

And how about the rates for room and board – including three nourishing meals, morning coffee, afternoon tea and bedtime tea or coffee – ranging from £8 (about $12) a day for full-time students and unemployed postgraduates, up to £17.83 (including tax) for those whose expenses are being paid or subsidized by non-church sources? 'Many pay £8 a day and it costs us £15,' said Mr. Jagger. 'At our prices we could fill our beds with people who want cheap holidays.'

He is not a rose-water cleric out of P.G. Wodehouse. This is a sturdy Yorkshire go-getter who not only studied theology for seven years, and history after that, but also burrowed deep into the techniques of business management. He welcomes conference groups, and he has performed miracles in getting tough business people to contribute services and odd bits of paving to St. Deiniol's. If he had just a little bit more loose change he would be delighted to upgrade the accommodations, and he also wants to build a quadrangle on the ground level for handicapped guests. 'If there's a Carnegie we'll call it the Carnegie wing,' he said, fixing me with a stern eye, as though I knew where the Carnegies spent their summer holidays.

Mr. Jagger is nonetheless a soft touch for hardship cases, or at least prepared to make the best of them. He gave some students room and board in exchange for their painting a back corridor. When the government cut off grants for library assistants, he kept several on as volunteers – again in exchange for room and board.

St. Deiniol's fills up at Easter, and is busy from June through September. There are fewer guests during the academic year, and the annual occupancy rate is about 60 per cent. Rank has no privilege here – the Archbishop of Canterbury, a member of Parliament and a secondary school student get identical accommodations. Michael Ramsay, who was to be Archbishop of Canterbury, wrote his first book here. Harold Wilson, one of Gladstone's successors as Prime Minister, wrote part of his Gladstone Prize Essay here. 'The great scholars get on with their work,' said Mr. Jagger. 'Some of the pretentious ones immediately let you know how important they are.'

I may or may not have rubbed shoulders at meals – served by waitresses – with a future prime minister, but I did meet a woman who was turning out a conscientious spot of homework. Dr. Ivy Oates, a sixty-nine-year-old general practitioner from Sheffield, came to St. Deiniol's for the first time ten years ago, and has been coming back regularly a week before her Open University exams, or for long weekends to prepare written assignments. 'At home you've got meals to get, and the house looks at you and the telephone goes,' she explained. 'Here it was quiet, it was beautiful, and the library has got the atmosphere conducive to study. You could work in peace and settle down without any trouble.'

In 1982 her course was the history of mathematics, in 1983 evolution, and in 1984, Science and Belief from Darwin to Einstein. 'You meet such nice people here,' Dr. Oates said. 'There was once an American lady here who got ill and called me in the night.'

Malcolm Lambert, who teaches medieval history at the University of Bristol, arrived for the first time in 1955 as a research student. 'I liked it because it was so cheap,' he said. 'It was three pounds a week, all found [room and board], and if you had a good feed once a week it was all right.' He stayed once for eighteen months, purchasing rare books he needed for his research that St. Deiniol's happened not to have, and he felt he was still coming out ahead.

Until thirty years ago women were not admitted as residents. Once they were, Professor Lambert met his wife-to-be at St. Deiniol's, and they eventually celebrated their silver wedding anniversary here. They now come to the library with their friends the Jarmans. Thomas Jarman wrote *The Rise and Fall of Nazi Germany*. 'Perhaps St. Deiniol's is a bit of a Shangri-La,' he said. 'You want to stay on. You don't want to leave.'

'In the old days they couldn't heat the place – didn't have enough money,' said Professor Lambert. 'It was a vicious circle – no money, no heating, no guests and no money.'

There is now effective central heating, and Professor Lambert had brought sixteen students – all paying their own way – who had just been admitted to Bristol to study history. The students were given assignments to prepare at St. Deiniol's, for example: 'Explain why the Kings of England were able to conquer Wales but not Scotland.' One seminar on medieval history was going to be held in the keep of

Hawarden's old castle. While I was at St. Deiniol's there was to be an after-dinner lecture on Franklin D. Roosevelt by John Kentleton, who teaches American history at the University of Liverpool. 'We have some of our lectures in the pub,' Professor Lambert told me, and his wife added: 'We thought we'd publish "The Fox and Grapes Papers."'

The Fox and Grapes is one of the three local pubs. At St. Deiniol's, going to the pub is known as 'choir practice.' Thus far Mr. Jagger has resisted pleas for a bar at the library, and for wine at meals.

So we all pressed our way to the pub bar for our drinks, and took them along into the small private room for the lecture. Having lived in the States during most of the years of the F.D.R. presidency, I arrogantly doubted whether I would learn much and expected a dry evening, but the lecture was informative and even gripping.

My neighbour and drinking partner at the talk, John Buchanan, is an Episcopal minister in Mount Pleasant, a suburb of Charleston, S.C. He was spending a six-month sabbatical at St. Deiniol's, along with his wife and his two daughters, who were attending Hawarden's secondary school. Mr. Buchanan's bishop, FitzSimons Allison, formerly of Grace Church in Manhattan, had stayed at St. Deiniol's, and recommended it. Mr. Buchanan was spending much of his time reading books on contemporary Christian spirituality.

Gladstone spoke of the purpose of St. Deiniol's as 'divine learning' – in which he included the classics. He wanted 'a house of study for the glory of God and the culture of man,' and 'intellectual hospice.' But he insisted that the hospitality 'should as far as possible be made available for persons beyond the pale of the Anglican Church or even of the Christian Religion.'

One of Mr. Jagger's predecessors tried to turn the library into a theological college, which was not the founder's intention, nor is it Mr. Jagger's. But the staff still prepares ordinands – over thirty years of age – for unpaid church service. 'We've trained lawyers, headmasters, schoolmasters, bank managers, doctors and engineers,' said Mr. Jagger, who acts as principal of the course.

The statutes require the warden-librarian to be a clerk in holy orders of the Anglican Communion, and he must abide by 'the rule of clerical subscription' – abstaining from diocesan or parish work. The first warden was Gladstone's son-in-law, and the cult of personality is still going strong: Mr. Jagger is working hard on a two-volume study of Gladstone as politician and Christian.

St. Deiniol's lives very much under the shadow of the great man. There are Gladstone portraits and statues, large and small, in halls, dining room, common room, floor hall, stairwell, gallery window and library proper. On the front lawn stands a huge Gladstone statue refused by Dublin, though Gladstone supported home rule for Ireland.

The very divisions that Gladstone imposed in the library still hold sway: *A* is prolegomena, *B* bible, *C* patristics, *D* philosophy, *E* doctrine, *F* spirituality, *G* godly worship, and so on, omitting *H* (hell?) and *I* (infidels? idolatry?), proceeding all the way to *W* – topography and travel. The library has open shelves, and readers can take books back to their rooms. There are no keys to bedroom doors, and there has never been a theft reported by any resident.

But this is not paradise. Gladstone's official correspondence – with the help of his secretaries Gladstone wrote 25,000 letters a year while Prime Minister – has been carted off to the British Museum, in 750 volumes. Most of the correspondence with the royal family is likewise in London, but that may be just as well. Gladstone was not precisely Victoria's favourite, nor she his – he called the Queen 'Her Infallibility.'

Sir William Gladstone, great-grandson of the founder, former Chief Scout of Britain, now lives in Hawarden Castle, acts as chairman of the library's management committee, and provides the library with passes admitting guests to his grounds.

St. Deiniol himself was not a Gladstone, but a sixth century Celtic saint. Despite all his miracles, he, too, would have had to submit a testimonial to get into this bookworm's heaven.

Applications and further information are available from the Booking Secretary, St. Deiniol's Library, Hawarden, Deeside, Clwyd CH5 3DF, North Wales; telephone Hawarden 532350.

MAKING TRACKS
THROUGH THE HIGHLANDS

John Chancellor

The wind off the Atlantic was Force 7, nearly a gale, buffeting the little train on the single track between the mountains and the lochs. The mountaintops were hidden in cloud; squalls stormed across the water; rain beat upon the windows of the train. It was cold and getting dark. Our destination was half an hour away.

But we were already at home. Six of us, in our own warm observation car, lamps lit, drinks in hand, watching the bad weather tumble across the spectacular Western Highlands of Scotland. We looked forward to a tasteful meal and a comfortable bed, all without leaving the train.

It was the fourth evening of a week's journey on our private train, a 640-mile trip from Glasgow north to the Western Highlands, to the islands of the Inner Hebrides, ending in Edinburgh. That night would be spent on a siding at Kyle of Lochalsh, a fishing village across the sound from the island of Skye.

We were a sextet of Americans travelling in two private rail cars, a day coach and a sleeping car. Regal accommodations. The sleeping car once had been part of the British Royal Train. The company that chartered the two cars said it was not permitted to publish the names of former occupants, but we could guess. The sleeper had been built in 1939, when George VI was King and Elizabeth (now Queen Elizabeth the Queen Mother) was Queen.

The day coach was built in 1920 for Sir Henry Thornton, general manager of the Great Eastern Railway, as his official coach. He was an American, and he ordered an observation platform, American style. British trains don't have them, and the platform – a rare sight in Britain – is called an open veranda. Inside, it is like riding in a very expensive cigar humidor. Everything is panelled in mahogany. Nothing has been changed since Sir Henry's day: exquisite woodwork, tufted black leather, sixty-five-year-old electrical switches, brass lamps, and flowers in cut-glass containers.

The two-car train is called the *Highland Belle*. The cars belong to a railroad museum in England and are the wheeled equivalent of landmark buildings; no alterations can be made, and they are to be returned to the museum. Gerard Morgan-Grenville, the British entrepreneur who started these charters in 1983, is searching for two cars of comparable quality, and hopes to run the train in 1986. If the service and accommodations remain as good as they were in May 1985, the passengers should be as happy as we were.

The trip began in Glasgow's Queen Street Station, where we were assembled under the courteous command of Captain Gerald Davie, a bearded Scot who is train director. Our two cars were attached to the afternoon train to Fort William. As it trundled through an enormous tunnel under Glasgow, we picked our rooms. The sleeping car has twin beds in the former royal sitting room, with buttons on the wall marked 'Waiter' and 'Valet.' There are four single rooms with washbasins, wardrobes and remarkably comfortable berths, and two large toilet/bathrooms with baths and showers. Fit for a king, I would think as I bathed.

The Glasgow-Fort William run took us through the hills above Loch Lomond and onto Rannoch Moor, a wild, barren, treeless plateau filled with peat bogs, small streams and tiny lochs. The rail line floats on a mattress of tree roots, brushwood and tons of earth and ash. Here and there stand shooting lodges, and, since there are few roads, hunters can arrange for the train to stop near the lodges.

Dinner that evening was served in the observation car's dining room. The car is fifty-eight feet long, with a lounge overlooking the open platform, a galley in the middle and a spacious dining area. The food was delicious, prepared by Sarah Leonard, a young English chef who learned her trade on barge charters in France, where she lives. The galley on the *Highland Belle* is small, but Sarah Leonard's talent is large. She can produce cheese soufflés served in tiny tomatoes while rocketing along at sixty miles an hour.

In addition to standard breakfast fare, she offered marvellous venison sausage, black pudding (a blood sausage that nobody liked) and herring in porridge. That sounds as though the porridge is served with bits of herring swimming in it, a combination we thought would be repulsive. It is not. The herring is breaded with porridge, then fried. It is only boring.

Dinners were sumptuous, beginning with crayfish or cock-a-leekie soup, proceeding to Scottish lamb, stuffed trout or salmon, delicious local cheeses, and desserts such as burnt caramel with mocha sauce or Scottish flummery. The wines were carefully chosen. We sometimes dressed for dinner.

The evenings were spent talking, going over maps or reading. A useful history of the Highlands and the clans is *The Scottish Highlanders* by Charles MacKinnon of Dunakin, laird of Dunakin Castle (St.

Martin's Press, 1984).

The rest of the train's staff consisted of a New Zealander, Joanna Maunsell, who served at table and made up our rooms, and Terry Atkinson, an intense young English technician whose passion is railroading on antique cars. Everyone was friendly and competent. Only Mr. Atkinson lives on the train. The others stay in bed-and-breakfast houses along the way. They leave the train after ten at night and return at seven in the morning. We thought that was a hard life, but they seemed to enjoy it.

The fifth staff member is Tom Wilson, a Scot who spends his evenings driving across Scotland so he can meet the train the next day and take the passengers on tour in his van. The *Highland Belle* is more than a train trip. It is a guided tour of parts of Scotland, and Mr. Wilson, a former ship's pilot, is the guide.

On our second day, he drove us from Fort William to one of the most beautiful places in Scotland, Loch Shiel, where the Glenfinnan Monument stands at the head of the loch. It was here, in 1745, that Bonnie Prince Charlie rallied several clans to fight in his ill-fated Jacobite rebellion.

The highlight of that day was a boat trip through the mist of the Hebrides to the island of Rhum. A picnic lunch was served as we cruised past the island of Eigg (Rhum, Eigg and a third island named Muck are sometimes called the 'cocktail islands'). There is a great Edwardian folly on Rhum, Kinloch Castle, a crazed extravaganza of a house built when the island was the private estate of the Bulloughs of Lancashire. The family's wealth was limitless and so was its taste for the latest gadgetry of 1901. There is a crude form of air conditioning in the billiard room that can clear the air of cigar smoke in twenty minutes. We were serenaded by a clamorous electric automaton that played drums, horns and flutes as we drank tea in front of a roaring fire.

So we passed our days, sleeping aboard each night, riding on the train or in the van each day. We became connoisseurs of rail yards, stations and sidings. The best siding was at Kyle of Lochalsh, with fishing boats on one side, a handsome station on the other, and the sparkling waters of Loch Alsh at the end of the observation platform. The worst location was in the centre of Inverness Station, where we were objects of understandable public curiosity.

On the third day we staged a rebellion. We had spent hours in the van, driving through the Tayside region in an aimless sort of way, part of the time in the rain and the rest in glorious sunshine. The day had ended at Scone Palace in Perth, where we were welcomed by a piper, given sherry and a private tour. It was very grand but we were very tired. When we finally boarded the train at Perth, we were exhausted.

We told Captain Davie that we felt overprogrammed, and he said we could spend all day every day on the train if that's what we wanted. Some previous passengers had done just that.

We settled into a slower routine that allowed time for relaxation. Some of us read, some stood on the observation platform, waving to local people and breathing the mountain air, and some took naps. We had found our rhythm. There is a special quality about a long ride on a private train. The train becomes a world in itself, distanced from the scenery, which rolls endlessly by, separate from the countryside outside. The passengers and the staff became a little community of eleven happy people.

There were smaller excursions: we were taken to Urquhart Castle on Loch Ness (the monster did not appear); to Cawdor Castle, where, according to Shakespeare, Macbeth murdered Duncan; to the battlefield of Culloden, where Bonnie Prince Charlie's army of tartaned Highlanders was defeated; and to Kinloch Hotel on the island of Skye, where we ate a superb lunch. One of the staff of the *Highland Belle* had telephoned ahead to make sure we were not fed what we would be eating that night aboard the train.

The terrain included broad river valleys, the rocky coves and sea lochs of the Atlantic coastline, and tall mountains. Ben Nevis, 4,406 feet high, is the highest peak in Britain; it towers above the handsome city of Fort William, which is at sea level on Loch Linnhe. At Balmacara Estate on the coast, warmed by the Gulf Stream, there is an enchanting woodland garden where the rhododendrons were in brilliant bloom. Palm trees lined the esplanade at Plockton. The West Highland Line rises to 1,350 feet at Corrour, surrounded by peaks twice that high, windswept and desolate. One of the few snowsheds in Britain is here, to protect the tracks from winter snowdrifts and avalanches. We were glad we had packed sweaters. We shopped for tartans and woollens in Perth and Inverness, Glasgow and Edinburgh.

Sometimes our two cars were attached to the end of a scheduled train, which meant stopping at every station. Travel by train is important in Scotland. The trains and the stations are spotless, and the railroad employees we met were unfailingly cheerful and courteous. Once in a while we would be pulled by our own diesel locomotive, which meant no stops until we reached our destination. The tiny train would speed along, clicking and clacking at what seemed to be ninety miles an hour. At one stop, the three men in our party were allowed to sit in the engineer's seat, and we acted like teenagers on an outing.

There is an awesome beauty about the Highlands, but a terrible history, which explains much. The Earl of Cawdor refers to his ancestors as 'gangsters.' The MacGregors and Colquhouns, the Campbells and MacDonalds made the Hatfields and McCoys of eastern Kentucky look like pacifists. And what the clan chiefs did to the crofters, the peasants, in the eighteenth and nineteenth centuries, was worse.

Before their defeat at Culloden in 1746, the Highland crofters paid their rent by serving as soldiers for their clan chiefs. But Culloden was the last land battle in the British Isles. When there was no further need for crofters as warriors, their chiefs demanded cash, which the crofters didn't have. The chiefs then leased the crofters' land to Lowland and English sheep farmers. The crofters were evicted from holdings some had occupied since before written history. From 1785 to 1854, the years of a tragedy called the Highland Clearances, the crofters were brutally removed from their land, forced into the slums of Glasgow or Edinburgh, or into ships that took them to Canada or America. A Scottish diaspora. By 1860, the Highlands were empty of all but the sheep and the shepherds.

That is what the Highland traveller finds today, a vast emptiness of great natural beauty, sudden rain, sudden sun, a sense of hidden territory, and something undefinably mysterious, dark and bloody in those high hills and deep lochs.

We came out of the Highlands on the final day, riding south from Inverness through the grandeur of the Grampian Mountains, down across the high moorland into the peaceful pastoral valley of the River Garry. The locomotive pulling our two cars slowed as Blair Castle came into sight. It belongs to the Duke of Atholl, who is the only British subject allowed to maintain a private army. On our private train, we saluted.

Most charters on the *Highland Belle* last one week, but it can be chartered for two. When we disembarked that afternoon, each of us would have stayed for another seven days, if not forever.

Train Lover's Guide
The railroads through the Highlands of Scotland remain, for many, the best way of exploring the wildest and most romantic countryside in Britain. Take the train to Wick, or Thurso – Britain's most northernly station and close to John o'Groats – and you will not see highway or house for tens of miles during its remotest section.

The watchful traveller will likely see deer, perhaps standing against the horizon, erect and proud like the subject of Landseer's painting; the lucky may spot an eagle soaring over the peat-brown bogs.

The most southerly of the routes into the Highlands, to Fort William and Mallaig, starts at Glasgow's Queen Street Station: The West Highland line threads its way through the suburbs of Scotland's second city, skirting the river Clyde, and turns abruptly north to run along the shores of Gare Loch, Loch Long and Loch Lomond, called the queen of Scottish lakes and the largest freshwater lake in Britain. The finest views of the loch may be had in fall and winter because its banks are heavily wooded.

Near the Inversnaid Hotel on the far side of the loch is the cave where Rob Roy, the outlaw romanticized by Sir Walter Scott, questioned his captives. From Glen Falloch – Wordsworth's 'vale of awful sound' – Crianlarich is reached, a junction where the lines to Fort William and Oban diverge. Taking the northerly route to Fort William enables the traveller to experience some of the most desolate scenery in Scotland, the wilds of Rannoch Moor. Along Loch Treig the sound of rushing water is heard continually, for in five miles there are 150 bridges over the watercourses that tumble down the hillside.

The character of the scenery changes dramatically as the train heads down the narrowing defile of Glen Spean to Monessie Gorge, where the railroad clings to a ledge above fuming water. As the train leaves Spean Bridge, the Commando Monument may be seen to the right, commemorating the area's use as a training ground during World War II. Old and new castles at Inverlochy are passed before the train draws to a halt in the modern station at Fort William, 123 miles from Glasgow. The largest town on this stretch of the coast, Fort William has many hotels and tourist facilities.

Among recent developments is the introduction of steam-hauled trains from Fort William over the forty-two-mile line to Mallaig, a gateway to the Western Isles. These specials, which run throughout the summer, in addition to the regular diesel trains, have proved immensely popular, combining the charisma of steam with perhaps the most beautiful rail journey in Britain. The railroad was one of the last to be built in Britain, opening as late as 1901. Crossing the southern point of Telford's Caledonian Canal, the train heads west to skirt the shores of Loch Eil with the dominant peak of Ben Nevis over one's shoulder. On a great horseshoe curve, the line crosses over Glen Finnan on one of the first concrete viaducts in the world.

As the line makes its sinuous way to the Atlantic at Loch nan Uamh, there is more than a touch of the South Seas to the scenery, with the deep blue of the sea, the brilliant colours of the trees and tropical plants that enjoy the warmth of the Gulf Stream. The islands of Rhum and flat-topped Eigg come into view as the train continues to Morar, where white sands stretch for miles along the sea. To the east, a glimpse may be had of Loch Morar, more than 1,000 feet deep and the deepest inland water in Britain, before journey's end at Mallaig, on the water's edge. The spot overlooks the Sound of Sleat to the island of Skye.

There are three trains a day in each direction between Glasgow and Fort William, and four between Fort William and Mallaig. An overnight sleeping car service is also available between Fort William and Euston Station in London, Saturdays excepted.

Farther north, Inverness, regarded as the Highland capital, is served by fast trains from Edinburgh and Glasgow, an overnight sleeping car from London and a daily high-speed train connection with London's

King's Cross. Inverness is an excellent starting point for a tour of the north of Scotland. The journey between Perth and Inverness goes through the heart of the Grampian Mountains, which offer winter sports based on the skiing and holiday resort of Aviemore. Summer visitors may relive the age of steam on the preserved railroad between Aviemore and quaintly named Boat of Garten.

The railroad to the isles – the line from Inverness to Kyle of Lochalsh – is another route much admired by train lovers. Built to serve the islands off the west coast and the few communities en route, the eighty-two-mile run passes through lovely scenery and terminates on the very edge of the water opposite Kyleakin on Skye. (The one-way fare on this one-class train is about $10.) There are three trains daily to Kyle, the second of which has an observation car. First they run through farmland and then hug the shoreline of Loch Garve. The central section of the line crosses peat bogs until Achnasheen. (Several stations on the line were originally either private or paid for by local landowners, who would head north from their English country houses to their shooting lodges for the annual round of deer-stalking and grouse shooting.)

The finest section begins at Strathcarron, at the head of the sea loch called Carron. The train is never far from the southern edge of the loch as it makes its way over the final ten miles to Kyle.

This part of the line cost five times as much per mile as the rest of the railroad because much of the track bed had to be blasted from solid rock. The view constantly changes as the train weaves along the shore. The fishing village of Plockton precedes the arrival at Kyle, where trains draw to a halt on the pier. Just a few minutes' walk from the station is the Lochalsh Hotel, with views across the water to Skye.

Another railroad could form an unusual route for the tourist to reach Ireland: the line from Glasgow Central to the ferry port of Stranraer. It enjoys scenery of great variety and is served by a frequent schedule of trains and an overnight sleeping car from London's Euston. Evidence of past and present industrial activity accompanies the early stages of the route from Glasgow, but agricultural land is soon reached and golf courses, such as Turnberry, Prestwick and Troon, are a feature of the Ayrshire coast. Ayr itself is a resort and the coastline to the south, which is followed by the railway, is protected for the scientific interest of its volcanic rocks.

The greatest attraction of the coast between Ayr and Girvan, however, is Culzean Castle, transformed by Robert Adam between 1777 and 1792 into a clifftop home of remarkable beauty. Between Girvan and Stranraer the line traverses wild and remote country, though it lacks the scale of the Highlands. Stranraer is on Loch Ryan, which saw intense activity during World War II when a major harbour for the importation of war material from the United States was developed at Cairnryan.

Train Passes

A wide range of travel passes and tickets are available on British Rail, which also sells hotel and travel packages through its own travel company, **Golden Rail Holidays** (Golden Rail Holidays, P.O. Box 12, York YO1 1YX, England). —Anthony J. Lambert

SECOND HELPINGS CHEZ GIRARDET

Barbara Gelb

Lunch was seven courses, not counting a little hors d'oeuvre of an onion tart; delicate and delectable, it was presented, smilingly, as an *amusebouche*. Lunch lasted from noon until three.

For dinner, the third course was a *consommé de langoustines*, an ambrosian broth made from crayfish, in which floated points of baby asparagus and franc-size ravioli stuffed with fresh caviar. The broth's purpose, our captain explained, was 'to wash the stomach, so that you can eat more.' We found – my three table companions and I – that indeed we could. Dinner, too, was seven courses and lasted from eight until eleven.

I had been hearing about Restaurant Girardet – 'conceivably the greatest French restaurant on the European continent' – from my old friend Craig Claiborne ever since Craig discovered and first wrote about it in 1976. Fredy Girardet, Craig said, 'has, solely on his own native talent, become one of the greatest creative forces in the world of chefs today, second neither to Bocuse, Guérard, Vergé or any of the other titans on the European scene.' Since then, other travellers I knew also came back sighing over the delights of Mr. Girardet's kitchen. And so I made it a point to plan a detour during a recent European trip that would allow me to eat at Restaurant Girardet.

Since the restaurant is in Crissier, a tiny Swiss village a few miles outside Lausanne, and not a place I am likely to visit often, I decided that I must make the most of my detour and dine at Girardet's twice. There are so many remarkable dishes on the menu (supplemented by Mr. Girardet's spontaneous embellishments) that once is not enough to get a fair sampling of what the restaurant has to offer – no more than is one swim in the Caribbean enough; you have to swim by moonlight as well as at sunrise. And since I was on a tight schedule, I arranged – well in advance – to have both lunch and dinner there on the same day.

Mr. Girardet is a showman as well as a chef, and he likes nothing better than to improvise a menu for an appreciative and adventurous diner. Not to put oneself into his hands is to miss the true joy of dining 'chez Girardet,' as the proprietor likes to refer to his establishment.

There is an ample menu listing a variety of seafood, meat and poultry dishes, and it should be studied as a jumping-off point – if you object to eating rabbit, say, it would be wise to mention that.

We were greeted on a Saturday noon by Louis Villeneuve, the white-coated maître d'hôtel. He was pleased when we told him we wished to put ourselves entirely in the hands of Mr. Girardet, and would welcome whatever he chose to serve us.

'Americans are often difficult to please,' Mr. Villeneuve said. 'We offer to serve them what Mr. Girardet has decided to prepare that day. We want to give pleasure. But often they want something different.'

Since we were to eat both lunch and dinner on the same day, the meals were designed by Mr. Girardet to harmonize with each other, to be unrepetitious and to be composed of small portions of light and subtly seasoned food, so that we could sample as many different dishes as possible.

The pièce de résistance of our lunch, and one of the restaurant's famous specialities, was *salade de foie de canard chaud* – hot duck liver served in a vinaigrette sauce. It's difficult to do justice to the taste of this delicacy; the exquisitely browned slice of liver gleams like a Fabergé enamel flower amid vivid swirls of emerald-green chive, slivers of jade lettuce, ruby-red radicchio and chips of topaz carrot – almost too beautiful to eat, but much too fragrant to resist. It's like being nourished on delicious air, a morsel so ethereal that you are barely aware of eating.

Knowing we would be wowed by this dish, Mr. Girardet sent to us for our inspection and admiration – part of the ritual and dazzle – a whole, raw duck liver. Our headwaiter, John Davey, explained that Mr. Girardet regularly sends a personal representative to the Landes district in southwest France to shop for the livers, which are about the size of a small cantaloupe (the duck must be the size of a kangaroo). The raw liver is pale and silky and glistens like platinum. The restaurant buys about thirty-five pounds of liver each week and makes it into terrines and pâtés, as well as serving it as a *salade chaude*.

Our headwaiter, who asked us to call him John, was chatty and good-humoured, like the rest of the dining room staff. He is from Bristol, England, and is married to a Swiss, and he seemed to regard himself as a combination master of ceremonies and ringmaster – but in a manner that was amusing without being at all intrusive. And that is another of the restaurant's unusual qualities. It is rare to find an establishment of such impeccable cuisine, so flawlessly presented, where there is not the slightest whiff of hauteur, or, for that matter, of subservience. The help are all young, with shining faces and open manners.

'We like anyone who likes to eat,' one of our waiters told us, when we commented about two groups that were admitted despite having dogs in tow. 'If the dogs sit quietly, we don't mind. We even allow infants in arms, if they do not cry and disturb others. We allow everyone to benefit from our kitchen.'

The restaurant's two dining rooms – the total seating capacity is about seventy – are housed in what was formerly the Crissier town hall, built in 1929 (the modest, three-storey building of grey and pale green stone still bears the words *Hôtel de Ville* chiselled into its lintel). It is on a lazy street where few cars go by and at its end, beyond a church, you can see a snow-capped mountain. Yellow and purple pansies are clustered at the restaurant's entrance, and there are boxes filled with flowers at all the windows.

In the larger dining room, where we ate, clear, soft light poured through windows hung with translucent ivory-coloured curtains. The décor seems as far as Mr. Girardet could get from the red velvet and oak panelling indulged in by some of the traditional establishments of French three-star cooking; but for Girardet's, the simplicity of a monochromatic setting works perfectly.

The walls are a pale cream stucco trimmed with dark wood. A few muted paintings adorn the walls. The floor is tiled in an amber colour and left bare. 'I don't like carpets; they are not clean,' Mr. Girardet says. The tables are covered with cloths of beige-on-beige, stamped with a discreet lower-case monogram (fg); the china is fluted but plain white – the better to display the subtle colours of the food – and the cutlery is utilitarian and includes the all-important flat, scalloped spoon for scooping up vestiges of sauce. The tall, cane-back chairs are just straight enough to encourage you to sit up and take your food seriously, but comfortable enough that you can linger without restlessness for three hours.

After the duck liver, we were served little daisy-shaped ravioli stuffed with grilled parsley, garnished with black truffles and sparkling in a gentle sauce of butter, port and what Mr. Girardet calls truffle essence.

The next course was a slice of red mullet decorated with scales cut from courgettes and seasoned with olive oil and herbs. And that was followed – we had assured John that none of us minded eating rabbit – by *aigulette de lapin au romarin*, slices of tender meat, not unlike veal, in a rosemary sauce, accompanied by pearly new potatoes, whole, tiny young carrots and a bracelet of snow peas and bits of sliced turnip, all grown nearby.

With lunch we drank local wines, a custom highly recommended by two of my dining companions, both knowlegeable travellers in Switzerland and both much better able than I to judge wine. The first was a tart white that almost sparkled, a Fendant de Sion, made from a grape called Chasselas; it tasted something like a Pouilly Fumé. The second was a Pinot Blanc de Clavoz, much appreciated by my companions.

We lingered at table over coffee, talking to Mr. Villeneuve. He asked if we would like to inspect the kitchen on our way out. It was nearly four, and we found the kitchen – spacious, with enormous windows that fill the room with sunshine – completely tidied and scrubbed spotlessly clean, with not only the floors and counters, but also the windows, walls and ceiling newly washed.

To fill in the four hours before we were to return to dinner, we drove a bit through the countryside, which resembles that of Burgundy, particularly in its fields of velvety green, overlaid with a blanket of brilliant yellow rape flowers, from whose seed an inexpensive cooking oil is extracted.

We followed Lake Geneva's northern shore eastward for about twenty miles, from Lausanne to Montreux. The drive was lovely on the golden, late spring afternoon, with the sun still high. On our right, the lake itself was serene, filled with darting white sails and the reflection of snowy mountains. On our left were the terraced vineyards typical of the region.

As we drove through Vevey one of our party exclaimed at the sight (missed by the rest of us) of a small sculptured figure standing, without a pedestal, in a strip of grassy park along the lakefront; he was sure, even from a quick glimpse, that it was Charlie Chaplin, probably Vevey's most famous citizen (and according to Mr. Girardet, at one time a good customer of the restaurant). None of us had heard of such a statue being erected after Chaplin's death, and we agreed to examine it on our way back.

We visited Chillon Castle, made famous by Byron's *The Prisoner of Chillon*, then headed back toward Lausanne. The area was crowded with cars and tour buses, and by mistake we turned the wrong way into an access road. A small boy on a bicycle scolded us in shrill Swiss-German for our error. 'Every Swiss is a cop at birth,' muttered the friend who was driving our car.

At Vevey's Quai Perdonnet, we stopped to inspect the statue we had glimpsed earlier. It was indeed of Chaplin, dressed in a cutaway and bowler, leaning on his crooked cane with one hand clutching a rose to his breast, the costume and stance of his character in *City Lights*. The statue, commissioned and paid for by the town of Vevey, was made by John Doubleday, a British artist, and was installed in 1982. We could find no plaque, but an official of Vevey later assured me that there is one inscribed '*L'acteur genial qui procura tant de joie a tant de monde.*'

Returning to Girardet for dinner at eight felt something like coming back for the second half of *Nicholas Nickleby*. We visited the kitchen again, to see it gearing up. There is a staff of eighteen and, like the dining room staff, they are young and amiable, ready – even in the midst of preparing dinner – to chat. The cooks, all men, are accustomed to being put on display, and they were wisecracking in several languages; they obviously take great pride and pleasure in the culinary performance. They are apprentices to a master and they know it. Mr. Girardet believes that 'four or five of the young people' in his kitchen 'will one day be excellent chefs.'

In one section of the kitchen the ingredients for pastries were laid out, but they would not be put into the ovens until much later; the preparation of the traditional petits fours, served at the end of every meal, would not even be begun until nine o'clock.

At the evening meal it is Mr. Girardet's custom to greet his guests. He came to our table, elegant and poised in his white jacket and tall, crisp chef's hat, to ask if there was anything special we wished to try for dinner. We said we would, again, leave the menu to him, and he smiled with an artist's pleased assurance. Later, he told us, 'This morning I had no idea what I'd make for you. It gives me great pleasure to prepare an individual menu, but the customer must open himself to us.'

As we ate our first course of *gelée de poulette au fenouil* – chicken and fennel in aspic, garnished with a whisper of leeks and radishes – John said that Mr. Girardet was considering making us a lamb dish, if that was agreeable, and one of my companions, who dislikes lamb, politely demurred. No problem, said John, and asked how we felt about kidneys – which Mr. Girardet likes to combine with sweetbreads. That sounded good to me, but another of my companions asked if the dish could be made with sweetbreads only, and John said he was certain it could be.

Again, we drank local wine, starting with a Dezaley. The second course was *saumon aux navets*, a small, deliberately undercooked salmon steak, accompanied by tiny sweet turnips and served with a chervil sauce. The fish, Mr. Girardet later told me, was 'wild' salmon, imported from Scotland. The seasoning was perfect, and I noticed for the first time that there were no salt or pepper shakers on the table; they were not needed.

The third course was the ambrosian langoustine broth, which John said Mr. Girardet very rarely prepared. One of my companions murmured that it was the sort of dish of which his European mother would have said, 'You must eat this with your head.'

Our second bottle of dinner wine, something special to accompany the consommé, was a 1978 Pinot Noir du Valais from Mr. Girardet's special reserve. It was an equally appropriate accompaniment to the next course, sweetbreads tenderly wrapped in succulent, garden-fresh lettuce. The portions, though large enough to be satisfying, were never huge, and all of us felt we could go on forever. But we restrained ourselves and had only two desserts: an exquisitely airy passion fruit soufflé, followed by an assortment of ice creams – pine nut, vanilla and caramel, purer in flavour and creamier than any ice cream I had ever tasted.

Mr. Girardet joined us over coffee. Most of the dishes he had served us, he said, were classics of French cuisine. 'But even the classics, in personal preparation, change,' he added. 'I deduced from your appreciation of the lunch what to do for dinner; this evening I did something completely different. I wish we could know all our customers, hear them talk about food. Then we could tailor menus for them.'

The restaurant does file copies of the menus served to its regular customers; members of the staff – if not always Mr. Girardet himself – try to determine a new client's preferences from a tableside 'interview,' if the client is not set in advance about what to order.

'I try to be pure and straight,' Mr. Girardet said. 'I want young people to take pleasure in my food, as well as the elite. Good cuisine is for all people who take pleasure in it. I like to do things sincerely. I may make errors, but they are not errors of insincerity. We have no formality here; no ties are required. A restaurant is part of life. If there are restraints, it is not a good restaurant. People come not for show, but to enjoy food.'

Chez Girardet is a family affair, with Mr. Girardet's wife, Muriel, and his mother, Georgette, both acting as managers. Mr. Girardet's father, Benjamin, ran a small restaurant in this same building when Fredy was growing up. 'My father had a great influence on my life,' Mr. Girardet said. 'He had great wisdom. I lived in an almost perpetual culinary discussion, but my parents tried to discourage me from being in the restaurant business. They said one could have no normal family life. So I began at fifteen to learn the trade of typesetting. But after two months, I couldn't stand it. I said, I have to go into the kitchen.' Mr. Girardet, who is forty-eight, was twenty-nine when his father died. He bought the building that houses his restaurant in 1969.

Mr. Girardet bicycles to stay fit and to clear his mind. He told us he was planning to leave at ten the following morning for Gstaad, by bicycle, a ride of three hours and forty-five minutes. His wife and daughter, who is seventeen, had preceded him there for the weekend. The time on a bicycle, he said, is 'a time you battle against yourself. You are alone with nature. You think of nothing.' Not even *foie de canard*.

CHEZ FREDY

Restaurant Girardet, 1 Rue d'Yverdon, 1023 Crissier, Switzerland (telephone 34 15 14), suggests that reservations for dinner be made three months in advance. For Saturday lunch, reserve two months in advance; for weekday lunch, two weeks. The restaurant is closed on Sundays, Mondays and some holidays. Prices at the restaurant are not low; they can easily run $50 to $75 a person with local wines.

If you have time, the best plan is to spend several days in the area, so that you can dine chez Girardet at least twice. Crissier is about a $10 taxi ride from the centre of Lausanne, which has abundant hotels. The **Lausanne Palace** (20 37 11) and the lakeside **Beau-Rivage Palace** (26 38 31) offer many amenities; both have double rooms for about $110, including breakfast and taxes. Rates at the somewhat more modest **Royal-Savoy** (26 42 01) and the central **De la Paix** (20 71 71) are about $90 for a double room with breakfast and taxes.

THE CITY BENEATH ROME

William Weaver

In 1956, the pastor of **San Pietro in Vincoli**, the Roman church that houses Michelangelo's *Moses*, decided that the basilica needed a new pavement. So he ordered the old floor taken up, to be replaced by the polished travertine marble found there today. Before the digging had gone very far, the workmen came upon some ancient remains; and the simple replacement of the floor turned into a complex project of excavation that went on for several years. Like almost every building in the heart of Rome, San Pietro in Vincoli was built over layers of other constructions. Somewhat to his dismay, the pastor found a cross-section of Roman history beneath his feet.

In their haste to see the *Moses* (and to get back to the bus and on to other sights), tourists scurry past the little iron railing under the portico of the church that marks the entrance to the excavations. Visitors with more time, and more curiosity, seek out a priest (ring the bell in the left nave) and ask to be shown the underground discoveries. The descent is not always comfortable. A certain amount of stooping is involved, and you have to watch out for scraped elbows, but with the priest's guidance, you can discern five layers of Rome: today's church; then traces of the fifteenth century church constructed by Sixtus IV; a fifth century basilica (its columns are embedded in the foundations of the later churches); fragments of a villa from Nero's day (perhaps an adjunct to his Golden House), and fragments of terracotta lamps and pots that give evidence of a more primitive settlement. At the Neronian level there is the outline of a Roman pool, but to reach it today you have to crawl on all fours across a stretch of dusty rubble. I took it on faith.

Everywhere in Rome there are patches of the subterranean city, or rather cities: an austere, special world, of which the catacombs and the excavations under St. Peter's are the best-known portions. Rome has its spelunkers who, armed with powerful flashlights, gumboots and cameras, drop down manholes, essay caverns or simply dig in open fields. But the sub-Rome is also accessible to less venturesome visitors. For a first glimpse of it, I recommend a visit to **San Clemente**, a subtly rich little basilica a short walk from the Colosseum.

The present church contains, among other treasures, a superb twelfth century mosaic of the Triumph of the Cross and frescoes by Masolino that include the much-reproduced St. Christopher, a friendly giant carrying the infant Christ. Today's San Clemente was built in the twelfth century, over a fourth century church that, naturally, stood over ancient Roman constructions.

Excavation beneath San Clemente began in the nineteenth century, under the direction of the Irish Dominicans who have long governed the church. As you descend the stairs to the lower levels, the first thing you perceive is the silence: It has a different, more intense quality than the hushed atmosphere of the street-level church.

The second level (today's church counts as the first) is the fourth century church, in use until 1100, with some just legible frescoes, among them a Byzantine-style scene of Christ sitting in judgement. On this level one of the most revered places is the presumed tomb of St. Cyril, who died in Rome in AD 869. With his brother Methodius, he was active among the Slavic nations and invented the Cyrillic alphabet (some modern marble plaques, in that alphabet, here mark the devotion of Eastern European Catholics).

Near this bare, cramped shrine, another staircase leads down to the third, lowest level. The walls of what was probably a large Roman house are now visible; this may have been the titulus of Clement (a titulus, in early Christian Rome, was a private home that served as a place of semiclandestine Christian meeting and worship, and was, in effect, the focus of a parish). A narrow street divides it from what is thought to have been an insula, the Roman equivalent of an apartment house. In its court was a temple to Mithras, a Persian god popular in Rome for the first few centuries after Christ. The temple included a triclinium, where you can still see the stone couches on which devotees of the cult reclined for the ritual feast.

At this level, the unearthly (or under-earthly) silence is broken by a sound of rushing water: a buried stream (you can glimpse it, at one point, through a grille), whose source is one of the mysteries of San Clemente. As I stood in the narrow street, so narrow that I could touch both walls, I was suddenly shocked to hear shrill, childish voices. If they hadn't been crying out in French, they would have seemed the friendly ghosts of children of Trajan's time, playing tag, as some kids of modern Rome were playing in the Via San Giovanni in Laterano, eight or nine yards above my head.

The sense of past life is also strongly felt in the catacombs, strangely, because the catacombs, after all, were cemeteries. But, just as in Italy today (especially in small towns), collective visits to the cemetery were an established practice in the early days of Christianity, religious but also social in nature. Frescoes in many of the catacombs depict the refrigerium, the funeral banquet or commemorative meal at which families gathered at a tomb to break bread together.

In my childhood, the ancient Roman movie was a genre as distinct as the Western; in those pictures the early Christians always seemed pious, boring and unreal, as, dressed in white, they died, singing hymns or smiling seraphically, while the luckier pagans ate grapes, drank wine, kissed girls and drove fast chariots. But the catacombs give you a different view of the early Christians. Some, indeed, were saints, but many were ordinary people with ordinary pursuits; near their graves (especially in the Sant'Agnese catacomb) you see the incised symbols of their trades – a trowel for a mason, a side of ham for a pig-butcher.

Nobody seems to know how many catacombs there are in Rome: one of my guides said sixty, another said more than a hundred. Besides the Christian catacombs, there are also pagan and Jewish ones. More are being discovered all the time, but many – for reasons of economy – are not regularly open to the public. Cynical travellers say that if you've seen one catacomb, you've seen them all. This is partly true, but the effect of visiting them is cumulative. In any case, asked to recommend one catacomb to stand for all, I would suggest the vast cemetery under the church of **San Sebastiano**, on the Appian Way. It is not the richest catacomb, but it is certainly the most famous; during the Middle Ages, while the other catacombs were forgotten, pilgrims still came to this spot to pay homage to the early martyrs.

The entrance to the catacombs is through a doorway in the walled forecourt of the little baroque church of San Sebastiano. My latest visit there was on a Monday morning (the catacombs here are open when Roman museums and galleries are closed); I was the only visitor, so I had the guide all to myself. He was an enthusiastic scholar and, I think, a priest; it was hard to tell, because he was wearing a woolly sweater. It was a hot day, but I, too, had brought a sweater along. In the sweltering Roman summer, the catacombs have the added attraction of a temperature reminiscent of the most enthusiastic American air conditioning.

We descended to the first chamber, with the tomb of St. Sebastian himself. The room is plain, except for a simple table altar and a marble bust of the saint, somewhat dubiously attributed to Bernini. Long a place of cult worship, the chapel is still the site of an annual pilgrimage on St. Sebastian's feast day, January 20. From there the real catacombs begin: rows and rows of shelf-like niches carved out of the porous tufa rock. Bodies were simply wrapped in shrouds, then sealed in a niche with a slab of marble or, with poorer families, brick. These graves can easily be dated, since Roman tax laws required brick makers to stamp their bricks with a device bearing the Emperor's name. The San Sebastiano cemetery was in use from the first to the fifth century AD.

As space was needed, the Christians simply dug deeper into the tufa, and the catacombs comprise many miles of passages – needless to say, the visitor is not conducted through all of them. Besides the niches, there are the grander arcosolium tombs, sarcophagi with an arch above them. At the end of the visit there are three impressive brick-faced mausoleums, pedimented like three miniature temples, their elegance in contrast to the more humble Christian graves.

Since the San Sebastiano catacombs were always known, they were subject to vandalism and are relatively bare (though some interesting and beautiful wall decorations do survive, including a charming fresco of an appetizing bowl of fruit with a plump bird pecking at a grape). But the **San Callisto** catacombs, nearby, were 'lost' for more than a thousand years and rediscovered only in 1849 by the pioneering Italian archaeologist Giovan Battista De Rossi, who found them while visiting a vineyard. Pope Pius IX bought the land at once, and excavations began.

The San Callisto catacombs are a short, pleasant walk from San Sebastiano. After crossing a busy road, you enter the Vatican's property, a flourishing farm, where you proceed between fields of corn and wheat, past a flourishing kitchen garden (I paused for an envious inspection of the fat artichokes and luxuriant tomato plants).

One of De Rossi's early discoveries was the important crypt of the Popes, with loculi containing the remains of nine Pontiffs from the third century, identified by marble plaques. He went on to bring to light frescoes, mosaics and carvings, still visible. Among the most striking are the frescoes of six praying figures (in a cell curiously misnamed 'The Five Saints') and an early third century fresco of Christ the Good Shepherd, a favourite theme in several catacombs. The excavation was fresh when Nathaniel Hawthorne visited the catacombs in the late 1850s and used them for a scene in his Roman novel, *The Marble Faun*: 'They went joyously down into that vast tomb, and wandered by torchlight through a sort of dream, in which reminiscences of church-aisles and grimy cellars – and chiefly the latter – seemed to be broken into fragments . . . The intricate passages along which they followed their guide had been hewn, in some forgotten age, out of a dark-red, crumbly stone. On either side were horizontal niches, where, if they held their torches closely, the shape of a human body was discernible in white ashes, into which the entire mortality of a man or woman had resolved itself.'

Torchlight has been replaced by electricity, but otherwise today's experience is much like Hawthorne's. His stern puritanism often made him an unsympathetic tourist: The accent on the grimy cellar is indicative. But catacombs are, indeed, not to everyone's taste. In 1788, the more sympathetic Goethe went to San Sebastiano, meaning to visit the catacombs, but he reported: 'I had hardly taken a step into that airless place before I began to feel uncomfortable, and I immediately returned to the light of day and the fresh air . . .'

The grottoes of **St. Peter's** are not catacombs exactly; rather, they are the result of a quarter century of excavation, begun in 1940 at the command of Pope Pius XII and concluded in 1965, after the discovery not only of the grave of St. Peter but also of most of a skeleton that is generally accepted as the saint's. Visit is by appointment, since groups have necessarily to be kept small.

Our party, about a dozen in all, met in the Piazza dei Protomartiri on the south side of the basilica, once the site of the Circus of Nero, where St. Peter – like countless other Christians – was probably martyred.

In exploring the substrata of Rome, it is often hard, even impossible to grasp the architectural sense of a complex site. To assist the visitor, in the anteroom of the grottoes there is a scale model, showing the relationship between the first basilica of St. Peter's, erected by Constantine in the fourth century, and the earlier aedicula, the little monument built to protect the remains of St. Peter not long after his death. The aedicula stood within a necropolis bounded by the so-called 'red wall' of monumental niches which provided evidence essential to authenticating the site of St. Peter's grave. Visitors are invited to take a long look at this model, which then makes the subsequent progress through the excavations more rewarding.

To build his basilica, Constantine had to level the Vatican hill, covering an ancient graveyard that had occupied the southern slope since the first century. The graveyard was not a catacomb; the tombs – like so many little houses – stood in the open air, lined up along narrow streets. The excavations disinterred two of these streets, parallel to each other; and if in your imagination you can remove the dark ceiling over your head (and the huge basilica above it), you can believe you are walking through a cemetery in the first century, when people who had witnessed Peter's martyrdom were still living. The red brick façades, after a millennium and a half, still have a warm glow, and here again, the sound of voices – those of the party of tourists ahead or behind your own – echoing along the street reinforces the sense of life.

For there is nothing gloomy about these tombs: Some are bright with frescoes of birds and fruit and animals, or with mosaics (one shows Christ as the sun, driving a chariot like Apollo's, against a glowing gold background), or with stucco decoration. The inscriptions tell us that most of the tombs are pagan, but some are Christian and some are both, suggesting that the family owning the little temple was converted.

Finally, you come to the Clementine chapel, built over St. Peter's grave (and directly below the great main altar of today's basilica) by Clement VIII at the end of the sixteenth century. This is where the excavations ordered by Pius XII began, and it is the heart of St. Peter's. Above the altar is a vertical porphyry slab flanked by slabs of plain white marble. This was the rear wall of Constantine's monument over the tomb of St. Peter. From the chapel, one person at a time can go and peer through a grille and see the site of the tomb, the simple, rough wall in which the bones were found and in which they rest today. At this point, the visitor's religious convictions (or lack thereof) are beside the point. You know you are in a holy place.

Then you go back into the chapel. Through other grilles above your head, you can see the floor of the present-day basilica. Not even the sound of shuffling feet, the click of camera shutters, the occasional flare of a flashbulb exploding, can totally erase the profound impression of what you have seen.

THE DREAMLIKE PACE
OF AN ITALIAN SUMMER

Sondra Gotlieb

It was late in June when my husband told me we would be able to take two weeks' holiday in August. 'And I want to go to Italy,' he said. 'Don't be foolish,' I replied. 'You're over fifty. Only eighteen-year-olds and backpackers have the stamina to push through the August hordes. Every sensible traveller knows that Italy in August is off limits to middle-aged people who like to maintain a dignified touristic pace. Besides, it's not chic to go to Italy in August, unless you own a villa in Tuscany, which we don't. Think of the trippers from Manchester and Tokyo cluttering the piazzas, overrunning the hotels with their cameras and little flags.'

I'm what is known as a poor traveller. My husband compares me to a rare but delicate Swiss white wine that turns sour after a fifty-mile voyage. It's not that I like to stay home. I want to travel, but, inevitably, disappointment sets in. Why wasn't the Parthenon whiter? Which corrupt guidebook gave that indifferent restaurant in Paris a star? Why do they have nasty blue jellyfish on the beaches in West Palm?

My husband, used to my finely tuned nature after twenty-six years of marriage, was not deterred. He knew an Italian, very well connected, related both to the leader of the Christian Democrats and to the head of the Italian Communist Party. The man likely had his suits made in Bond Street and was seen only in the best holiday places at fashionable times of the year. 'Let us rely on his judgement,' my husband said.

Six weeks later we found ourselves in **Asolo**, a small hill town about forty miles from Venice, within an hour or two's drive of Vicenza, Verona and Padua, and five minutes by car from the great Palladian villa, Villa Barbaro at Maser. Happily (it takes me three days to recover from jet lag), there is nothing to do in Asolo except walk up and down the narrow arcaded streets, stare at the high medieval walls that protect the summer villas – some of them former palaces – of prosperous Italians and read plaques commemorating Eleanora Duse and Robert Browning. Duse, who died in Pittsburgh, is buried in the rather more romantic cemetery of Sant'Anna in Asolo; Browning lived in the Villa Cipriani for several months. The Cipriani, now owned by the Ciga hotel chain, is where we, too, were advised to stay.

The Cipriani has only thirty-two rooms and is designated in red (meaning especially pleasant) in the Michelin red guide. This means linen sheets, antique and pseudo-antique furniture, a bed that is turned down every evening and a garden with a superb view of the hills of Veneto. The concierge, Pepino, was Mr. Cipriani's right-hand man when the former was alive and running the Hotel Cipriani and Harry's Bar in Venice. Pepino is keen on maintaining a chic international style for the Cipriani in Asolo.

The Michelin red guide also awards the Cipriani a star for food. But the first advice Pepino gave us was not to order Italian style: 'Who needs soup, pasta, meat and cheese and dessert every day? Just order a little mozzarella and tomato salad if you like.' Pepino personally deplores overeating. For two days I sipped mimosas on the terrace and watched the Italian families ordering the Cipriani's famous *tagliarini verdi gratinati*, that rich and creamy preparation of green noodles, the local fragrant porcini mushrooms with *filets* of beef, and every kind of dessert known in Italy. The third day I abandoned my chic, international-style grilled chop and salad and ordered Italian style.

When we were not eating we read, walked and slept. The only flaw was my unspoken quarrel with one of the other guests over the single deck chair. I reserved it for myself each morning by placing a book ostentatiously on the seat. After my stroll, I found that the chair had disappeared and that my book had been left on the grass. I complained to Pepino about the lack of deck chairs. He shrugged and muttered about the Villa Cipriani becoming too commercial. 'Next thing people will be asking for is a swimming pool.'

Asolo in August was not crowded. Most of the shops were closed – *Chiusa per Ferie* the lopsided signs said. (The locals like to take their holidays in August, too.) There were just enough beautiful Italian girls to make our strolls interesting for my husband. The only stressful moment of the day occurred when we had to decide which of the two cafés in the handsome central square would be the more suitable for drinking a glass of Prosecco, the sparkling local wine. It cost about fifty cents at either. After we had spent four days in idleness and quiet, Pepino decided we needed more excitement in our life and suggested a tour of the Brenta Canal.

In earlier centuries, during the hot months of summer the Venetian patricians used to retire to their villas, true pleasure palaces that they built along the banks of the Brenta River. They made the slow, dreamy trip from Venice in a luxuriously canopied boat called a *burchiello*, which plied the **Brenta Canal**, which still links Venice and Padua. We took the modern version of the *burchiello*, a covered motor launch furnished with a bar, which leaves from Padua early in the morning and arrives in Venice about sunset. The slow pace of the boat, the sun, the passage through the reedy waters and the unhurried visits to the villas, including Palladio's Villa Foscari and the eighteenth century villa of Stra, made those hours the most memorable of our trip. We grabbed seats (not without a certain pushing and shoving) in the uncovered front of the craft, where we had the coolest breeze and finest view.

The boat stopped every fifteen minutes or so during the voyage and waited placidly for the locks to be opened. Although it was certainly the largest craft on the Brenta, and keeps a most regular schedule, arriving punctually at each lock, at more than half the locks the captain was forced to honk and signal a child hanging over the bridge to run and fetch the lockmaster from more important doings. While we watched the elaborate turnings and manoeuvrings, and the gradual descent of the water, the passengers in the launch, who were mostly Italian, drank their capuccino and cheered each time a lock creaked open.

Stra was one of the most important stops. We straggled out to view the Villa Pisani, now called the Villa Nazionale because it is owned and maintained by the Italian Government. The guidebooks consider Stra to be the queen of the villas on the Brenta. It is certainly the most monumental, with its immense classical proportions, huge vestibules, side courts, stables and ornamental lake, all set within a thirty-two-acre park. The key attraction for most tourists is the Tiepolo frescoes in the ballroom, which depict the apotheosis of the Pisani family and are remarkable for their freshness. But for us Stra was a symbol of splendour fighting dilapidation. There was an almost heroic attempt to re-create the sweet, grand summer life of those eighteenth century Venetians. The hedges that formed the great maze were clipped most precisely; the rose garden, parched and filled with dandelions. Superficially, the struggle of maintenance evoked a charming confusion, but the desperation of these efforts to keep the past fresh made the strongest impression.

It is difficult to provide a perfectly timed, delicious lunch for a group of trippers like ourselves on a tight schedule – the boat had to reach Venice before dark so we could catch our bus back to Padua. We docked behind an inn – I never did learn its name – where the waiters had already set the correct number of tables on a vine-covered terrace. The moment we arrived, bottles of red and white wine were placed in front of us and we dined on homemade tortellini, fresh local fish and cheese and fruit – all within the hour. It was an idyllic and efficient production which left one of our companions, a French doctor, completely unimpressed. He was sunk in gloom because of the recent election of Mitterrand. Neither the villas nor the meal could keep his mind off what he considered the destruction of France. Tears welled in his eyes as he spoke, and we hoped our next stop, the Villa Foscari, would take his mind off the fall of Giscard d'Estaing.

The Villa Foscari, built to the designs of Andrea Palladio and finished about the middle of the sixteenth century, is also called La Malcontenta. Tradition claims that a member of the Foscari family banished his wife from her friends and her purportedly sinful life in Venice to this retreat among the marshes. The villa and town take their name from her displeasure. The name seemed to fascinate my husband, and for weeks afterward he would repeat the word *malcontenta* in a most irritating and knowing manner.

This was our first visit to a Palladian building. In Italy, most of Palladio's villas and palaces are relatively inaccessible. They are spread around the Veneto countryside, off the main roads, and concentrated in Vicenza, a small town about twenty miles from Padua. Yet Palladian neo-classical design caught the imagination of a great part of the western world; Thomas Jefferson, for one, owned a copy of Palladio's *Four Books of Architecture*, which inspired his design for Monticello.

La Malcontenta is not the grandest of Palladio's designs, but it is typically Palladian in the absolute harmony between structure and landscape. The porch has high Ionic columns and the stairs ascend on two sides. We approached the front from the river through the weeping willows bending over the bank. It couldn't have been a more fitting temple for an unhappy goddess. The plan of the Villa Foscari is a cross, with a great central hall, high ceiling and a spacious room at each corner. The effect is one of sobriety, coolness and light. The walls and ceilings are covered with carefully restored frescoes, which were begun by Battista Franco and finished by a collaborator of Paolo Veronese, Battista Zelloti. The two most appealing frescoes in the villa are masterpieces of trompe l'oeil, with figures beckoning welcome through a nonexistent door.

We entered Venice at sunset, cruising slowly through the Grand Canal. Until the boat docked at San Marco, it was possible to believe that we were eighteenth century Venetians returning to our city palazzi. Reality began when we disembarked into the August crowds choking the piazza. It took one hour to reach the bus station and determine which bus was designated to take us back to Padua. Our only desire was to leave Venice as quickly as possible. 'One panicky hour in a perfect day,' my husband said, 'is not bad for Italy in August.'

After a day of rest in Asolo (necessary for me) we drove to **Vicenza**, a sleepy provincial town where a great body of Palladio's designs can be seen just by walking through the streets and squares. Unfortunately, many of the palaces were closed and unmarked, which made it difficult for tourists like ourselves to know if we were gazing at a true Palladian structure or not.

The Teatro Olympico, however, was open and it was worth the trip to Vicenza all by itself. The theatre, which opened in 1583, is modelled after a theatre of antiquity, described by Vitruvius. It has remained an active theatre; Joseph Losey filmed his movie version of the opera *Don Giovanni* there several years ago. Streets painted in trompe l'oeil and statues superimposed within niches high on the walls fill and surround the stage. The false depths and bewildering foreshortened streets, depicting a city at dawn or dusk, reminded us of one of De Chirico's early and enigmatic street scenes.

It was a good thing that we visited the theatre in the morning, because we lunched at an informal restaurant named the Tre Visi. I chose the house speciality, *bollito misto*, a heavy platter of boiled meats with four kinds of sauces, with polenta and wine. It was exactly the wrong thing to eat on a hot day. After lunch my husband dragged me to another Palladian delight, the Municipal Museum, considered one of the architect's most original buildings. I don't remember seeing it at all.

Italy in August was not the fearful experience I had anticipated. Except for that nasty hour in Venice we never encountered hordes of tourists – Vicenza, for example, was almost empty. In fact, on reflection, it wasn't bad at all. I might even return.

IF YOU GO

The **Hotel Cipriani** in Asolo charges about $100 a night for a double room with bath; a meal in the restaurant, with wine, costs about $30 a person. In Vicenza, a three-course meal should cost less than $20 at the **Tre Visi**.

During the summer months, the Brenta Canal excursion can be made from Venice (Tuesday, Thursday, Saturday) or Padua (Wednesday, Friday, Sunday). The return is by bus. The fare, about $45, covers admission to the villas, lunch and return bus journey. Apply in Venice to **C.I.T.**, Piazza San Marco, in Padua to **C.I.T.**, Via Matteotti 12, or to **Siamic Express**, Via Trieste 42.

WÜRZBURG: JEWEL BOX OF ROCOCO

Olivier Bernier

A great golden palace, its gates opening onto a sleepy little town; rooms decorated with paintings of almost magical beauty; enfilades of apartments built to honour a passing emperor: It all sounds like the setting for one of those stories the Grimm brothers collected at the end of the eighteenth century. Add to that a majestically terraced garden, a chapel decorated with dazzling fantasy and, not far away, a medieval fortress frowning from the top of a tall hill, and you will find yourself in Würzburg, a mere sixty miles from the bustling international city of Frankfurt.

In the eighteenth century Würzburg was only one of the vast number of independent states that eventually became Germany. When, in 1802, an attempt was made to impose some political unity, Würzburg, like other states ruled by a prince-bishop, resigned itself to a change of status. But, unlike Liège or Mainz, to name only two examples, it did not lose its independence. Instead, it became a grand duchy: Its palace was simply too splendid to waste.

That this immense pile was built not for a king or emperor, but for a succession of bishops is only the first paradox. Its very appearance embodies a stylistic contradiction: The twenty-odd years that passed between the laying of its first stone in 1720 and its completion in the mid-1740s saw the triumph of the rococo everywhere in Europe, and most especially in Germany; but in place of the rounded, oval forms or the wavy outlines we might expect, what we see from the huge square plaza separating palace and town is an almost severe building that follows a rectangular plan.

There is a simple reason for this uncharacteristic restraint. Bishop Philip Franz von Schonborn, like the eighteenth century connoisseur he was, sent Johann Balthasar Neumann, his architect, to Paris. There, Neumann was so impressed by what he saw that, after thorough study he asked a French colleague, Hardouin Mansart, who still practised the grand style of Louis XIV, to help him with his plans. As a result, what we see in Würzburg is an enchanting combination of rococo ornaments and a clear, easily understood shape. It is a blend of elegance and flamboyance to be found nowhere else in Germany.

Facing the town the wildly exuberant pediment of the central pavilion follows a wavy outline, topped by trumpeting angels, putti and a crown surmounting a lushly draped coat of arms. On the garden front, the long white wings are enlivened by a three-sided, domed central pavilion, adorned on the ground floor by a colonnade and topped by another wavy pediment. The tall windows and strong verticals of the ornamented third-floor pilasters provide strong rhythms which are taken up in turn by plain pilasters on the wings, creating a feeling of unity despite the palace's great size.

But it is in the gardens that the paradoxes multiply. We think we are looking at a grand, formal eighteenth century park, when what we actually see is something akin to a theatre set. Of course, there are real flowers, real trees, real fountains; but what we take to be distant perspectives are in fact sharply angled terraces receding toward a vanishing point to create the illusion of depth. The town of Würzburg was enclosed by fortifications, and Bishop von Schonborn was forced to build close to the walls; anxious to have at least the appearance of a park, he used the very rampart as the foundation for his artful trompe l'oeil.

Illusion is the key concept at the **Residenz**. Even inside the palace, where space is hardly in short supply, walls vanish and ceilings melt into artificial skies as we enter a rococo heaven. There is, for instance, the Gartensaal (Garden Room) on the ground floor of the central pavilion, where Neumann brilliantly solved the problems created by a comparatively low ceiling and relative darkness. Since nothing could be lighter or more gardenlike than a tent, he simply designed one, using delicately adorned stucco instead of canvas.

Held up by pink marble columns that march around the room, this canopylike ceiling makes us feel that we are, at the same time, indoors and out. The stucco is then made lighter still by twisted blue and white rocaille motifs and small mirrors that reflect the sky. This is further topped by a frescoed ceiling where deities prance across a wide-open sky. Altogether, this is more like the most sumptuous of summer-houses than the usually dank ground floor of a huge palace.

The Gartensaal is full of charm. The grand staircase rising to the main floor, however, takes us into a completely new, far grander realm, that of genius. Here, Neumann developed a new, dazzling treatment of a familiar scheme, the staircase that, after rising to a landing, divides into two branches. Normally, the first flight is made as light as possible; here, we are made to feel the weight of the structure as we approach it. The vestibule, on the ground floor, is almost cavern-like, dark, vaulted, each archway resting on a thick, plain column; then, as we walk up, we enter a new space, flooded with light so that the stairs almost seem to float upward.

From the first landing on, we find ourselves in an enormous rectangular volume, adorned with freestanding sculpture on the balustrades and bas reliefs along the walls. The walls are further decorated with tall pilasters that advance slightly into our space. There are stucco draperies, pediments above the windows, a great coat of arms topping the main door, all in dazzling white: We might well be in a ballroom, not a staircase, especially when we look up to discover the greatest masterpiece of all, Giambattista Tiepolo's vast and glorious fresco.

An apotheosis of Prince-Bishop von Greiffenklau, painted around 1750, this enormous fresco – it covers a space ninety by fifty-six feet – is also arguably Tiepolo's finest. From the first landing, we can already see Apollo rising to the zenith in a glory of golden light; and, as we walk up, the rest of the world is revealed little by little: The Four Continents, one to each side of the ceiling, pay homage to the ruler of Würzburg in a melting glow of brilliant light and soft colour, playful exoticism and dazzling composition. There are Moorish princesses and their camels, alligators and Indians, as well as portraits of Neumann, of Tiepolo's son Lorenzo and of the artist himself.

But even though the details are so varied, so infinitely entertaining, what matters here is the virtuosity of that greatest of rococo masters. The figures sweep across the heavens, colours sing, spaces communicate: The ceiling vanishes to make room for the vast expanses of Tiepolo's world, and even then, the figures spill over the edge of the picture frame, beyond the front plane right into our very own world, so that our space and theirs become one. As we reach the top step, we enter not so much the first of the Residenz's state rooms as Tiepolo's universe, a world full of sophisticated and amiable splendour.

At this point, our pleasures have merely begun. Crossing the top landing, we enter another rococo enchantment, the Weissersaal (White Hall). Deliberately designed as a contrast to the lush colour that precedes it, the Weissersaal, decorated only with pure white stucco, is a lesson in monochrome virtuosity. Everywhere we look, above the doors, along the pilasters, in the corners, all across the ceiling, we see a riot of curved, twisted, contorted ornament. There are shells, garlands, putti, rocaille motifs, draperies, frames, all spilling into one another. Nothing, in fact, could be less simple than this plain white room, the crowning achievement of Antonio Bossi, the artist responsible for most of the Residenz's stuccos.

Turning now to the left, we go through another doorway into the most dazzling room of all, the Kaisersaal (Imperial Hall). Here Neumann, Bossi and Tiepolo worked together to create perhaps the most magical setting in Europe. Once again, we feel we have been transported to a fairy-tale palace as we see the pink and white marble floor, the tall windows opening on to the park. Pink marble columns with gilded bronze Corinthian capitals are lined along the walls and linked by gold stucco rocaille and statues gesticulating in their niches; but, best of all, at each end of the room a scintillating Tiepolo is draped in stucco swaths painted to look like golden damask; on the domelike vault, another Tiepolo opens up a limitless sky. There are green monochrome paintings in the lunettes, mirrors that reflect the light, stucco figures and golden garlands. And yet, with all this splendour, the Kaisersaal is a triumph of graceful, easy elegance, partly because of the white ground of the walls, which keeps the space open, partly because the room is octagonal – it is the piano nobile of the garden façade's central pavilion – so that its surface is broken into many facets.

On either side of the Kaisersaal, along each of the long wings, stretch more eighteenth century enfilades, where the emperors Joseph II and Leopold II spent the night on their way to coronations at Frankfurt. They are full of charm, but they come almost as an anticlimax after the glorious succession of staircase, Weissersaal and Kaisersaal. There remain an impressive number of charming rooms in which, however, the quality of the detail is not often up to the standard set by French artists at this period. Still, the green-and-gold lacquer room is handsome, and the collection of white and gold porcelain stoves worth seeing. The suite in the style of Louis XVI, with its literal neoclassicism, is all the more appealing in that it tends to shade off into painstaking imitation of the French ornamentalists – complete with urns, chains and lions' heads.

Leave the Residenz and enter the Residenzplatz. Look back; in the middle of the left wing, there is a door framed by two columns; behind it is one more rococo masterpiece, the Hofkirche.

It is perhaps curious that in all those acres of palatial apartments, only a small space was reserved for the chapel, although it should be said that Würzburg already boasted a good many churches, so there was no need for a great space to accommodate the faithful. No matter: good things come in small packages, and the **Hofkirche** is undoubtedly the most dazzling of all German rococo churches.

At first, we notice detail – the twisted columns, gilt capitals, pink marble balconies and gold-and-white rocaille ornaments – but we quickly become enthralled with the intricacy and sophistication of the interior spaces. Five unequal ovals break into one another so as to give the walls a feeling of waviness and openness, reinforced by tall windows that lead the eye up to a series of frescoed domes and half-cupolas. There is movement everywhere; unexpected volumes lead us from section to section as marble gleams, gold glitters and stucco putti hold drapes, clouds and architraves. The ensemble is breathtaking and each detail of extraordinary quality.

The Residenz, its chapel and gardens can easily justify a two-day visit; the same cannot be said of much of the town. Würzburg was heavily bombed during World War II and rebuilt with competence but little charm. Still, there are suvivors like the pleasing (if heavily restored) rococo Haus Zum Falken on the market square, or the fine Gothic Marienkapelle. And the eighteenth century Neumunster should not be missed; its façade, with its curving baroque pediments, is especially fine.

Then there are the typically German tree-lined promenades, especially the Sanderring, a perfect instance of that widespread German amenity the Linden Allee, where, on fine days, people still walk up and down chatting and holding hands. This in turn leads us down to the river. The Mainbrucke, with its fifteenth century arches and baroque statuary, is worth crossing; but even if you don't feel like leaving the centre of the town, be sure to take a tramway.

Tramways, in fact, are yet another of Würzburg's links with its past; in caravans of two, three or four cars, depending on the hour and destination, they rattle along majestically down the middle of the streets. Although they seem to belong to the 1910s more than the 1980s, they somehow fit in perfectly with the carefully arranged shop windows where every inch is packed with awesome, violently-coloured goods.

The buildings may be postwar neutral, but the old spirit of small-town Germany has taken them over; any doubt as to this resurrection will be instantly dispelled by a stop at any of the frequent pastry shops and tearooms. Baroque architecture still lives in the volumes of shaved chocolate soaring from whipped cream foundations.

And if you yearn for something less sweet, you could do much worse than to spend a little time in a tavern. The wood panelling and long bars still shine cosily, the wooden chairs and benches have been polished by decades of use, and you will no doubt enjoy the same down-to-earth cheer that has attracted travellers for so long.

At this point you will probably feel up to further exertions, so take a tramway to the opposite bank of the Main. You will be on your way to visit the fortress of **Marienberg**, the residence of the bishops before the palace was built, which looms majestically from the top of the hill. Its Main-Franconian Museum holds some fine Gothic sculptures – among them an Adam and Eve – by Tilman Riemenschneider; but if time is short it may be best to remain resolutely within Würzburg's most glorious period and pay a visit to the **Kapelle**.

While you can drive up to this hilltop rococo church, you should, if you have the energy, walk up the clearly marked hill road. Soon, you will enter a park and climb up twelve terraces, each marked by a little open chapel displaying one of the scenes of Christ's Passion. As you toil up, you see little but earth, rock and vegetation. After much panting, you suddenly emerge on the terrace around the Kapelle: There, at your feet, is the town of Würzburg, with its vine-covered hills in the far distance and the fortress in the foreground. After that, the little rococo church with its bulb-topped tower comes as a pleasant contrast. Once again, you enter a world of fantasy; but this time, it looks specifically German, with its more complicated, more abandoned, wilder stuccos. Here we can feel directly the full, almost naïve enthusiasm of the local artists.

After that, nothing is left for us but to come down to earth again. There, revived by a glass or two of the local white wine (just ask for *Würzburg Wein*), we can imagine, for a moment, that life is just as brilliant, as exuberant and as colourful as the buildings of Würzburg.

IF YOU GO
Getting There
Würzburg has no airport, but there are frequent train services from major German cities. The journey from Frankfurt (there are 29 trains a day) takes about an hour and a half and costs about $15 one way in first class, about $10 in second. From Munich, there are 43 trains a day; the trip takes just under four hours and costs about $30 one way in first class, $20 in second. Sleek, fast Inter City trains leave both cities hourly; there is a surcharge of about $2 for either class. Cars may be rented from any of several agencies at the Frankfurt or Munich airports; average rates for a small car are about $35 a day, with unlimited mileage. Frankfurt is about 75 miles, Munich 170 miles.

Hotels
The **Rebstock**, at Neubaustrasse 7 (telephone: 50075), is installed in a charming eighteenth century house within easy walking distance of the Residenz. Room rates are about $40 for a single room and about $65 to $100 for a double, including breakfast. More modest establishments near the Residenz are the **Amboger**, 77 Ludwigstrasse (50179), about $30 single, $50 to $60 double; and the **St. Josef**, 28 Semmelstrasse (53141), about $20 single, $30 to $40 double. The **Walfisch**, near the centre of town at 5 Am Pleidenturm (50055), offers exceptional views of the Main and the Marienberg fortress. Double rooms are about $65.

Food and drink
Würzburg is full of taverns, many of which serve wines from their own vineyards. Try one for lunch or a snack: A glass of the excellent local white wine or equally excellent local beer, a pair of the highly recommended local sausages and sauerkraut and coffee should run about $5 to $10 at any. The **Backofele**, Ursulinergasse 2, is within five minutes' walk of Residenz, while the **Hofkeller** is directly on the Residenzplatz. The **Ratskeller Würzburg** (Bei Gratennechart) specializes in the local beer.

For something more substantial, the **Hotel Rebstock** has a well-regarded restaurant where a dinner of such specialities as veal schnitzel and game, perhaps roast venison, in season, should cost about $25 a person. Prices are similar at the **Walfisch Stube** in the Walfisch Hotel, which specializes in grilled dishes and fish from a nearby lake. The **Zur Stadt Mainz**, at Semmelstrasse 39 (53155), has been a restaurant since 1460 and maintains a traditional kitchen offering such typically hearty Franconian dishes as oxtail stew and roasted spareribs; meals range from $10 to $25 a person, and reservations are a necessity.

Hours and fees

The **Residenz** is open daily, except Mondays, from 9 am to 5 pm, April through September, and from 10 am to 4 pm the rest of the year. Admission is about $1.50. Hours are the same for the **Marienberg Fortress**, but the hours of the **Main-Franconian Museum** are 10 am to 5 pm; admission to either is about $1.

Excursions

Würzburg is the starting point for the **Romantic Road**, which runs from the Main to the Bavarian Alps, through wooded hills and vineyards, past ruined castles and old towns. The whole route is just over 200 miles in length; if you do not have time to make the entire journey, a day trip can be made to **Rothenburg ob der Tauber**, about 60 miles from Würzburg, which preserves a number of splendid Renaissance buildings and squares. There are also a number of Main River excursions, among them a cruise to **Veitshöchheim**, the summer retreat of the prince-bishops, with its rococo décor and park. The trip takes 45 minutes each way and costs about $3 round trip; boats leave every hour from 10 am on from the Alter Kranen. The palace is open from 10 am to 5 pm, and the palace gardens are open until 8 pm from May to September. During the summer, there are also trips to the old fortified vineyard towns of **Ochsenfurt** and **Sulzfeld** on various days of the week. For information, schedules and other excursion possibilities, write to **Kurth und Schiebe**, Sandflurweg 19, 8702 Margetschheim, Würzburg (telephone 58573).

OSLO: MEET ME AT THE CAFÉ

Joseph Heller

I am no longer a person who looks forward to travel. It is easily demonstrated, I believe, that with the exception of paintings, three statues by Michelangelo and the city of Florence, everything looks better on picture postcards than in reality, and I can no longer understand why people who do not relish confusion and physical discomfort will travel long distances to gape at something more easily viewed in a magazine or newspaper travel supplement. And until a Scandinavian trip in November 1984, which included stays in the capital cities of Norway, Sweden, Denmark and Finland, too, I was complacent in my conviction that there existed nowhere in the world anything that would be a treat for me to discover. But I had not reckoned on the **Theatercafeen** in Oslo, about which I never had heard.

Imagine if you can – it will take a large stretch – a café with a blended ambience of Sardi's, Elaine's and the Russian Tea Room. Imagine as well – I warned you it would not be easy – a room that is larger in floor space and in number of tables than all three combined, probably, that is as animated and populated at any hour as all of these at their peak, and that is nonetheless always comfortably informal and relaxed, and there you have the Theatercafeen.

I have been to Scandinavia before, always with the brazen objective of elevating into an unqualified success the publication of novels by me whose debut in my own country has inevitably been marred by a fair – or unfair – amount of belittlement and indignant disapproval. My days are busy with interviews, the evenings with dinners and occasional parties, the usual kinds of conversational literary debauchery. But before this trip, I had never been in Scandinavia, or in any other foreign country as an author, without a full schedule of appointments and activities awaiting me.

This time, however, through some quirk in the planning, I arrived in Oslo from London on an early Sunday flight, to discover myself in a foreign city in the strangest and most disconcerting circumstances: I had no one to meet and nothing to do that whole day and evening. And

I could think of no place to go or anyone I wanted to see. What I desired strongly in this depressing state of affairs was a good stiff drink. That proved impossible to obtain, for in Norway, a land keenly sensitive to the beguiling effects of alcohol, distilled spirits are not sold on Sundays. What I wanted next was a congenial place with convivial people. Here my luck was good. I found exactly what I hoped for right there at the Continental Hotel: the Theatercafeen, a spacious and bustling eating and drinking haunt that is known throughout the city as the busiest place in town and throughout the country as the place to go when in Oslo.

The Theatercafeen was first opened in 1900 to accommodate, as its name suggests, the actors and audiences of the newly established National Theatre, which still functions just across the street. The proximity to the National Theatre, the concert and recital halls and to other theatres no more than a block or two away remains part of the attraction for actors, directors and musicians, as well as for those others who enjoy being in places frequented by such celebrities. On the walls are drawings of actors, authors, journalists and other individuals of eminence who have been regular patrons over the years. An American who looks intently will identify a stunning portrait of Lauren Bacall and another of Marlon Brando at his most charismatic – and he will be mistaken. The resemblances are vivid, but all of the pictures are of Norwegians, and each time a new face is added to this gallery of fame, which happens only rarely, there is a big ceremony.

But theatre people and their followers can account for only a small percentage of the tremendous daily flow, from 10.30 in the morning, when the Theatercafeen opens, until midnight, when it closes. Only on Christmas Eve are the doors shut. Even between meals, the tables are almost always taken, although I never had to wait for one, and any decline in volume from the peak hours for lunch and dinner was not discernible to this naked eye.

After a while it dawned on me that close to half the journalists with whom I had interview appointments elected to meet at the Theatercafeen, despite a noise level that was always rather high. In addition to its popularity with locals, the Theatercafeen is the place to which businessmen, journalists and travellers from other Norwegian cities are likely to head when they arrive in Oslo, to see who is in town and to disclose their own presence. In this respect, it serves much the same bulletin-board function as the Russian Tea Room at lunchtime and Elaine's in the evening. Everyone talks, and everyone smokes. But the hubbub is never so loud that one has to shout, nor are the fumes from tobacco more noisome than those from a single cigarette on the largest aeroplane.

Miss Aase Gjerdum, my editor at the Norwegian publishing firm of

Cappelen, confides that she has spent a good deal of money at the Theatercafeen over the past three decades. Apart from the allure of notables who might be present, she told me, the room is one in which a woman can sit with other women without appearing to be there to attract the attentions of men.

Strictly speaking, the Theatercafeen cannot be described as a drinking place. Except for the first hour, the rules of the house dictate that no one be given a table who is not prepared to eat, and resolute headwaiters make certain the rules are enforced – regardless of how much money a patron might be prepared to spend on rare wines and expensive champagnes. Everybody present between meals is therefore eating between meals. In more ways than one, this is my kind of place. Because open sandwiches and cups of tiny local shrimp in Russian dressing are always available and ingested so easily, the problem of ordering a snack with a coffee or nightcap is far from insurmountable.

Distilled spirits, banned throughout the country on Sundays, are not served until three in the afternoon on weekdays. This means no whisky or cocktails for lunch, ever. But it was not at all uncommon for me at the Theatercafeen to find myself surrounded at 10.30 in the morning by men carrying on lively discussions as they began their days with beer and bottles of wine (while I was having my third and fourth cup of coffee – along, perhaps, with a little piece of pastry or a taste of bread and cheese).

But the menu, I must warn, is limited by most standards and appears never to change, from meal to meal or day to day. And between meals an American palate can begin to tire of such basic snacks as herring, shrimp and smoked or marinated salmon and dishes of poached or pan-fried fish, reindeer and overcooked beef. It happened even to me: After three or four consecutive days of stopping in to see what was going on, I could feel the edge of my appetite starting to dull.

There is live music for much of each day, I am compelled to reveal. It is performed by a group of four or five instrumentalists stationed on a wooden balcony high above the dining room. The music is neither as bad nor as good as the best or the worst in contemporary American popular music (much in that statement depends, of course, on how one feels about contemporary popular music). I can say with certainty that the music savours of old-world European, as does the design and décor of the room. But in the presentation of that music at the Theatercafeen lies a story of tenacious ambition involving the *Guinness Book of World Records*, a story that seems known to every grown-up in Oslo, and even perhaps in all Norway.

The central figure in this epic of dogged perseverance is the ensemble's piano player. His name is Reidar Thommessen, and he is also known popularly as Valsekongen, which means 'King of the Waltzes.' Mr. Thommessen will soon be ninety-six years old, and he has been obsessed for more years than anyone can remember with the goal of getting his name in the *Guinness Book of World Records*. His sights are set on one or all of three categories: oldest active public performer, public performer with the longest history (he began playing when he was sixteen or eighteen, which gives him a span of about eighty years) and composer of the greatest number of published songs. His output totalled 157 when last counted and most of them, God forfend, are waltzes. Typical titles: 'I Love Your Smile,' 'The Most Beautiful Rose,' 'City of My Dreams.' His latest composition was released last year on his ninety-fifth birthday, which was celebrated at the café (where else?) with much pomp. The title is 'Longing for You' and was dedicated to his wife, who had died, they say, a short time before.

Do not misunderstand me when I tell you he looks his age. He enters and leaves under his own steam and ascends the steep staircase to the bandstand without assistance and with no visible difficulty. It is simply that Mr. Thommessen, at nearly ninety-six, plainly does appear a bit older than the average man or woman of ninety-four or ninety-five, although a good deal healthier and more sanguine. Had I said to him, as once I was tempted to do, that I hoped to be able to hear him playing again if I returned in three or four years, I felt he might have responded amiably with the retort of George Burns: 'I don't see why not. You still look like a healthy young man.'

The prediction heard most often on everyone's lips in Oslo these days, after the distressful conjecture that neither Norman Mailer, I nor Gore Vidal will win the Nobel Prize this year, is that Mr. Thommessen is going to achieve his wish in the next edition of the Guinness book, at least as the oldest active public entertainer. With the death of Eubie Blake at one hundred, he now seems a sure thing. And if the oddsmakers are mistaken, no one doubts that he'll keep on trying.

On my last evening in Oslo, I was tired and still had packing to do after returning from a cinema at which, to my astonishment, one could make reservations by phone and have numbered seats reserved. But I was drawn one more time into the Theatercafeen, just to see who was there. It was as busy at eleven in the evening as it had been at eleven that morning. And, of course, my companion and I had to order at least a snack to be permitted a table. I began with another delicious plate of gravlax and followed that up with a main dish of poached trout. (The coffee in all Scandinavian restaurants and hotels, by the way, is superb and puts much of the rest of the Western world to shame. I should also mention that I've since met English and American sailors, fishermen, hikers, campers and cross-country skiers who have gone to Norway for different reasons than I did and were not disappointed, but I would be telling a lie if I pretended to know anything about that.)

A portly and jolly engineer from the city of Bergen was there; he never fails to come to the Theatercafeen his first day in Oslo, he told us, just to find out who else is in town. One in a party of three women stopped as the group was leaving, just to tell me quickly with a blushing smile that they'd recognized me from my photographs in the newspapers and were happy to find me in their city, and that they hoped that I was having a good time and would want to return. Yossarian would like it there, I reflected, but Bruce Gold would find it too placid – undistinguished by the presence of anyone but me he recognized, and it's made to order for me, King David, and Bathsheba, who likely would want her picture on the wall. And I knew that when I did come to Oslo again, I would stop in at the Theater-cafeen the very first evening, just to make sure I was in town.

OSLO CLASSIC

The **Theatercafeen** is on the ground floor of the **Continental Hotel**, 24-26 Stortingsgaten, Oslo 1 (telephone 02 41 90 60). Double rooms are about $90, and suites cost up to about $220, including breakfast. The hotel's **Annen Etage** restaurant, to which Michelin recently awarded one star, has such seafood specialities as turbot braised in wine and lobster fricassee as well as such game dishes as grouse in cream or red wine sauce and reindeer in cream sauce with lingonberries. Set menus are about $25 a person for three courses without wine and about $35 a person for five courses without wine. A five-course dinner with wine, coffee and liqueur is about $55 to $65 a person. The restaurant is closed on weekends during the summer. Plan to spend about $25 for a light meal with wine at the Theatercafeen.

COPENHAGEN: CHILD'S PLAY

Margaret Atwood

'Should we go to Tivoli?' I asked our Danish friend. This was a rhetorical question, as I intended to go no matter what he said. I had already seen Tivoli from the outside, at night, lit up and looking like an upside-down chandelier from the 1890s. What could keep me away?

Our friend was driving with us in a horse-drawn carriage through a beech forest on the outskirts of Copenhagen. It was early May, and he was showing us the beech leaves, which had just come out. These new leaves, bright green and glossy, have deep romantic and emotional significance for the Danes. I later noticed that in our hotel the jardinières were filled, not with flowers, but with fresh beech branches.

'The beech trees and Tivoli,' he replied. 'These are two things you should see.'

'Do the Danes go?' I asked, with the tourist's usual anxiety about being merely touristy.

'Everyone goes,' he said. 'Rich, poor, old, young, it makes no difference. Everyone goes to Tivoli.'

'Why?' I asked.

He smiled. 'You will see,' he said. 'It is done well. With a charm.'

'We'll have to take our daughter, of course,' I said.

Travelling with a child is a good excuse. You can do things you really wanted to do anyway, without having to apologize to yourself for your childish tastes, and if other adults look at you funny, you can always grin and jerk your head in the direction of the kid.

Why did I think I needed such a passport? Because Tivoli Gardens is an amusement park. A famous one, of course – it's been in operation since 1843 – but still an amusement park, and these days I don't go to amusement parks much. What I visualized were midways, barkers, gangs of roving, raucous adolescents, boys in black leather, gum-chewing girls in ponytails (an image left over from the 1950s), Ferris wheels, candyfloss and garbage. In short, a North American fun fair. Tivoli is like that, but unlike it as well. It's in a different dialect, a different language even. Its assumptions about its own raisons d'être are not the same.

You deduce the differences at first by the absences. Compared with the North American equivalent, Tivoli is relatively quiet. There is music, true, here and there, and even screams from those being whirled around in devices no sane person would ever get into. But there is no uproar. After a while you realize that there is no hard sell; no one is yelling at you to buy things. Even the politeness of the ticket taker seems to imply that you are there to enjoy yourself, not to be sold things. The element of carny, that sly art of extracting loose change from your pocket, is minimal, and the feeling of transient illusion – tomorrow the tents will be struck, the magic will have moved on – isn't there at all. Tivoli is an illusion, too, but it's a permanent one.

Then there's the geometry. Tivoli is large, but the scale is human and the layout circuitous, so that wherever you are inside it, there's an intimacy – few linear vistas but many corners, which, when you turn them, reveal a small lake perhaps, with children riding in tiny boats, or an intricate fountain or a layout of flower beds with little white wrought-iron benches. The condition of the flowers is noteworthy: No one seems to pick them, step on them or throw ice cream wrappers on them. What Dane would cut down the beech wood or pick the flowers in Tivoli? An amusement park, yes, but also a national treasure.

But also an amusement park, which means rides. In Tivoli there's no midway as such. The rides are spinkled about, and you get tickets for them at central booths, as if for the underground. Or you can buy a pass, which gets you into everything. Since we were with a child, we got a thorough tour of the rides. Nothing flashy here or gigantic; and though there were more violent ones for those hardier than we, we stuck to those that appealed most to our eight-year-old. Boats you could steer yourself, replicas of antique cars you could pretend to steer, a merry-go-round, a preposterous pirate ship with little dinghies plunging up and down around it – all these got visited twice.

When we weren't looking for rides, we spent a lot of time just wandering around. It was early May and Tivoli had just opened, and the Danes were just wandering around, too, with the air of relief northern peoples always assume at the return of spring. Nobody was in a hurry; tolerance reigned. One of the great pleasures of Tivoli is the Danes themselves, who, if our experience is any example, display a kindly civility toward strangers that is uncommon. Someone in Berlin once told me that Denmark was 'good for *Menschen*,' good for people as people, and this certainly appeared to be true. One young woman actually got up to offer us a chair, and a man of about twenty, seeing our daughter's interest in a booth where you were supposed to hammer a nail into a piece of wood in five whacks or less, insisted on staking her to a try. He even stayed to watch, with great patience, while she hammered away, and at the end the booth attendant solemnly presented her with a plastic necklace even though she hadn't quite got the nail in.

The nail hammering took place in one of several booths devoted, it seemed, to the Danish sense of the absurd. Nearby was a Mouse Circus, one of the silliest things I've seen in some time, though what you laugh at it yourself, for shelling out the few kroner necessary to get into it. I won't give it away by telling what goes on there, but children adore it. Elsewhere, you can get a Polaroid photograph of your head (looking oddly shrunken) on Mona Lisa's body (or a ballerina's or a washerwoman's or just about anything else), with a trompe l'oeil panorama of Tivoli in the background. This proved such a draw that we had to do it four times. The Danes appeared to like it, too; there was a waiting line.

In the European game of who loves whom, the Danes love the English and are, in this propensity for slightly pinheaded whimsy, surprisingly like them. The White Knight in *Alice*, with his gentle melancholy, his gangly benevolence, his absentmindedness and his addiction to apparently ridiculous inventions of his own making, is practically Danish. And few other countries in Europe could have thought up the courageous fairy-tale ploy of putting yellow stars on everyone to protect the Jews, as the Danes did under Hitler. Few other countries would have believed it could work.

But Danish affiliations are not all English. 'The Norwegians and the Swedes call us the Italians of Scandinavia,' our friend had told us.

'Meaning what?' I asked.

'That we are frivolous, I suppose,' he said with a shrug that was indeed Italianate, and there is certainly a theatricality about Tivoli that would not be out of place in a Fellini movie. As we wandered around, lost but not worried about it, a parade appeared, composed entirely of costumed children, band and all. In the middle was a golden state carriage with a miniature king and queen inside. This apparition turned out to be the famous Tivoli Brigade of Guards, founded in 1844, though we didn't know it at the time.

After a while we got hungry. Our friend had told us that many people went to Tivoli just to eat, which would strike a North American as odd. Are the Danes, then, junk-food junkies? Not at all. When I was young, I thought that the Danes ate nothing but blue cheese, sardines and toasted Danishes, because these were the only culinary exports I had noticed. But they are, in fact, exacting about their food, of whatever kind. Tivoli contains a wide range of eating and drinking possibilities, including several top-grade restaurants, and we strolled about reading their menus. Divan I and Divan II (both founded in 1843) appeared to be the most accomplished.

But eight-year-olds aren't noted for their devotion to marinated salmon, so we ended up in the hot dog nook. The hot dogs were long and thin and an alarming shade of red, but they tasted fine and could be eaten while walking around, which enabled us to catch the free show in the open-air theatre. This consisted of an acrobat who fell off his tightrope, then did it again and got it right. That he'd missed the first time only made the Danes more sympathetic to him. 'He was wonderful,' said my daughter, who had been relatively unmoved by the flawlessness of the Peking Circus.

The acrobat's fall was part of the charm of Tivoli, along with the Mouse Circus and the shooting gallery with ducks that looked home-made and the test-your-strength machines that were like something from a 1940s country fair in North America, where young men stood about in groups, joking and hanging back, then baring their forearms and hoisting the huge wooden mallet. There's a homeliness about Tivoli, a modesty, something touchingly human. It does not glitter. Instead, it glows.

We'd arrived at Tivoli in the late afternoon and stayed on through the long sunset and the lingering northern dusk. Now, in the semidarkness, Tivoli was showing its lights, and it is a view that should not be missed. Every curve and curlicue of the original nineteenth century ironwork structures, the ornate gateways, the towers and spires, the Arabian Nights Palace, the pagoda – the skeleton of Tivoli, if you like – is outlined with small coloured lights, red, orange and yellow. These illuminations were once candles, then gaslights; now they're electrical. But apart from that, you're seeing the form of Tivoli as it once was and has been ever since.

In this light Tivoli seems to float, like a school of fragile jellyfish or the interior of a Venetian glass paperweight, suspended in time. Tivoli in the daylight is fun, but Tivoli at night is like something from the inside of your head. You go out through the gates, and nostalgia sets in at once.

TIVOLI TIME

Tivoli is open from 10 am to midnight from May 1 to the third Sunday in September. Admission is about $2. Many events, among them fireworks displays (Wednesdays, Saturdays and Sundays), shows on the open-air stage (daily except Mondays) and concerts by the Tivoli Guards, composed of boys between the ages of 9 and 16 (Thursdays and Saturdays), are free; admission is charged for some other stage, concert and ballet performances. Daily programmes are posted inside the grounds. There are 25 rides and other amusements, which range in price from about 40 cents to $1.20. A Tivoli Tur-Pas, good for one day's unlimited use of all rides, is about $7.

Dining

Tivoli is in the heart of Copenhagen, within easy walking distance of all major hotels. Within the park are more than two dozen eating places, ranging from cafeterias and a pizzeria to a traditional coffeehouse and luxurious international restaurants. A short list of establishments open for both lunch and dinner and offering particularly good food or a particularly charming setting includes:

Belle Terrasse. An airy, light-filled restaurant, decorated with chintzes and overlooking Lake Tivoli. Predominantly French menu. Dinner for two with wine about $50.

Divan I. A glass-enclosed room, filled with flowers and plants; founded in 1843. Danish and international menu. Dinner for two with wine about $50.

Divan II. Flower-filled restaurant opening onto a garden, also founded in 1843. French and international menu. Dinner for two with wine about $50.

Faergekroen. A fairy-tale farmhouse with a flowery terrace, built over Lake Tivoli. Simple Danish cooking. A meal for two about $20.

Kinesiske Tarn. The restaurant occupies two floors of the Chinese pagoda, outlined in lights at night. Varied menu, with a few Chinese dishes. A meal for two about $20.

La Crevette. The only restaurant in Tivoli specializing in fresh seafood, often in nouvelle preparations. Dinner for two with wine about $50.

Nimb. Large international restaurant installed in the Arabian Nights Palace, with terrace and enclosed garden room. Music for dancing in the evening. Dinner for two with wine about $50.

SICILIAN HIGH NOTES

Harold C. Schonberg

It was supposed to be a nonworking vacation in Sicily, which we were visiting for the first time. Forget opera, concert and symphony. Instead, concentrate on pasta and the local wines. Ruins and mosaics. Churches and monasteries. Driving here and there. Walking among the ruins left by the Greek and Norman and Spanish and Moorish settlers, who for millennia had made Sicily the crossroads of the Mediterranean. Perching on a fallen pillar in a Greek pantheon, preferably at sunset or under the full moon, and thinking the appropriate thoughts.

But the first stop was Palermo and, as I said to my wife on our arrival, Palermo after all has had a distinguished musical tradition and it would do no harm to look into it. Just a little look. A teeny-weeny look. Hey?

I also said this while driving to our hotel and getting lost. Some people have a sense of direction. Others don't. But how can a music lover get mad at a city that has streets and squares with such names as Via A. Scarlatti (Alessandro Scarlatti was born in Palermo in 1660)? Or the Piazza Verdi? Piazza Bellini? Via Alfredo Catalani (the composer of *La Wally*)? Via Umberto Giordano (the composer of *Andrea Chénier*)? In Palermo they even name streets after great singers of the past, as witness Via Mariano Stabile.

It so happened that, on the day we arrived, the Teatro Massimo was giving a performance of Donizetti's *Lucia*. Who could miss a *Lucia* in Palermo? These days the Teatro Massimo is not playing in its own house in the Piazza Verdi. That has been closed for ten years or so, pending renovation. Instead, performances are being given at the Politeama Garibaldi, another big house, built in 1891, and originally designed for spectacles.

This *Lucia* was a performance, at 6.30 pm, for children, and the place was thronged with kids, most of them accompanied by their parents. Like so many European theatres, the Politeama is an enormous building with an auditorium that is small by American standards, seating about 1,300. Between the acts, the kids rushed to the bars – ice cream bars, candy bars, soda-pop bars – and then dispersed to the rest rooms. During the performance they were very well mannered. But once in a while, when their parents did not like the leading baritone, and vented their disapproval with whistles, the kids enthusiastically joined in. They also applauded and bravoed when their parents applauded and bravoed. These kids are being brought up right.

The performance was not bad. Indeed, it was provincial opera at its best, and certainly nothing to be ashamed of. Alfonso Gubernati, the house manager, explained that Palermo traditionally was host to young singers on their way up. And most of the singers were indeed young.

The soprano, Mariella Devia, had a clear and well-focused voice of attractive timbre. She probably is more a natural lyric than a coloratura; she did try for some of the acrobatics, but above a high C the voice suddenly took on a hard, unpleasant sound that had little to do with her natural scale. Antonio Savastano, the tenor, was thoroughly reliable. He appears to have the ambition to match Luciano Pavarotti in girth, and he is certainly well on his way. Less interesting was Carlo Desidere, the hollow-voiced Ashton.

It was a traditional staging, with production by Sir Peter Hall, and the acting was equally traditional, of the outstretched-arms school, the lurch and stagger, the back of the hand over the eyes to express great emotion.

We made arrangements to see what was going on at the old Massimo, and the following morning the house manager, Alceste Tagliarini, took us through the building, leading the way through totally dark corridors and backstage areas with a flashlight.

The Teatro Massimo, opened in 1897, is huge. Originally it contained 3,200 seats. Today the building is gutted, work is going on, and Mr. Tagliarini hopes that it will reopen in about three years at a cost of something like $8.5 million. At that time it will not have 3,200 seats. Posteriors and the human frame have grown since 1897, and only some 2,000 seats are planned. The pit also is being opened up, and will be able to take a Wagnerian orchestra.

But it will have some of the amenities of its predecessor, including the royal box with its elaborate antechamber and private stairway. The Massimo is a horseshoe-shaped structure with five tiers of boxes and a balcony. The murals on the ceiling will be restored, the statuary all over the place polished up, the marble cleaned, the exterior – now in shocking shape – repaired. This is a very classic building with Corinthian pillars, a pediment with Greek masks on either side, and a big staircase leading to the building flanked on both sides by huge lions, on each of which a muse is comfortably seated.

On the pediment a few noble thoughts: *L'arte rinnova i popoli e ne rivela la vita* – roughly 'Art renews the people and thus reveals life.' Underneath: *Vano delle scene il diletto ove non miri a preparar l'avvenire* – 'The pleasure of the appearance is in vain if not addressed to the preparation of the future.' Or, in less poetic words, if there is no substance, appearance is without meaning.

In Palermo we fell in love with the marionettes in a tiny theatre at 6 Viale Nicolo Ragusi. Il Teatro dei Pupi Ippogriffo, it is called, and it can seat about seventy-five on wooden benches. Not very comfortable, but the little place, with its colourful primitive curtains, its marionette models hanging on the wall (for sale), its provisions for musical accompaniment (an old music box and even older player piano, painted like a Sicilian wagon), makes you feel wonderfully at home.

This theatre is strictly a 'mom-and-pop' affair, run by the same family for generations – a *famiglia di puparo*. Sicilian marionettes have a long tradition, going back to medieval times, and usually the operation of a marionette theatre passes from father to son. At this Teatro dei Pupi Ippogriffo, mom was at the box office. During the performance she synchronized the player piano with the stage action. Her sons were manipulating the puppets. Her grandson, a handsome seven-year-old named David, helped at the box office, turned the crank of the music box for the overture, and then disappeared backstage to help his big brothers and uncles operate the marionettes. He also could be heard as the Voice of an Angel during the harrowing scene when the hero went to heaven.

Propped against the stage were signboards in English and German telling the action. The hour-long show was named *Death of Ruggiero della Aquila Bianca:* 'Charlemagne sends Ruggiero to Rome. On the way he meets a dragon and kills him, then rescues Aladina, a lady being held captive by a giant, who intends to sell her as a slave. He kills the giant, whose soul is taken by a devil . . .' And so on through the adventures and eventual death of the young, gallant Ruggiero of the White Eagle. All Sicilian marionette theatres seem to have shows based on Charlemagne and his knights, and their battles with the Saracens. The knights always win.

When the curtain goes up, the illusion is extraordinary. Intellectually we know that these marionettes are no more than three feet tall, but they look life-size on the tiny stage, and the intellect is suspended. We believe in their substance, their reality, their flesh and blood. They wear armour, knightly regalia, regal clothing, brandish swords and spears and go clanking around the stage with great thumps. The backstage handlers were virtuosos. They even had Ruggiero sheathing and unsheathing his sword, and that takes an awful lot of practice.

Sicilian marionette shows are great for battles. Here was Ruggiero expertly dispatching a dragon, the poor beast (who never had a chance) expiring with a final sad, despairing twitch of its tail. Here is Ruggiero lopping off the head of a giant, said head landing about five feet away. Here is Ruggiero in battle with another knight, an epical example of sword play not seen since Errol Flynn faced down Basil Rathbone in *Robin Hood*. Such thrust and parry! Such noise! Such sounds of steel against steel! Such thuds and stamps from the backstage puppeteers! And finally Ruggiero splits his opponent's head in half. At which point the audience cheers. At marionette theatres the audience (largely made up of tourists) is part of the act, cheering the hero and hissing the villains.

During all this a stentorian voice from backstage narrated the action, in Italian, of course. If Ruggiero was Errol Flynn, the narrator was a cross between Lionel Barrymore and Charles Laughton, reciting in an orotund voice heavy on exaggerated emotion. As the action progressed, other backstage voices took a variety of roles. In a way, this was a real play. The background music was lovely. All of it was salon stuff, turn-of-the-century inconsequentialities, some of it with a faint Italian flavour. So it did not have any Redeeming Social Value, but it sure was fun. Whenever a battle scene took place, the same music was repeated. It sounded like this:

In Taormina there also is a puppet theatre – I Pupi Siciliani di Macrí, of course run by a *famiglia di puparo*. We saw *The Adventures of Roland and the Rout of Roncesvalle*. Here the synopsis was shorter. Roland kills giants, dragons 'and many snakes.' The Taormina marionette theatre operates out of the Cine-Teatro San Nicolo, off the Corso Umberto, and was founded in 1887 in Acireale by Mariano Pennisi. At his death, Emanuele Macri took over. The Cine-Teatro San Nicolo is a real theatre, seating about two hundred, with white walls and a rather antiseptic flavour. It had nowhere near the charm of the Ippogriffo. Nor was there any music.

Palermo had spoiled us. In Taormina they seemed only to be going through the motions, without the expertise and consecutive sweep of the Palermo puppeteers. Only one voice recited the action, so this was basically a pantomime where the Palermo performance approximated a real play.

But one amusing thing happened at the Taormina performance.

Roland's visor kept slipping down, covering his face. During one of the scene changes there was the sound of great backstage hammering. Somebody was trying to fix the errant visor. When the curtain went up, Roland and his knights were being received by Charlemagne. Roland's visor still kept slipping down. And every time it happened, Charlemagne gravely lifted his arm and pushed it up.

Not far from the Cine-Teatro in Taormina is the lovely little Church of San Nicola di Bari. It has a pipe organ. Behind the organ console is a cassette machine with six eight-track cassettes inserted and ready to go at the punch of a button. Perhaps these cassettes are used by parishioners who do not wish to pay for an organist when they have to use the church facilities. Or perhaps they supplement the organist.

On two of the cassettes were the wedding marches of Mendelssohn and Wagner. That took care of weddings. On another two were Handel's *Largo* and Schubert's *Ave Maria*. That took care of funerals. On the last two were the Frescobaldi *Toccata* and Bach's *Toccata and Fugue in D minor*. That took care of ceremonial occasions.

GETTING SEATS FOR THE SHOWS

The best way to obtain tickets for the opera in Sicily, as elsewhere in Italy, is to ask the concierge of your hotel to telephone the box office a day or two ahead of time. Unless a superstar is singing, there is hardly ever any trouble in reserving seats. The price of seats in Sicily runs roughly from $10 to $25. The marionette theatres, though popular, never seem to be sold out. Just get to the box office about 15 minutes before a performance. Tickets cost about $3.

HOTELS AND RESTAURANTS

The following listing is highly selective and should be taken only as a point of departure. An effort has been made to list establishments in different price categories. It should be noted that not all establishments accept credit cards; it is a good idea to check ahead.

Hotels

Rates quoted are approximate, for two in a double room, including continental breakfast and tax. Most also include private bath or shower. In addition to the establishments listed, the Jolly Hotel chain has hotels in several of the larger cities. These are comparable to such American chain hotels as Holiday Inns, and are dependable and clean.

Taormina

San Domenico Palace Hotel: The hotel is installed in a fifteenth century monastery, with a calm inner courtyard, antique furnishings, private gardens. Ask for a room with a view of the sea or of Mount Etna. Swimming pool. (5 Piazza San Domenico; telephone: 23701. 117 rooms, about $145.)

Hotel Timèo: Tranquil hotel near the ruins of the Greek Theatre. Rooms overlook the coast and Mount Etna; many have small balconies. Public rooms are airy and comfortable. Lunch can be taken on the terrace, with extensive views. (59 Via Teatro Greco; 23801. 55 rooms, about $115.)

Excelsior Palace Hotel: A comfortable hotel with a long terrace extending to a large swimming pool. Views of Mount Etna and the coastline. Open March 15 through December 11. (8 Via Toselli; 23975. 89 rooms, about $50.)

Villa Belvedere: Friendly, comfortable hotel, with a garden and views of Mount Etna and the sea. Swimming pool. Open March 23 through October. (79 Via Bagnoli Croce; 23791. 41 rooms, $40.)

Palermo
Villa Igiea Grand Hotel: Large, traditional hotel with turn-of-the-century décor, set in a garden facing the harbour; ask for a room on the port side. Rooms are spacious; there is a quiet terrace where one can have light meals or a drink. Swimming pool. (43 Salita Belmonte; 543744. 123 rooms, about $110 to $125.)

Grand Hotel et des Palmes: Large, comfortable, slightly old-fashioned hotel, near the centre of the city. Good service. (398 Via Roma; 583933. 205 rooms, about $55.)

Politeama Palace Hotel: A dependable and clean hotel in the centre of town. Rooms are of adequate size and the service is good. (15 Piazza Ruggero Settimo; 322777. 102 rooms, $50.)

Trapani
Astoria Park Hotel: Modern hotel on the beach; ask for a room on the sea side. Rooms are efficient and clean. Swimming pool, tennis court and children's play area. (Lungomare Dante Alighieri; 62400. 94 rooms, $60.)

Agrigento
Villa Athena: In the Valley of the Temples, with an extraordinary view of the Temple of Concord; ask for a room facing the ruins. Service is friendly and cheerful though the décor is somewhat shabby. Garden, swimming pool. (Via dei Templi; 23833. 41 rooms, $50.)

Ragusa
Hotel Montreal: There are few places to stay on this part of the island. This hotel is small and clean and useful to know about if you need to stop overnight. The rooms are small. (6 Via San Giuseppe; 21133. 65 rooms, about $30.)

Catania
Excelsior Grand Hotel: Large hotel on an imposing piazza in the centre of town. Comfortable rooms are decorated in a style reminiscent of the 1930s. Good service. (Piazza Verga; 325733. 164 rooms, $70.)

Restaurants
Prices are approximate for a meal for two with wine. Service is often included, but it is customary to leave a little more.

Acireale

Panoramico: Two-storey restaurant on a hill looking out over a valley of country villages toward the sea. Pasta dishes with tomatoes, olives and aubergines and other local fare; good seafood. Ask for a table upstairs. Closed Fridays and November. (Route 114, about two miles north of town; 885291. About $25 to $30.)

Taormina

Da Lorenzo: Pleasant family-run restaurant. Fresh seafood, especially swordfish, and other typical Sicilian specialities. Good Sicilian wines include a light rosé from vineyards on Mount Etna. Eat on the terrace if the weather permits. Closed Tuesdays. (4 Via M. Amari; 23480. About $30.)

  La Griglia: On the main thoroughfare of the town and sometimes crowded with tourists. Notable seafood and such local specialities as pasta with sardines or pasta with herbs. Closed Tuesdays and from November 11 to December 20. (54 Corso Umberto; 23980. $30.)

  La Ciclope: Also on the main street but less noisy. Menu lists pastas with seafood, including one with an aubergine sauce and fish; good mixed antipasti. Closed Wednesdays and January. (1 Corso Umberto; 23263. About $25.)

Palermo

La Scuderia: A tranquil and beautiful setting on the edge of the eighteenth century Parco della Favorita. The cuisine is more inventive than is usual in Sicily; specialities range from grilled fish to wild game. Save room for dessert. Good service. Closed Sunday evenings. (Viale del Fante; 520323. About $40.)

  Charleston le Terrazze: Summer quarters of the Charleston restaurant in Palermo (which is open from September to mid-June, closed Sundays). As close to nouvelle cuisine as Sicilian fare comes, with such specialities as Sicilian risotto, fresh grilled fish, meats with various herbs. Ask for a table on the terrace. Open from June to September. (Seven miles north of the city in the village of Mondello, on Viale Regina Elena; 450171. $40.)

Trapani

Dell'Arco da Enzo: Serve yourself from a wide array of antipasti, then order something prepared on the grill for a second course. Good local wines. Friendly service. Closed Fridays. (110 Via Nino Bixio; 27796. $20.)

  P & G (di Gallo Paolo Giuseppe): Crowded with local businessmen at lunch. Try pasta with a sauce of four cheeses or one made of tomatoes, aubergine and garlic. Good fresh fish. Afterward, walk a block to the promenade and stroll along the sea. Closed Sundays and August.(1 Via Spalti; 47701. $20 to $25.)

Agrigento

Le Caprice: Cold antipasti, fresh fish, good local wines. A house speciality is a dish of pasta en papillote, a cross between macaroni and gnocchi with a sauce of tomatoes, aubergine and herbs, cooked in aluminium foil.

The view over the Valley of the Temples worth a visit all by itself. Closed Fridays and July. (51 Strada Panoramico dei Templi; 26469. $20 to $30.)

Siracusa
Jonico-a Rutta e Ciauli: On a hill looking across the harbour to the old town; try to eat on the terrace. Tranquil atmosphere. Owned by four brothers who use traditional Sicilian ingredients in an inventive style; fish dishes range from squid to swordfish. Personal and helpful service. Closed Tuesdays. (194 Riviera Dionisio il Grande; 65540. $25 to $30.)

Bandiera da Lino: Just across the bridge from the old town. May be crowded, but has a warm atmosphere and friendly service. Choices include a hearty fish soup, local fish, other Sicilian specialities. Closed Wednesdays and from September 20 to October 20. (2 Via Eritrea; 68546. $25 to $30.)

Catania
Pagano: Don't be put off by the exterior. A house speciality is rigatoni with a tomato, aubergine, basil and ricotta cheese sauce; veal dishes are worth sampling. Good antipasti and vegetables. Closed Sundays and August. (37 Via de Roberto; 322720. $25 to $30.)

SIGHTS NOT TO MISS
Aci Trezza
A seaside fishing town between Catania and Taormina; park your car and take a walk along the ocean promenade. Unusual rock formations just outside the harbour are called the **Cyclops reefs**; legend has it that they are the rocks Polyphemus threw at Ulysses. In the late afternoon, one can observe fishermen repairing their nets and families enjoying the day.

Cefalù
A fishing town near Palermo, it is best known for its mosaic-decorated **Norman cathedral**. The church is being restored and much of it is closed off, but it is worth stopping even to see a small part of it. Afterward, walk down the cool, cobbled streets to the old port.

Palermo
Among many sights, be sure to see the twelfth century, Arab-Norman **Palatine Chapel** on the first floor of the **Norman Palace**, which is decorated with highly detailed and exquisite mosaics. Open from 9 am to 1 pm and from 3 to 5.30 pm on Monday, Tuesday, Thursday, Friday and Saturday, and on Wednesday and Sunday mornings; closed on some holidays. The hours vary in winter.

Segesta
The ruins of the **Doric temple** stand alone in a somewhat barren mountainous countryside. Best times of day are early in the morning or just before sunset when the light plays on the temple.

Erice
The narrow mountain road bends in hairpin turns and offers extensive

views of the coastline, Trapani and the sea beyond. Exceptionally lovely at sunset as the mist rises over the mountain. The town, which is medieval and resembles a fortress, is unusual in Sicily.

Siracusa
The archaelogical area is open from 9 am until about 5 pm (later in summer) and closed Mondays. Even if you don't arrive in time to wander among the ruins, the views from the walkway to the Paradise Quarry and from the Viale Rizzo looking down into the Greek Theatre and out toward the harbour are worth the stop.

SHOPPING
Handicrafts
The local handpainted and glazed pottery is good value. Prices range from a few dollars for a small dish to more than $500 for an antique platter. Be wary of anyone selling a so-called antique at a low price. If you are driving on the northern coast, stop in Santo Stefano di Camestra. The main road is lined with one pottery shop after another and looks like a colourful street fair. One can buy quality pottery in either traditional or more modern designs at reasonable prices.

Placemats, tablecloths, napkins and clothing decorated with fine petit point work are a bargain, though not cheap (four placemats were $25). If you do buy needle-point crafts, make sure they are handmade and from Sicily. Some shops carry less expensive goods from Taiwan and the quality tends to be inferior.

Safety Tips
Lock your car, even when in it, and pack luggage and valuables in the boot, out of view. Do not leave anything in an untended car. Leave valuables in your hotel. If your hotel has a safe, deposit any item of great value in it. Do not carry all your money with you and do not carry your wallet in an accessible pocket. Women with shoulder handbags should wear them across their chest.

INFORMATION
For more information go to the tourist offices found in all the major cities on the island. There is one at the Palermo airport, but the main one in Palermo is the **Azienda Autonoma Turismo**, Villa Igiea (540 141). In Taormina, the main office is the **Azienda Autonoma Soggiorno**, Piazza Santa Caterina (23 243).

– Carol Plum

HIGH LAND OF THE CONQUISTADORS

Frederic Raphael

I first went to Spain more than thirty years ago. It was then a forbidding and, if you had a strong liberal conscience, a forbidden land. Many of those who loved it had sworn they would never return while Franco remained in power; they had a long wait before the accession of King Juan Carlos in 1975 restored his country to the European community and to democracy.

On my way to Spain that first time, I stopped on the French Riviera, where I was lucky enough to be asked to tea by Somerset Maugham. He was eighty years old, but he found generous time for an unknown and unpublished writer. When I left Maugham's Moorish-style home on Cap Ferrat (now the site of a bungalow colony), he gave me a letter to a man in Madrid who would, he assured me, 'open all the d-d-doors.' I was, and remain, grateful for his courtesy, and I regret that somehow I managed to lose the precious document and never made contact with the sublime porter who might have given me the key to the city.

On that first trip to Spain, and on many subsequent ones, I followed the starriest route in the guidebook and headed south. For young writers of my generation, Andalusia was at once romantic and highly practical: it had the stylish poverty of the primitive, sun-glazed local colour and gypsy music, and one could stretch a small publisher's advance into months of simple living. Today that whole harsh southern coast has taken on the lineaments of Miami.

For the real Spain, you have to look elsewhere, which is why we went recently to Estremadura. The very name of this little-visited area, with its intimations of remoteness and its hint of hardness, has always fascinated and slightly intimidated me. Estremadura clicks no snappy castanets, promises no orange groves or somnolent beaches: it has hardly been touched by the great tourist avalanche that falls directly south onto the Costa del Sol or topples eastward to the Costa Brava. Those who can bear to absent themselves from serried pleasures should head due west from Madrid.

The road to Estremadura drives like an arrow into the eye of the setting sun, toward the Portuguese border. Roman legions paced out the long miles to Mérida (they called it Emerita Augusta) and Napoleon's armies tried to turn this sullen plain into a French province before the Duke of Wellington burst out of his Portuguese redoubt, beat them at Talavera de la Reina and Salamanca and drove them back through the Pyrenees, not without a little help from Spanish guerrillas, who paid the French back for their atrocities with their own mercilessness. Goya was the great witness of that savage war, and, even after the experience of our own vicious century, it is a callous eye that does not wince at his scintillating accuracy. Geography is history here; and landscape is art. You cannot appreciate what you see unless you have some taste for books and battles and pictures.

Estremadura begins under the southern lee of the Sierra de Credos. The crests of these mountains rarely lose a quiff of snow, and they usually glare in the brilliant sky like a jaw full of gigantic incisors. We made our first halt at the looming castle of Oropesa, the gateway to Estremadura, where, as it happens, there is a framed citation from my old friend (as I now dare to think of him) Willie Maugham. It declares that he came for a single night but stayed for several days, captivated by the superb austerities of the fortress in which the modern *parador* has been ensconced. I am not usually to be recruited among Franco's admirers, but the chain of state hotels that he encouraged, which are installed in one magnificent site after another, have transformed touring in this country. You may not, in high season, stay for more than three nights, and advance booking is usually essential, but castles in Spain were never so welcoming before, and only a dull dog or a very heavy sleeper could fail to have brave dreams under such historic roofs.

I had an idea (inspired perhaps by the film *Spanish Earth*, for which Hemingway, the greatest of Hispanophiles, wrote the heroic commentary) that Estremadura was an irredeemably arid and depopulated region, its peasantry ground down by the lazy tyranny of absentee landlords. Was I disappointed or relieved to find instead a varied terrain, often rich with wheat and tobacco and olives, and studded with prosperous pueblos? There is, no doubt, a good deal of hardship here, but it no longer feels like a place from which to escape. For centuries this great landlocked expanse, breaking finally against the ramparted mountains behind Badajoz, exported its sons – or had them thrown out – to the farthest corners of the world. Not only did conquistadors ride or march from every Spanish village where poverty armed ambition and primed audacity, but the very names of the places themselves were carried across hazardous oceans and planted in the New World.

It is one of those bizarre twists of fate or providence that the conquistadors found in Central and South America a rich and desirable landscape that, in aspect and vegetation, almost exactly mirrored the Iberian Peninsula itself. There are three cities called Trujillo in what was once the Spanish empire, all named after the sturdy Roman town that so delighted us we made it the centre for our travels in the region. (Here, again, there is an excellent *parador*.)

The Plaza Mayor in **Trujillo** is dominated by a strutting equestrian statue of the town's most favoured son, Francisco Pizarro. The greening bronze horseman is the work of two Americans, Charles Runse and Mary Harriman. Although set up only in 1927, it symbolizes perfectly the proud and opportunistic character of the little city. Pizarro looks as if he is about to step off his plinth and charge into acquisitive battle. The son of a swineherd, he was the most daring and grasping of those who took stout Cortez's example to heart and left a bleak hearth in the quest, as Sir Walter Raleigh put it, 'for gold, for praise, for glory.' In Peru Pizarro found such profusion of the first that it secured him an easy option on the others.

Trujillo's main square is hedged by an asymmetrical assortment of buildings, badged with the heraldic devices of noble families, but it is more like a parade ground than a civic amenity. As you sip your oloroso and stab a succulent olive, before climbing to watch the sunset from the battlements of the Moorish castle that commands the town, you are reminded that there are times when the sword is mightier than the pen. Trujillo was founded by a gambler – Julius Caesar, who crossed the Rubicon in an all-or-nothing dash for supremacy – and spawned other gamblers who did not hesitate to risk everything against the odds: Pizarro and his crew crossed a vast sea, daring dangerous storms and Englishmen to take the cross (and the lash) to Peru. They pillaged that orderly Inca state of everything valuable that could be transported to a galleon and shipped home for Spain's enrichment and, in the event, her ruin. (Pizarro married an Inca princess; you can see her image next to his on a wall in his brother's palace in Trujillo.) The realm of Philip II, the gloomiest man to be blessed with the Midas touch, lorded it over Europe and made Spaniard a byword for arrogance.

Everywhere in Estremadura you see the evidence of *folie de grandeur*, nowhere more dramatically than in the mountain monastery of **Guadalupe**: God, too, demanded grandiose tribute, His portion of worldly wealth and show. Guadalupe is as central to a certain idea of Spain as is Delphi to ancient Greece. As you climb into the Sierra de Guadalupe, you leave modernity behind. When you reach this great sanctuary of *hispanidad* – the essence of Spanishness – with its turreted and crenellated monastery, you are aware, whatever your beliefs, that God is not mocked with impunity in this superstitious, fatalistic and unsentimental land. Looking up through the massive hoops of the Moorish cloister at the exploding rose window of the monastery church, you realize that Spanish Catholicism is not only a creed but also a cause. The Moorish style here defers, however grandly, to the crusading conquerers Ferdinand and Isabella. Just as in Córdoba the Great Mosque wears an outsize Gothic jacket, a Sunday suit of Christian cut, so Guadalupe is a vote of victorious thanks, heaped in ochrous and elaborated stone, to the Lord of Hosts. The Franciscan monk who guides you past the rather morbid collection of Zurbaráns will show you a lantern taken from a Turkish ship at the battle of Lepanto and now used to illuminate an antechapel. Cervantes pulled an oar at Lepanto, Don John of Austria's great (and finally futile) defeat of the Turks, and did not get home before serving several years as a slave on the Barbary Coast. His *Don Quixote* (an infinitely odder book than the casual reader may think) is the grandest gesture ever made in the art of ridiculing grand gestures. Rather than the latest protracted thriller, the traveller in Spain should limit himself to the Don and, say, the poems of García Lorca and Juan Ramón Jiménez.

It is perhaps only fair to warn that there is not a lot of fun to be had in Estremadura. Even the bars are seldom garnished with the rows of tapas that turn every drink into a small meal in places like San Sebastián or Barcelona. The local ham and cheese, however, are excellent for picnics, and the wines of the Marquis de Cáceres – which should have been grown in the enchanting town of the same name but are not, coming instead from Rioja – are light and delicious. **Cáceres** sports an old quarter where 'Santiago,' the war cry raised by Pizarro's men, has its birthplace, so to speak. In this perfectly preserved precinct the Military Order of the Knights of Saint James (Santiago) was founded in 1170 to safeguard pilgrims on the arduous way north to Compostela. (Those who completed the journey often sewed scallop shells onto their cloaks, hence the culinary term 'coquilles St. Jacques' for a delicacy that my Sephardic forebears would be ashamed to know is a particular favourite of mine.)

The churches and noblemen's houses of medieval Cáceres make a tawny maze through which the tourist can walk back several centuries in a few minutes. It is rather a shock to come suddenly upon the Palacio de los Golfines de Abajo where, a plaque informs us, Francisco Bahamonde Franco was proclaimed head of state. It is a sign of the changing times that you can hardly read the inscription for the large splat of pitch that someone has tossed against it.

At **Mérida**, a bustling and not very engaging town, we travelled even further back in time. Its Roman aqueduct is, like all the pinnacles of the area, the exclusive residence of storks, which peer proprietarially from wherever their bristling nests can find purchase. (Their unlikely anatomy reminds you that nature, too, is capable of bold and fanciful flights and that Spanish architecture, with its insolent inventions and outrageous anatomy, is not necessarily unnatural.)

Sometimes I wonder, as we climb up, and down, our umpteenth set of Roman ruins, whether I'm really adding to my stock of indelible memories. However, Mérida's ruins merit a detour. The amphitheatre (where gladiators fought wild animals and one another) and the theatre – where actors did their buskined stuff – are closely adjacent. Their proximity jolted me into seeing how much they had in common: the same crowd thrilled to literal blood in one place and was purged by sanguinary metaphors in the other. Those who laughed at the gladiators' genuine fear in the arena had only to go a few yards to be amused by the simulated panic of a slave in a play by Plautus. The modern bullfight, however degenerate, is a singular mixture of both of these elements, with an audience that can go from pious admiration to heartless derision in no time at all.

As garrison towns went, Mérida, with its watered civility, was probably what used to be called a 'cushy billet,' but it was a long way from Rome, and the legionaries did their best to deck its remoteness in familiar forms. It is frequently in frontier posts that men preserve most obstinately the habits and petty pretensions of the distant homeland: Englishmen dressed for dinner in the jungle when they had ceased to do so in Mayfair.

Theatregoing in Roman Mérida was, of course, a matinée business (there were no footlights in the ancient world), but the handsome odeon, with its wedding-cake double-decker backdrop, must have given the privileged classes the illusion that they were as well entertained as their metropolitan cousins. Spain furnished Rome with several men of letters, including the spicy Martial, and the actors who performed the plays of Seneca or Plautus on provincial tours could expect a sophisticated and critical audience, even at the western limits of the empire.

Estremadura demands a certain effort of the imagination from the traveller, a decisive willingness to walk and look and learn. Its countryside is dauntingly varied, surging from placid fields into rock-strewn uplands where cleft boulders raise heavy grey haunches above the nibbling goats. Battlements top the peaks of exaggerated hills, and Roman roads stride straight over bouldered gorges, while Gothic bridges rear up and over, for the sheer show of it, or so it seems. There are petty pleasures as well as demanding sites: the little town of Plasencia offers a Plaza Mayor where a living documentary of provincial life parades endlessly before the sipping tourist, a perfect setting for a production of *L'Elisir d'Amore*, brassy with busy character.

And when you have done with *hispanidad* in its more uncompromising form and are ready to leave Estremadura, let me recommend a night or two at **Salamanca**, not far up the road. The Plaza Mayor is one of the most gracious squares in Europe. Like the Piazza San Marco in Venice, it creates a garrulous drawing room in the heart of its city. The brothers Churriguera, who were responsible for some of the flightiest flights of baroque imagination, here surpassed themselves. The tiered façades of the square are of a ginger-coloured delicacy, and on sunny days, crowds move round the arcaded cafés, agile in pursuit of shade. Not far away are the peaceful courtyards of the ancient university, the oldest in Spain. The Patio de las Escuelas has a modesty in accordance with the spirit of the place and sports a statue of the poet and mystic Fra Luis Ponce de León, whom Willie Maugham often quoted for his sage and tolerant remark that a man fulfilled himself best by acting in accordance with his nature. A few steps take you to the lecture room where Miguel de Unamuno, hardly a rabid revolutionary, delivered his bitter rebuke to the fascists, whose slogan *Viva la Muerte* ('Long Live Death') struck him as so shameful that it broke his heart. In Salamanca's russet streets, in the shadow of its two soaring cathedrals (the Churrigueras were busy on the new one as late as the eighteenth century), you gain a comforting sense of the liberalism that, often battered and beleaguered, has survived so obstinately, and begins again to flourish, in a country where nearly everything has a tendency to go to extremes.

THE MANY SURPRISES OF STOCKHOLM

William Howard Adams

I knew by the envious glance of a friend that I was not the only one who considered a ten-day idyll in Stockholm equal to a stay on a tropical island, a cruise in the Mediterranean or a trip to Istanbul on the Orient Express. The Swedish capital shares nothing with such exotic places, yet its consoling northern qualities – the soft, changing light and shadows, depending on the season and weather, the human scale of its setting and the shimmering presence of water on all sides highlighting with its reflections the baroque palaces and churches – seem to me unmatched as a civilized environment to which one can escape.

Nor is it necessary to give up any essential amenities or fumble with an unknown language, since the entire country seems to speak perfect, colloquial English. The shining efficiency of everything from buses, subways and boats to shipshape hotel rooms with automatic trouser pressers that really work confirms all of one's expectations of neatness and order. As for the Swedes, they take their small domestic luxuries as routine.

The reference to water, light and baroque palaces may sound vaguely like a travel folder for Venice, and indeed these superficial similarities are apparent from the moment you arrive in the middle of the city. There may not be any Grand Canal, or gondolas darting about, but the commanding presence of the harbour in front of the Royal Palace, lined with an array of boats and vessels from the small private motor launches to the elegant white liners from the Baltic tours that stop there regularly, underlines Stockholm's historic role as an ancient capital of a seafaring race in the same way that Venice's lagoon serves as a reminder of its historic connections with the sea.

The strong dollar has taken some of the sting out of Stockholm's high-priced reputation with an exchange rate, at this writing, of about seven kroner to the dollar and, given the superb and mitigating quality of both accommodations and food, the old complaints about the expense of the place are not as loud as they once were, especially in the restaurants.

To shake jet lag painlessly, and at the same time grasp a sense of Stockholm's geographical setting, I would first recommend a long boat ride through the hundreds of islands that make up the archipelago to, say, Vaxholm or even farther to the island of Sandhem. Never mind the two or three quiet hours that the elegant little ferry takes. Gliding past the first pine-covered islands and watching the dark green forests gradually recede as one moves farther toward the open waters of the Baltic is unparalleled therapy. Not only does it clear one's head of whatever accompanying baggage of anxieties remain from travel or from the chaos of former existence, but it also establishes an appreciation of the physical environment that has shaped Sweden's destiny from the days of the Vikings. Sandhem is a very special place, without cars and with a beguiling cluster of cottages and buildings strewn along the narrow, winding paths of the settlement.

The boats for the islands in the archipelago leave from the quay running along the north side of the city's harbour in front of the Grand Hotel and National Museum. Both are sober Renaissance Revival buildings matching at a distance the scale, if not the stolid grandeur, of Nicodemus Tessin's Royal Palace just across the way. Stockholm may not glitter with an array of architectural jewels, but the ancient merchant houses appear very much as they did in the seventeenth and eighteenth centuries, and the numberless churches with their resolute Lutheran spires punctuate the cityscape in all directions.

The heart of the capital is the Old City, stretching away from the palace and the cathedral standing at the top of the hill where the first settlement was planted in the thirteenth century. Since the palace now houses a complex of museums – state rooms, armoury and Royal Treasury – you might as well begin your introduction to Swedish history by exploring the incomparable collections of artworks in one of these institutions.

The present palace was designed by Nicodemus Tessin the younger, born in 1654, the remarkable architect with Renaissance interest in all manner of art and design. His collection of 10,000 drawings in the National Museum – of everything from buildings, gardens and silver to water pumps for fountains assembled in Paris under his direction – is one of the great resources for students of French architecture and design at the end of the seventeenth century.

When one visits the royal collections and the great private castles now under the care of the state, one is convinced that the Swedes have never thrown anything away. These places, situated in a country with modest physical resources and having been spared invasions and destructive revolutions, are literally piled high with the accumulations of artworks, furniture, silver, porcelain and even linen stretching back over three centuries.

I was drawn to a handsome decorated cupboard in one of the remoter bedrooms at the Gripsholm Castle. When I asked what it held, the doors were opened to shelves stacked with fine linen table-cloths, napkins and sheets, the household dowry of an obsure German princess who had married a Swedish prince in the late seventeenth century. It reminded me of the ancient Egyptian fabrics displayed in the new galleries of the Metropolitan Museum. There is something ineffably royal in luxurious piles of folded linens – whether it is of the Middle Kingdom of 1060 BC or the seventeenth century Vasa dynasty.

Even when things have been accidentally destroyed as the original Royal Palace was in a disastrous fire in 1697, at least a shadow of the old castle remains if you know where to look. As I approached the main entrance to the palace, walking through a perfect Italian square complete with the baroque rear of the cathedral on one end and Tessin's residence opposite and centred on a Piranesian obelisk, I noticed a peculiar irregular line laid in black stone running in the white pavement paralleling the formal façade of the palace. My companion explained that it was the outline of the foundations of the original medieval castle. Somehow that subtle silhouette gave form to the Swedish attitude toward the presence of the past in daily life, unremarked but there nevertheless.

To enjoy Stockholm, it is not necessary to plunge into an exhausting round of sightseeing. Rather, the rule ought to be to look at a few things at a time and to savour the small pleasures, since there are few four-star world-class artworks demanding to be seen and admired whether or not you are really interested. This freedom from guidebook despotism is to my mind one of the secrets of a real idyll in an unfamiliar foreign city.

The superb collections of the palace – the finest assembly of crown jewels in Europe and a roomful of royal coaches and rare equipment, princely costumes from every regime, beginning in the sixteenth century – can be taken in small doses. There is no reason the tours of the royal apartments cannot be postponed for a rainy day.

When the call of the countryside becomes irresistible, you can take a boat to Drottningholm, only an hour away, or go out to Haga on the northern edge of the city and linger over a delightful lunch in one of the festive painted-copper tents put up as barracks for the royal guards by Gustavus III in 1787, from designs by Louis Jean Desprez. Haga is a wonderful English park with rolling meadows, magnificent trees and a lake that would be the envy of Capability Brown. The park was laid out in the 1780s by a friend of King Fredrik Magnus Piper, who had spent a year in England studying Stourhead and other English picturesque landscape creations.

One of the nice things about Swedish parks is the un-American restraint in not mowing the grass to within an inch of its life. Perhaps it is an unspoken gesture of the Swedish love affair with nature, and nature responds with waves of tall, golden grasses and wild flowers.

Gustavus ushered into Swedish life an uncharacteristic theatrical quality when he came to the throne in 1771. He loved the theatre and was a patron of all the arts, so his assassination at a masked ball in the old Opera House in Stockholm in 1792 seemed to be the appropriately flamboyant final scene to his operatic career. Sixty years later, Verdi based his opera *Un Ballo in Maschera* on the King's tragic end. His sinister costume of a Venetian cavalier and the mask he was wearing on the fatal night can be seen in the Palace Museum.

Gustavus was planning a splendid neoclassical palace on a hill in the middle of the park at Haga, but only the enormous foundation had been laid at the time of his death. Like the outline of the old castle wall in the palace pavement in town, the foundation is still there, buried in overgrown weeds and grass, a reminder of former dreams of royal megalomania.

The King left for the ball from his small, almost bourgeois pavilion that still stands in the park near the lake. Its exquisite rooms are furnished with all of their original furniture and, as an ensemble, it is the best series of Gustavian interiors to have survived. The Mirrored Room in the wing facing the lake was designed so that the mirrors flanking the windows also reflect the view of the lake, creating a momentary confusion between the illusion and the real view.

During Gustavus's life Swedish decorative arts reached a cohesive high point, drawing heavily on French fashion of the period, but ultimately uniquely Swedish in their elegant restraint coupled with an earthy quality that is difficult to convey in words. My recollection of a later afternoon meal in a simple, whitewashed dining room at Gripsholm Castle, where the scrubbed pine table was set with fine Gustavian silver, 1930s black glass Swedish plates and a few pieces of Mariberg faience from the late eighteenth century, captures something of that blending of refinement juxtaposed with a rustic air. It is a quality one finds nowhere except, perhaps, in a few Italian country palaces and Sicilian villas, where an intoxicating whiff of field or barnyard can heighten your perception of the ceiling frescoes.

The tangled threads of Swedish folk and court cultures can be straightened out in Stockholm's folk museum and in the decorative art galleries of the National Museum. An understanding of the Swedish devotion to folk art puts the fine late eighteenth century cabinetwork of the Haupt family and others into the context of a tradition of craftsmanship. The Nordiska Museum presents the most complete collection of objects illustrating the development of Swedish culture since 1500.

Just beyond and farther into the island park is the outdoor museum of Skansen, where examples of early Swedish vernacular buildings have been moved from all over the country. It was the first museum of its kind in Europe and has set professional standards for such well-known American museums as Sturbridge Village and the Shelburne Museum.

Gustavus's taste for the arts was no doubt the result of the strong influence of his formidable mother, Lovisa Ulrika, sister of Frederick the Great, who came to Sweden determined to play a leading role in the country's fledgling cultural life. Her court soon became the centre of Swedish literary and artistic talent. Leaning toward French court fashions, she founded the first Academy of Letters in Sweden in 1753, and inspired the building of the superb little court theatre at Drottningholm, where operas and plays are still performed in the summer.

At the far end of the English park at Drottningholm, placed at one side of the formal French gardens, stands Lovisa's Chinese Pavilion, a magic place capable of telling you more about the taste and manner of mid-eighteenth century court life than almost any other building I know of. The tall, elegant blue room in one of the wings, lined with painted black chairs in the style the English give to Queen Anne, must be, along with the Mirrored Room at Haga and the splendid Throne Room of the Royal Palace, among the most memorable interiors to have survived in Europe.

I would have to add to the list the theatre at Gripsholm commissioned by Gustavus, where even the neoclassical stage sets have been preserved. Built in one of the domed seventeenth century towers of the old, somewhat rattletrap castle south of Stockholm, again one confronts that special illusionist quality of faux marbre and deceptive architectural perspectives that seems to have fascinated Gustavian artists.

The tragic death of Gustavus III in the Opera House chilled the court's taste for theatre and may have contributed to the preservation of both the theatres at Drottningholm and Gripsholm. The former building was boarded up and forgotten until 1921, when it was rediscovered and restored to its present glory the following year.

At Drottningholm there is a very pleasant restaurant set back from the edge of the lake so that you can view the palace and watch the boats coming and going at the same time. Gripsholm, on the other hand, is a perfect place for a picnic, and the local bakery produces some of the best bread in Sweden.

Stockholm is, to be sure, not without its shortcomings. Of course it rains, but it does also in Dublin, London, or even Paris for that matter, and with some regularity. When it does pour in Stockholm, I grab a good book and stay close to the hotel, or drop into the National

Museum, where I could never tire of looking at its unequalled collection of French eighteenth century paintings.

Others may find the fall and winter twilight depressing (and many Swedes would agree), but there is a fascination in the mellow light and long shadows of October and November that can inspire quiet walks in the dusk before sitting down to a meal that in many restaurants ranks with the best to be found on either side of the ocean. Who couldn't stave off mid-winter Scandinavian depression with Baltic caviar or herring and dill, followed by a snowgrouse mousse or reindeer steak, with cloudberries for dessert?

It is easy for the casual traveller to misread appearances. But the signs of extravagant consumption and waste in Stockholm's streets, shops and restaurants seem less virulent than in most Western cities. This impression – that it has not yet fully succumbed to the shoddy, the synthetic and the vulgar in material qualities – contributes to a visitor's sense of well-being. It may have been a mirage, but it was still there when I left for the airport and the return flight.

STOCKHOLM SAMPLER
Hotels

Rates are for a double room with private bath, including taxes and service charges. Most hotels – a notable exception is the Grand – have weekend reductions of up to half on their room rates.

Grand, 8 Blasieholmshamnen (phone 22 10 20), 352 rooms, about $125 to $175. Traditionally the hotel for visiting leaders, Nobelists and other celebrities. Harbour view, opposite Royal Palace. Best rooms with water view, balcony. Large winter garden, French restaurant and bar with good smorgasbord.

Sergel Plaza, 9 Brunkebergstorg (22 66 00), 408 rooms, about $130. A building, formerly for members of Parliament, that was recently converted into an apartment hotel. Lobby bar, express checkout, two restaurants.

Strand, 9 Nybrokajen (22 29 00), 150 rooms, about $130. Recently renovated central quayside hotel. Suites with period furniture and fine restaurants, one in Italian-style piazza.

Royal Viking, a deluxe hotel opened in late 1984 near the central station (14 10 00), about $130.

Reisen, 12-14 Skeppsbron (22 32 60), 125 rooms, about $120. In the medieval Old Town, facing harbour inlet. Fine restaurants, including piano bar, and good sauna.

Boatell Malardrottningen, 4 Riddarholmskajen (24 36 00), 59 rooms, about $100. Large former luxury yacht once owned by Barbara Hutton, moored next to Old Town with splendid porthole views. Most cabins are small but smart, with showers. Deckside restaurant.

Diplomat, 7C Strandvagen (63 58 00), 132 rooms, about $125. Central and quiet though on main quayside avenue. Has teahouse cafeteria catering to shoppers.

Lady Hamilton, 5 Storkyrkobrinken (23 46 80), 35 rooms, most with shower instead of bath, about $110. Situated in Old Town alley next to Royal Palace and cathedral. Naval atmosphere, like Lord Nelson Hotel nearby under same management, which is on a bustling main thoroughfare.

Grand Hotel Saltsjobaden, Saltsjobaden (7 17 00 20), 100 rooms, about $125. Beautifully situated old-style hotel sitting on a yacht harbour in the suburb of Saltsjobaden, 20 minutes by train or car to city. International conference site.

RESTAURANTS

Prices are approximate for dinner for two with a drink and glass of house wine each, including service charge and tax.

Coq Blanc, 111 Regeringsgatan (11 61 53), about $65 to $80. Housed in a former theatre and recognized by the Michelin guide in 1984 with a star. Lunches are bargains.

Eriks, 17 Strandvagskajen (60 60 60), about $70 to $100. In a converted barge floating at central quayside with upper deck service in summer. Considered the best seafood restaurant in town, also with a Michelin star. Oyster bar on bridge.

Diana, 2 Brunnsgrand (10 73 10), about $65. In a cosy medieval Old Town cellar, with a wide range of good French and Swedish food. Lunch offerings include fish smorgasbord.

Operakallaren, the Opera House (11 11 25). A national gastronomic institution. Actually three restaurants – old-style French main one with terrace and fine food; a rotunda café in studio-type nightspot; and a small, moderately priced brasserie with Swedish specialities. About $60 in the brasserie and $100 in the main restaurant.

KB (Konstnarsbaren), 7 Smalandsgatan (11 02 32), about $50. Swedish and French cuisine and a popular bar. Literary atmosphere.

Finsmakaren, 9 Rasundavagen, Solna (27 67 71), about $60. A small neighbourhood restaurant about 10 to 15 minutes by taxi out of central Stockholm that serves French and Swedish food. Moderately priced.

Ulriksdals Vardshus, Ulriksdals palace park (85 08 15), about $80. Beautifully situated whitewashed wooden inn on city's northern outskirts, with high-priced French cuisine as well as fine smorgasbord (also as lunch Sunday). Swedish style.

MUSEUMS

Museums are generally open seven days a week, year round. Admission prices are nominal.

The **Royal Palace**, Old Town. With 600 rooms, the palace dominates the Old Town. There is a museum, treasury, armoury and hall of state.

The **Vasa**, Djurgarden Island. A 64-cannon flagship that foundered on its maiden voyage in 1621, the *Vasa* is almost completely restored. There are parks and amusements on the island as well, and maritime, ethnographic, technical and biological museums.

Skansen, Djurgarden Island. This is an open-air museum showing Swedish life in past centuries. There is also a zoo and aquarium. Restaurant.

Millesgarden, Lidingo Island. The home of the sculptor Carl Milles features his own works and collections, partly on a scenic terrace.

Hallwyl. In the centre of Stockholm, this is a palatial nineteenth century residence with a theatre courtyard.

DAY TRIPS
Archipelago Tour

Take a scenic steamship tour through a bit of Stockholm's archipelago of thousands of islands and islets in the Baltic east of the capital. The Vaxholm Steamship Company offers scheduled service to a number of destinations, including the fortress of **Vaxholm**, an hour's boat ride. Vaxholm has an inn; lunch (beef or flounder) is also served on board. Alternative, longer trips (three hours each way) include the island of **Uto** to the south, which also has an inn, or the yachting centre of **Sandhem**. Price about $5. (Telephone 14 08 30.)

DROTTNINGHOLM

A 30-minute trip by steamer or boat to the seventeenth century **Drottningholm Palace**, where the royal family resides, and its original theatre. Leaves from Town Hall bridge. Price is about $4, half fare for children.

FURTHER INFORMATION

In Stockholm, the city's **Information Service** is in Sverigehuset (Sweden House), Kungstradgarden park.

— Richard Soderlund

ADRIATIC CLIFFHANGER

Henry Kamm

When most of us think of Yugoslavia, our mind encompasses a Slavic, Balkan people, eastward-looking, dominated once by Byzantium and the Ottomans, coveted now by the Russians. We think of the cupolas of Orthodox churches and the minarets of mosques that are a legacy of the Turks.

True, all of it, but so incomplete as to falsify the vision. It leaves out the Latin aspects, strongest in the Roman Catholic lands of Slovenia and Croatia, and the most characteristic glory of those lands – the marvellous east coast of the Adriatic Sea and the islands offshore.

Weaving along the 435 miles of twisting, sometimes frightening road from Trieste to Dubrovnik, the traveller will encounter startling natural beauty as well as the evidence of many civilizations, from the worn stones of villages to the remnants of a Roman Emperor's palace, now part of the fabric of a lively city.

The Turks occasionally held to tribute limited areas of the coast, but never occupied them for long. Roman ruins abound, and later, not only Venice but Florence, too, stamped the coast indelibly with their architecture, sculpture, painting and urban vision. Occasional reminders of the Hapsburg Empire, which relieved Venice as over-lord, also crop up. On this coast the Slavic and Latin cultures intermingle under Mediterranean skies.

The languages – Slovenian and Croatian – are Slavic; so are the names of people and places. Both men and women tend to a burly Slavic physique that goes well with the names and the idioms. And yet the visitor knows himself to be amid a people and a culture that are more of the Mediterranean than of the world of the Russians, Poles or Czechs, or even of the Yugoslavs farther inland. Complexions tend to olive tones and hair is dark; gestures speak as volubly as words. People move as if they were of lighter build than they are.

Food is more aromatic than heavy; the thick sauces that in other Slavic cuisines are used to cover the poor quality of raw materials and other inadequacies are mercifully absent, disclosing ingredients of savoury freshness and tender consistency. Wine and distillates of grapes or other fruit are indigenous, taking the place of beer and the spirits of grain or potatoes prevalent among the Slavs of the north. Is it lighter drink that accounts for the absence of the public drunkenness that so marks Moscow, Warsaw and other Slavic cities to the north? Or is it perhaps that Mediterranean sense of moderation and equilibrium – qualities that have enabled proudly Slavic peoples to create a culture that is entirely at home among the old Hellenic, Latin and Byzantine civilizations of the region, a culture in which tongues speak Slavic while stones speak Italian?

Trieste, at the head of the Adriatic, was the region's dominant city, a place where all its ethnic and linguistic streams flowed together, until the collapse of the Hapsburgs joined the largely Italian port city with its nation. Today's Triestini cherish a special quality that it has become fashionable in Italy these days to call *Mitteleuropa*. In the Italian meaning, the German term suggests a sense of sympathetic understanding of the literature, music and art of late-Hapsburg central Europe, an appreciation of the Slavic and Jewish contributions to civilization, an awareness of having shared in a cultural melting pot – in short, a sense of being Italian-plus.

Confirming Trieste's claim to a diversity that is rare in Italy are a blue-domed Serbian Orthodox church, a large Greek Orthodox church and one of the world's biggest and, since the German occupation, tragically emptiest, synagogues.

What four and a half centuries of Hapsburg rule have most visibly bequeathed is the main square, a splendid expanse open to the waterfront called Piazza dell'Unita d'Italia. The name is somewhat ironic because each of the great palaces on the piazza's three sides was built late last century in the style of the Viennese Ringstrasse, that architectural incarnation of the Hapsburg Empire. Also reminiscent of a bygone age are the clusters of more or less venerable ladies who gather late every afternoon at the piazza's equally venerable Caffè degli Specchi, dressed, coiffed and painted for stately occasions that have been cancelled forever.

The Yugoslav border is ten miles away, and there are road signs in Slovenian on the way, in consideration of the minority that remained on the Italian side when the border was redrawn in 1954, after a long dispute. Italian and Yugoslav border officials seem to vie in casualness. The Italians hardly deign to look at one's papers. The Yugoslavs seize upon an American passport to show their authority, but the document is instantly returned with a no-questions-asked visa, free of charge and good for three months.

Having crossed the border, the visitor is faced with a choice. The impressive Roman, Byzantine and Venetian sights of the Istrian Peninsula may be sampled on a sinuous, 150-mile road around the peninsula, or one may take the straight, 50-mile stretch to Rijeka, the northern terminus of the coastal road to Dubrovnik. I succumbed to the lure of the south.

The road offered a hilly, wooded landscape and one special Hapsburg reminder: the proximity of the village of Lipica, where the Lipizzaners, the famous white horses of the Vienna Imperial Riding School, were bred. I resisted a visit to the stud farm in my haste to return to the coast and **Rijeka**, a port city with a great history.

The Italians, who still call it Fiume, battled over Rijeka with Austria and Hungary for centuries. In 1919, Gabriele d'Annunzio, the poet, marched in at the head of a legion he had formed and claimed it for Italy. That didn't last, and the city wound up divided between Italy and Yugoslavia until World War II, during which it went entirely to Italy and then entirely to Yugoslavia.

Ironically, Rijeka under Communism has far surpassed in activity free-enterprise Trieste, under whose shadow it always lived. While Trieste has seen its port and much of its urban activity decline in competition with Italy's other Adriatic harbours, Rijeka has become the undisputed principal port of its country. For the tourist, Rijeka's chief interest lies in its animation rather than its churches and medieval walls. Architecture of greater splendour awaits a traveller in the towns to the south.

With its wide-open private enterprise coexisting with the state economy, its relaxed waterfront cafés and its animated, Mediterranean people, Rijeka is an eye-opener for those accustomed to the dour and disciplined cities of other Communist countries. Slovenes, the most Western of Yugoslavs, pretend to find this altogether natural, but in longer conversations their pride in this considerable achievement of swimming against the current cannot quite be disguised. And conversations are easy; any language one knows comes in handy. The reason lies not only in the region's multilingual past but also in Yugoslavia's present. It is the only Communist country that allows its people to work abroad, and throughout Yugoslavia one meets people who have benefited from that policy.

About ten miles out of Rijeka comes the first small disappointment on a journey that offers a preponderance of great pleasures. Beside the lovely medieval town of Bakar, nestled in a small bay at the foot of mountains that drop steeply to the sea, stand the chimneys and storage tanks of what looks like a major petroleum refinery, as well as other artefacts of an industrialization that has not spared either side of the Adriatic. But the overwhelming impressions of a drive along the Yugoslav coast are of the land itself, its wondrous interaction with the sea and the survival of beauty that man has created through the ages.

A factor that prevents at least the driver from getting totally overwhelmed by the sights during the 375-mile drive from Rijeka to Dubrovnik is the often spectacular character of the road. It is well surfaced, but it conforms to a coastline that curves, rises, drops (or at least dips), with Nature at her most capricious. It demands the utmost concentration from drivers and should also demand a measure of restraint from passengers, who tend to utter cries of alarm, if not predictions of imminent doom, that distract drivers intent upon avoiding those very disasters.

Two colours dominate: the blue of the sea and the greyish white of the austere mountains, which is also the colour of the towns and villages built from their stone. In Dalmatia, between Zadar and Dubrovnik, pine forests, palm trees and cypresses soften the austerity and add a third colour, completing an image that charms as the French and Italian Rivieras did before so much of them fell into the hands of 'developers.' Yugoslavia is not that capitalistic, but it may arrive at a similarly destructive result by a different route, as my first overnight stop indicated.

I approached **Zadar**, a city on a promontory with a history going back more than two and a half millennia, with thoughts of a drink at the hotel, a stroll through town and dinner, followed by another stroll by moonlight. But the authorities who planned the tourist sector of Dalmatia's economy decided, the way central planners do, to concentrate. They created an appalling tourist complex of six hotels and some camping grounds that is far enough out of town to discourage any acquaintance with it.

The hotels, a representative of the local tourism office regretfully agreed, are nothing more than factories receiving prepaying masses of pale West Germans and Italians and discharging them a week later pink, red or brown and no closer to the real Yugoslavia than on arrival. The attractions are sun, sea and rates lower than hotels at home.

'Meat! All meat!' the representative muttered as we pored over a map to find more pleasant accommodations. An excellent lunch at the privately owned fish restaurant he recommended made up for the dreary dinner the night before in a state establishment – a meal punctuated by a German paterfamilias ordering the waiter to let the running and screaming children run and scream because he was paying good marks for their meal.

Although Zadar suffered much destruction in the last war, it remains a city eminently worth visiting, above all for St. Donat's Church, a ninth-century edifice that is Dalmatia's outstanding early-Christian monument and a marvellous setting for concerts during the summer. The city also has St. Anastasia's Cathedral from the Romanesque period, examples of Gothic and baroque church architecture and a fine archaeological museum. Its anthropological museum is housed in a delightful sixteenth-century building sporting an elegant clock tower right out of a child's set of building blocks for a medieval town.

Two towns should detain the traveller on the hundred-mile drive from Zadar to Split – **Sibenik**, with its celebrated cathedral, and **Trogir**, on its own tiny islet. The road to both of these towns, however, is frequently slowed during the summer by an echo of the Hapsburg days: caravans of cars from Czechoslovakia proceeding at a snail's pace on a road that for most of the way makes passing unthinkable. When the landlocked people of Prague and Pilsen belonged to the same realm as Dalmatia, they were drawn to this coast as their holiday spot on the sea. That habit has continued, surviving all political vicissitudes and limited only by Czechoslovakia's poverty in the currencies that Yugoslav hotelkeepers will accept and the Prague Government's stinginess with passports. But enough Czechs get out, driving low-powered cars and curbing their speed further to save costly petrol, to make the coastal drive torture for Italian and West German speed merchants.

Almost nothing seems to have been added to the town of Trogir since the Renaissance. This unity makes all the more clashing the unceasing effusion of disco music from the tape recorders that are apparently as important to the many small private cafés as their espresso machines. Most memorable of all Trogir's glories is the portal of the thirteenth-century cathedral, a treasury of Romanesque sculpture by Master Radovan. But everywhere one walks in the town, even at the height of the tourist invasion, when today's world is decidedly too much with us, one can relish the expressions in glowing stone of a sense of beauty that is timeless.

Split's charm is the very opposite of Trogir's. Where the miniature town enchants with its unaltered harmony, the bigger city delights with the way it has absorbed into its everyday life a monumental masterpiece of classical antiquity, Emperor Diocletian's Palace. Built at the beginning of the fourth century, the palace is far from intact; a city that has renewed itself through the ages has penetrated it from all angles, grown into it and within it, made it its centre. Yet enough of the palace is still standing to suggest its original grandeur.

The immense complex that the Emperor built as his retirement home is now a warren of bustling, narrow streets. Palace arches have become parts of houses, and washing hangs from them. A modern bank has a central antique pillar on which customers can lean while waiting. Diocletian's mausoleum has with minimal transformation become a cathedral, and the Temple of Jupiter its baptistry.

Tradition is taken seriously in Split. An ordinary dinner became an event when seven local men strolled into the restaurant to sing old

Dalmatian songs, secular and religious, in well-rehearsed though amateur harmony. Not to pass the hat, not because a Ministry for Folklore paid them to entertain tourists – just because, like their fathers and grandfathers, they enjoy singing these songs. About $12 paid for dinner for two and an extra litre of wine for the singers, who continued their concert in a palace square, causing heads to pop out of surrounding windows, before they retired late at night.

One of the special delights of the coast is the chain of islands that remain in view all along, creating the charming illusion that the traveller is himself on an island. They also serve as an ever-present refuge when one feels that too many other travellers are pursuing the same itinerary. The island of **Hvar** was my twenty-four-hour getaway, a two-hour ferry ride from Split.

Like those around Venice, most of the Dalmatian islands have been inhabited and built upon – nobly, very often – as long as the coastal lands have. The ferry to Hvar takes one almost to the foot of a great Renaissance square, complete with cathedral and arsenal. Hvar's beaches, as rocky as those of the mainland, have the compensating charms of even more limpid water and a sparser summer population.

So rich are the marvels of the coast that I reached **Dubrovnik**, that fabled destination of so many voyages, enchanted once again by its Venetian beauty but seeing it also for the first time as a single gem, perhaps the brightest, in a long chain. I understood more deeply the flow of civilization in all its varied waves that had formed this precious amalgam.

Within its battlemented and turreted walls, punctuated by stalwart fortresses that have remained inviolate through many a siege from sea or land since the fourteenth century, Dubrovnik is as civil and urbane a town as the Mediterranean offers. The Placa, or Stradun, which divides the Old City's neat grid of streets like a central corridor, invites strolling for the simple joy of being there; each side street extends an irresistible offer to explore.

Because earthquakes and fires have spared little of premedieval Dubrovnik, today's city bears the preponderant imprint of the High Renaissance and baroque. The architectural diversity is harmonized by the consistent use of the same materials – the region's grey stone and red tile. Successive governments, no doubt inspired by Dubrovnik's exceptional unity, have discouraged architectural vandalism and preserved the integrity of an entire town that the United Nations Educational, Scientific and Cultural Organization has declared a cultural monument.

Leaving Dubrovnik was made easier by the knowledge that I was heading for a city of supreme beauty. And when, twenty-four hours after casting off, the ferry sailed slowly into Venice on a bright morning, I experienced not only the customary thrill of that matchless sight, but also the sense of encountering a source that has nourished untold beauty elsewhere.

SEASIDE YUGOSLAVIA
SETTING OUT

Travelling along the coast of Yugoslavia is fraught with special problems. Accommodations in such towns as Zadar, which are geared to mass tourism, are unattractive. There, as in Hvar, I would recommend taking a room in a private house; in both towns I would further recommend avoiding the tourist complexes to eat in privately owned restaurants, where the food is better, the choice is greater and the service is faster and more obliging. The Tourist Office in each town can make recommendations; at most private establishments dinner for two with local wine should be no more than about $15 to $25.

Prospective travellers should make their reservations for both hotels and private rooms well in advance. Prices are higher during the crowded summer months.

BEGINNING IN ITALY
Trieste

The **Grand Hotel Duchi d'Aosta**, 2 Piazza dell'Unita d'Italia 2 (62 081), is a nice, centrally situated hotel. Double rooms cost up to $90. Somewhat less expensive and also pleasant is the **Jolly**, 7 Corso Cavour (76 94), with double rooms ranging up to $70, including breakfast.

Excellent restaurants are the **Sacra Ostaria**, 13 Via di Campo Marzio (74 4968), and the **Antica Trattoria Suban**, 2 Via Comici (54 368). Both specialize in seafood and offer fine fish soup and seafood risotto. About $40 will cover dinner for two with house wine.

Along the coast
Zadar

Try to stay in a private house and ask the helpful people at the **Tourist Office**, Pave Cingrije (25 948), to recommend a restaurant.

Split

The **Marjan** (42 866) is a good modern hotel with double rooms costing about $60. The **Park** (515 411), with double rooms at about $55, has an agreebly old-fashioned air and a terrace for meals and afternoon coffee with superb Central European pastries. The **Tourist Office** (2 Trg Republike) or the hotel concierge should be consulted about restaurants.

Hvar

The **Amfora** (74 202) is a big modern hotel, with double rooms at about $40, but rooms in a private house are plentiful and cheap. They can be obtained through the **Tourist Office** in Stari Grad, the Old Town. The private restaurants on the waterfront are pleasant.

Dubrovnik

Two good hotels within easy walking distance of the Old Town are the **Excelsior** (23 566) and the **Argentina** (23 855), both with double rooms at about $60. A good restaurant is the **Domino**, 3 od Domina Ulica (32 832), which specializes in steaks and other grilled meats but also has a way with fresh Dalmatian fish and shellfish. It's a good idea to reserve a table on the terrace, which fills up fast. Good fish specialities are also served at the **Riblji**, 1 Siroka Ulica (27 589). The **Cavtat**, 29 od Puca Ulica (27 499), has a particularly nice décor and serves fragrant Dalmatian specialities and wines.

— H.K.

FROM THE MEDITERRANEAN TO THE INDIAN OCEAN

A WALKER'S ROMANCE WITH SYMI

John Wain

The Greek islands, famous through the centuries in poetry and legend, have been the focus of many a powerful daydream. I have known people whose lives have been changed by one visit to any of the three island groups (Sporades, Cyclades, Dodecanese), who went home immediately and began to plan a strategy for transferring their lives to one or another of them. The magic is particularly strong for those of us of northern European stock, and many a biscuit tin has seen at least the beginnings of a savings hoard aimed at resettling the whole family on a Greek island. And yet after all they are nothing but a few lumps of rock sticking up out of the sea.

All over the Mediterranean region, for that matter, one is ceaselessly aware of the contrast between the richness of the sea and the stony poverty of the land. These arid Greek islands are the despair of man the cultivator and harvester. It is man the seafarer, the fisherman and trader who has built an important civilization on their stone-riddled hillsides, where a few sheep and goats bite industriously at anything green and growing, and only the all-bountiful olive tree gives nourishment, and wood, and shade.

The island I have most recently visited is Symi (pronounced, more or less, 'seamy'), a steep, gnarled knob of a place reached by sailing two hours due north from Rhodes. Rhodes, the largest of the Dodecanese, is close to Turkey, a fact that has played a decisive part in its long and crowded history. Symi itself is so jammed up against Turkey that one can see Turkey's mysterious purple mountains from most of the island. Symi is a fascinating, beautiful place, and I would recommend it to anyone who likes a quiet holiday and can do without mass amusements, loud discos or smart cocktail bars.

If ever I saw barren land, I saw it there. Some of the hillsides, particularly those facing out to sea on the eastward side, are almost completely without vegetation – except that, when you get close to them, you see and smell the exquisite wild flowers that root and bloom everywhere in the crannies. For the rest, the creatures most at home among these sun-baked stones are lizards, cicadas and patient, clambering tortoises.

That is one face of Symi: rock, stone, and more rock and more stone, with the blue sea washing around it and the blue sky arching above. That the human race has for so long been able to flourish there is because of the sea, and because of the inexhaustible energy and inventiveness of man. The ancient craft of boat building still goes on. Quiet, patient men, with broad skilful hands and sun-dried faces, work every day along the foreshore with lengths of timber and saws and knives, constructing caiques to a design that was probably familiar to Homer. A boat is built from its rib cage outward and each stage is painted and left to dry as it is made, so that the foreshore always has two or three orange-painted rib cages, reminding one each morning of man's ancient dialogue with the sea.

I walked past these slow, attentive boatwrights every morning with a friend with whom I was renting a small villa on one of the steep hillsides running down to the harbour. We found that our days quickly fell into a pattern. We like to walk, and there are rough but (in stout shoes) manageable paths leading over the hillsides in several inviting directions. These walks vary from the gentle stroll to the best-foot-forward expedition. We could amble up from Symi town to the monastery of St. George Drakountiotis ('he who has to do with dragons') and then down the short slope to the Bay of St. Irini, where there was a stone jetty, very handy for getting into the sea without having to walk over the rough shingle; this was our favourite bathing place.

We could take the more difficult walk up out of the town, past a row of squat, mysterious towers crowning the line of the ridge, which suggested fortified lookouts but had obviously doubled as windmills, and down into the Bay of Marina. If we wanted to walk along a surfaced road, we could take the short stroll to the deep inlet of Pedi. In addition, one of the few proper roads led down the spine of the island, all the way to Panormitis with its monastery – a walk we planned to take but, with the heat and our lazy mood, never did. We visited the place by boat.

The main thing is not to miss seeing Panormitis ('All-Harbours'), a gentle, wooded inlet where the island shows, for once, a welcoming face to the seafarer. The monastery, cool and white and tranquil, protected from the sun by stately trees in the courtyard, breathes that calm acceptance that the Eastern Orthodox version of Christianity seems to generate. A few yards outside its walls, a plinth commemorates the execution of the abbot of the monastery, one of his lay staff and a Greek resistance fighter, who were shot by the Germans in February 1944. Their crime: having allowed a group of British commandos to hide in the monastery and set up a radio transmitter.

Contrast, always contrast, in this part of the world is the law of life; even in this solemn and lofty place, war has left its pools of blood.

The sun (in mid-April) was, in the central hours of the day, far too hot for walking; we could have spent these hours strolling in the town or sitting in the waterside cafés, but this is also the part of the day when Symi town fills up with holidaymakers on day trips from Rhodes. Sleek, modern ferryboats, each holding 300 or 400 passengers, begin depositing their loads of humanity at mid-morning and begin taking them up again at mid-afternoon, and while these visitors were perfectly nice people, they tended to swamp the place for the small number of us who were staying on Symi, and therefore we clung to the usual belief of the visitor that for the length of our stay the facilities of the island belonged to us, the regulars. We had no right to this belief, of course, but then people have no right to half the beliefs they hold.

So we would go down early to the shops on the waterfront, and in the shadowy little streets behind, and lay in our day's stock of food and wine – oranges, feta cheese, delicious bread, olives, and large bottles of the local retsina, light and refreshing and only faintly resinous – and decamp to our eyrie to spend the middle part of the day on our balcony, eating, drinking, reading, talking, till the boatloads began to churn slowly out of the harbour and the tide of cool shadow to advance over the hillside. Then it would be time for an exploration, and the walking would bring on an appetite and the appetite would lead us to one of the pleasant small restaurants for red mullet or pork or lamb, with Greek salad, and another installment of retsina or perhaps some of the smooth red wine from Rhodes. Or sometimes I would have a glass of Fix, that good Greek beer whose name is arrived at by translating Fuchs, the name of the original Austrian brewer, into Greek letters and then transliterating it back again.

Most of the things that Symi has to offer could be found on any Greek island – sea, sun, rocky coasts, steep little streets, good things to eat and drink. What made it unique for us was the town of Symi itself rising up from the harbour. For Symi is two towns. The day visitors from Rhodes rarely climb to the upper town; indeed, the longer-term visitors go there very little unless they are sound in wind and limb, for it involves climbing many stone steps.

The climb is abundantly worth the trouble. Step by step, as one rises, more and more houses come into view. The upper town is only partly visible from below; some of it is over the crest of the ridge, and it makes no great spectacle from a distance. The main street, partly flights of steps and partly a smooth, not too steep gradient, leads upward to a maze of side streets, a secret city high above the bustling little harbour with its tourist shops and restaurants. There are shops in the upper town, too, and restaurants, but mainly it is the local people who use them.

Up there, not only are you away from tourism – a rare enough thing in any Greek territory – you are also amid a setting that mingles dignity and stateliness with brooding melancholy, and with a bright everyday cheerfulness, in a way I have never encountered in any place before. The houses are very handsome. All are beautifully proportioned, all are made of the finest materials, full of white marble and mosaic paving; and about half of them are empty, and not only empty but derelict, roofless, with trees growing up inside the rooms. What were obviously the mansions of prosperous merchants, with dates from the 1870s and 1880s still clear above their doorways, are now abandoned shells, sometimes with the black marks of fire still showing on their stonework.

It is a sight to remind one of W.B. Yeats's lines:

> *When all those rooms and passages are gone,*
> *When nettles wave above a shapeless mound*
> *And saplings root among the broken stone.*

The reflective, melancholy mood aroused by these ruins, however, is continually dispelled by the cheerfulness of the houses that are inhabited. Everywhere these are spick and span. Children run in and out of doorways; citizens bring chairs out into the lanes in the cool of the evening and catch up on the day's gossip; the inevitable canned Greek music rings out from the tavernas. And there is always the chance that, rounding some corner between high walls, one will suddenly come upon the elegant shape, stately yet welcoming, of one of Symi's many monasteries, usually with its courtyard shaded by trees.

Obviously the present-day inhabitants of the town are living in what remains of a much richer and more populous centre. But being Greeks and therefore great survivors, they see no reason why this should make them depressed. About half the houses are empty shells; in the other half, life surges along, though where the inhabitants get the income to keep up their attractive homes is a mystery to me. Perhaps they all own businesses down on the harbourfront.

The obvious thing, to anyone on the shortest of visits, is that Symi is half the town it was, in population, and probably not a tenth of what it was in richness. This is the work of two predators: war, and specifically in this case World War II; and progress, that impartial giant who has flattened as many communities as he has lifted up.

Progress struck first. The wealth that built these fine houses was founded on sponge fishing. The Symi people had excelled at this painfully difficult trade ever since the fourteenth century when as a result of some astute bargaining, they made a separate peace just before the Turks conquered Rhodes and were allowed to carry on their trade, custom and religion unhindered. For over 400 years they harvested the sponges as the American Indians harvested the buffalo – at a pace slow enough to allow the creatures to keep up their numbers so that the resource was always there. At last, with the technological jump forward of the nineteenth century, the sponge suffered the same fate as the buffalo, and during roughly the same time span.

Originally, sponges were gathered by divers who held their breath and sank to the sea floor holding on to a heavy stone. Once down, the diver groped around for a sponge, cut the root or stem that bound it to the rock, and put it in a basket to be pulled up on a line. Since even the hardy fishermen could dive for only about sixty seconds without coming up for air, a man was lucky if he gathered a few good-size sponges in a day. But there were a lot of divers, and a lot of boats – under Turkish protection, the people of Symi fished all over the Mediterranean and all over the oceans of the Ottoman Empire – and it was enough. Before the invention of foam rubber, every household bathroom in Europe and America, and every seraglio in the Middle East, had its sponges.

Then in 1819 came the invention of the covered diving-suit with air-tubes, which was to the sponge what the rifle was to the buffalo. The suited divers cleaned out the shallow sponge beds; had to go deeper; finally had to go down into the cold darkness of forty fathoms. In those days nothing was known about nitrogen narcosis, and when a diver signalled that he wanted to come up, it was thought helpful to whisk him to the surface as fast as possible. Many died in the agony of the bends; many survived in a crippled state. But there were always others to take their place, for the sponge trade was booming and the fine new houses on Symi were going up as fast as the craftsmen could work.

The 1880s were the good years, when, exactly as in a gold rush, the lure of wealth seemed more dazzlingly important than human lives, certainly other people's lives. It was said, though reliable statistics would be impossible to come by, that one man in three on Symi was either dead, or dying, or crippled before his youth was over. Then the peak began to slope down. Men would not undertake the work. The fleets carried on, recruiting divers from nearby Kalymnos; if it comes to that, I believe some sponge fishing goes on even today. But in a world that can so easily make sponges from rubber or plastic, there is no longer any point in paying that human price.

As for World War II, the story is told more shortly and is in any case in all the history books. First Italian, then the grimmer German occupation; British aerial bombardment; guerrilla and commando action. When the Germans finally pulled out in December 1944, they gathered all their ammunition and detonated it to keep it from falling into Allied hands. This was normal military practice; whether it was normal practice to keep the ammunition in Symi's finest church, standing high on the promontory that is the town's Acropolis, is more doubtful.

The dreadful explosion was timed to happen an hour or two after the German forces put to sea. The original orders were that the whole thing was to be kept secret from the townspeople, which would have resulted in hundreds of deaths in the shattered houses around. But a decent man, a corporal, risked his neck by tipping off the inhabitants, and all that day the houses were quietly evacuated, treasured possessions being passed out through back doors and over balconies. One of the ships taking off the soldiers was mined or torpedoed a few miles out to sea, with the loss of most of those on board, including the corporal. At least he was in a better position to meet his Maker than the higher officers who gave the original order.

A strong argument for spending a holiday on Symi is that it involves, on the way there and the way back, visits to Rhodes. This, the largest and most easterly of the Dodecanese, has always been a special place. In the third century BC it was the richest of all the Greek city-states; and since then it has known wealth, poverty, peace, war, but never insignificance.

Even as part of classical Greece, Rhodes was very highly differentiated, with its own way of looking at things. In religion, for example. The ancient Greeks had very localized minds; gods and goddesses tended to be associated with specific places, and the cult and the temples for each one grew up in that place. The heavenly bodies, though they were undoubtedly thought of as divine, were given the tribute of a vague general respect rather than an actual cult, because they were not associated with a particular place. Except in Rhodes. There, Helios the sun god was worshipped with temples and a full-scale cult. Now that the worship of the sun has returned to earth in a different form, when so many people feel deeply emotional about the sun as they hardly do about anything else, Rhodes, with its glittering harbour, swimming pools and beaches, and its cool groves of trees beneath the huge medieval walls of the fortress, is still the ideal place for the worshippers of Helios.

THE ISLAND IN FOCUS
BASICS

The best time to visit Symi is between April and October, but the island of 2,300 inhabitants is usually crowded in the peak months of July and August. Symi is seven miles long and six miles wide, has only one coastal village and has a limited choice of accommodations. The best way to get there is to take one of the five daily flights from Athens to the island of Rhodes, a 35-minute trip costing about $40 one way, then take one of the four daily ferries to Symi. The trip costs about $10 round trip and takes two hours each way.

ACCOMMODATIONS
There are three hotels, all small, the **Aliki**, the **Dorian** and the **Nirefs**. At the Aliki a double room with a sea view and air conditioning costs about $40, including breakfast; without a sea view, about $35. Two suites, each sleeping up to four persons, are about $50. The newly built Dorian is a bit less expensive. The Nirefs was due to reopen in 1986 after closing for a season to expand its facilities threefold, to sleep a total of 65 persons.

Rooms in private homes and entire houses are available for rent. Houses vary in size from one to four rooms and can accommodate between two to six people. Prices run from $10 a day for two to $25 for the house sleeping six. Each place has a kitchenette.

RESTAURANTS
The island has a score of tavernas and restaurants, most of them offering a variety of local and international dishes. The best known is **Katerinetes**, which has a varied menu but specializes in fish. A fish dinner costs about $25 for two, including wine. It starts with soup (fish or meat), goes on to a shrimp dish, continues with grilled fish or lobster, and ends with fresh fruit or ice cream and after-dinner drinks. A more moderate meal with a few appetizers, a steak for two, fruit, salad and wine will cost about $18.

Most restaurants will have fresh fish and appetizers such as squid, octopus and *taramosalata* (fish roe paste), and include such Greek dishes as moussaka and stuffed vine leaves. Prices average $12 for two, including wine.

The island also has a few bars and two discothèques.

ISLAND ART
A small museum exhibits Dodecanese island art, with an emphasis on the area's maritime history. It is open daily except Sunday from 9 am to 2.30 pm; admission is free, though it is customary for visitors to make a small contribution.

NEW EYES IN AN ANCIENT WORLD

D. M. Thomas

I could have wished to see the treasures of Tutankhamen under better circumstances than these: peering over a throng of tourists while our officious Egyptian guide shouts, 'Hurry up, please! Keep together!' She rebukes me sternly when I veer off toward an exquisite figurine, recognized from an art book. It's not on our tour of 'highlights,' and I might lose touch with the group. I could get lost in the labyrinthine museum, and there is no time for the bus to wait for stragglers. Trapped in Cairo, I would be yet another victim of Tutankhamen's curse.

Lingering perilously after our party has rushed on, I press my face to the glass case to see the golden throne on which the queen, with still-living tenderness, is offering a flower to her husband. I have described it in a novel I'm writing, and I want to confirm that such timeless beauty exists. It does. I rush to catch up with the mob. 'Back inside quickly! We are going to have a speedy lunch, then you will see the famous Pyramids . . . '

The lowest level of ochre stone is head high; when I strain my neck to gaze up, the stone ranges 'tease me out of thought,' to paraphrase Keats. The Pyramids are awesome, but no more so in reality than they were in my imagination. I cling on to the humanity of the queen's flower. The myriad toilers in Cheops's time have yielded to myriad camel drivers and pedlars of junk souvenirs. One cries 'Tally Ho!' when he learns I am English, and claims improbably to be Yorkshire born. He presses bangles on me, for England's sake, then somehow extracts a £5 note from me, 'for Allah's sake.'

April dusk falls as our coach inches toward the city outskirts. We pass the walls of a graveyard, shadowed by waving, grinning, barefoot boys and girls. They live in a cemetery known as the City of the Dead, yet appear happy. My real discovery in Egypt is its people's inexcusable gaiety and vivacity. These hungry, houseless children have no right to wave and dance and smile at us sleek tourists. Nor do Egyptian girls have the right to be so beautiful without health charts, controlled diets and dentistry. I see two or three slender Nefertitis on every street;

and evidently they change gracefully into plump and dignified matrons.

Five hours later we are disgorged back onto our cruise ship, a Greek liner called the *Atlas*. No time for a shower or a change . . . we rush to dinner. The food on board is good, the service first class. But there is, in fact, hardly time to feel the pleasant timelessness of cruising. We are 'doing' the eastern Mediterranean in a week, and it's all go. The first day, we had an afternoon stop at Rhodes. Unseasonable clouds and cold (in England it is unseasonably cloudless and warm) suddenly became a Mediterranean spring, and red flowers blazed on a slanting field. That is my memory of Rhodes. The second afternoon gave us the culture shock of Alexandria, as foetid, squalid, crammed and mind-blowing as Lawrence Durrell painted it in his *Alexandria Quartet*. Tomorrow, after Cairo, we must rise again at six for a day's tour of Israel. Maybe we won't bother with it, we say, as we collapse onto our bunks.

I have never particularly wanted to go to Israel. I would have preferred seeing one or two more Greek islands. Moreover, last week some bombs were planted on Arab buses. Tomorrow happens to be Good Friday: a perfect day, we decide, for a reprisal in Jerusalem.

Bonnie, a charming American-Israeli guide, welcomes us with a rose each, to thank us for visiting her troubled country. The sky is cloudless, for the first time; the coach air-conditioned, the road smooth, the hills and citrus groves peaceful. We have, in Bonnie, an intelligent woman who obviously takes pride in her work. She notices straightaway that our seven-year-old son is sitting uncomfortably on his mother's lap and tactfully rearranges the seating without offending anyone. The talks she gives are informative and amusing, and she senses when we would prefer silence. Passionate about her newly discovered homeland, she points out the wayside monuments to dead soldiers and tells us that a jet can cross Israel from south to north in fifteen minutes and from west to east in fifteen seconds – a graphic illustration of Israel's fragility.

Nevertheless, she makes me squirm with some chauvinistic remarks. The Arab mayors who were blown up? They really had themselves to blame. The Palestinian problem? She will explain it to us very simply, in just two minutes . . .

But there was peace, an indefinable serenity, that Good Friday in embattled Israel. I could see that this was, indeed, the Holy Land. I had used this terrain, but only metaphorically, as a setting in my novel *The White Hotel*, yet it would never have occurred to me that one aspect of my metaphor could be borne out in contemporary reality: a holy stillness.

'All journeys,' writes Martin Buber, 'have secret destinations of which the traveller is unaware.' The discoveries of my foreign journeys have usually not been the ones I anticipated. Thus, I first saw Venice only because I wanted a break during a monotonous Yugoslavian holiday; astonishingly, I expected little of Venice, believing I would find a cliché. Imagine gliding in a hovercraft toward San Marco when one hasn't expected anything! I gasped with wonder. In Leningrad, the revelation was not the Hermitage and other palaces but an Orthodox cathedral service. In Egypt, not the majesty of the Pharaohs but the living majesty of poor people.

And in Israel, where I expected fear, I found serenity. Where I expected a distasteful blend of ancient fanaticisms and modern commercialism, I found Jerusalem the Golden . . . It came into view like a mirage, shimmering, poised between matter and spirit. As Venice seems to balance air and water, so Jerusalem seemed as rooted in the azure sky as it was in its rock. When we entered the city, I couldn't believe how still it was – and on such a day.

Again our guide helped, by leading us to Bethlehem in the morning, when the crowds at the sepulchre would have been greatest. The Church of the Nativity was almost deserted. I liked the idea of thinking about Jesus' birth when everyone else was thinking about his death. Before we filed into the grotto traditionally accepted as the birthplace, Bonnie asked if any of us could sing. Frank, a tall, burly American, eagerly said yes, and together they started up 'Silent Night.' We all joined in uncertainly. It was very moving. There was even a young woman with a child on her lap, sitting in an alcove.

Frank, gaining confidence, transported with religious joy, struck up a second carol and then a third, in his strong but wavering voice. I was reminded of Delius waspishly observing of the liturgical composer Parry that he would have set the whole Bible to music if he could. Frank, I suspected, would have liked to sing the whole *Oxford Book of Carols*. Sensitive as ever, Bonnie steered Frank out, still singing. She had noticed a priest who wanted to be alone for a few moments, in quietness.

As we took our seats in the coach, an Arab boy jumped on, waving postcards. Bonnie put her hand firmly on his head and pushed him out. With a sheepish smile, he vanished. The Arabs generally were subdued. In that respect, the contrast with Egypt was disturbing.

After a relaxed lunch at an Arab restaurant overlooking the Mount of Olives, we moved on to Christ's Passion. Around the cross, in the Church of the Holy Sepulchre, it was crowded and sombre; old women in black habits wept. Our son became uncomfortable in the candle-flickering gloom, and his mother took him outside. Like me, he showed a preference for the place of birth.

Together, he and I covered our heads to go to the Wailing Wall, wrote our prayers on slips of paper and pressed them into cracks. I looked at the stately, sober-suited long-bearded Jews and saw why they are indestructible. Later – too late – our son opened his tiny fist and showed us a prayer slip that, he claimed, had fallen out of the wall. We debated with our consciences whether to post it to the Chief Rabbi, Jerusalem, but decided that God had probably read it already.

Our ship, which had disembarked us at Ashdod, would meet us at Haifa. We set off to complete the triangle. How amazing to be told that, just over there, by the roadside, was Rachel's grave! And to be entering the valley of Sharon. The Song of Songs was all around us. The Rose of Sharon . . . I would have loved to glimpse Galilee and the Dead Sea. But by the time we had passed swiftly through compact, affluent Tel Aviv and reached Haifa, we seemed to have covered much of Israel, without undue hurry and without terrorists. I knew I wanted to come back some day to see it properly.

Yet what, after all, is seeing something 'properly'? As well ask of the travellers to Emmaus if they had seen Christ 'properly.' For any with eyes to see, we were being shown daily miracles. I wondered how many, though, were fully aware of the ocean of experience, human and divine, they were crossing; from the Acropolis in Athens to the Pyramids and Tutankhamen (and you could, if you had superhuman endurance, take a quick flight to Luxor), on to the Old Testament and the Gospels. Nor had we finished. There were still the Revelations of St. John, written on Patmos, and the Greco-Roman ruins of Ephesus.

But between Christ and St. John we were grateful for a full day's sailing. Almost for the first time on the cruise, I felt in touch with myself at the age of fourteen, when my family emigrated to Australia. I had always wanted to taste again that month-long, mythic voyage round the globe. The thirst to rediscover is as powerful and unslakable as the thirst to discover.

Strangely, my Australian adolescence was brought close to me when, after a swim at dawn on holy, barren Patmos, we landed on the Turkish mainland and were driven to Ephesus. The first poetry that ever thrilled me had been projected from a cinema screen in Melbourne – some lines, as I discovered much later, of John Donne:

> *I wonder, by my troth, what thou and I*
> *Did, till we loved? Were we not wean'd till then?*
> *But suck'd on country pleasures, childishly?*
> *Or snored we in the Seven Sleepers' den?*

I came to learn, almost unnecessarily, that the incomprehensibly moving line about the Seven Sleepers' den referred to seven youths of Ephesus found alive after sleeping in a cave for 200 years. And now our learned guide was saying that over there, in those volcanic hills, the seven young men of Ephesus had slept! Einstein was right – the universe is curved; we don't move in straight lines.

If I had been asked before the cruise which places on our itinerary interested me least, I would have said Israel and Ephesus. I might easily have passed up both excursions. But Ephesus proved to be as stunning, on a smaller scale, as Israel. The past is so intact there that I really felt I was walking along a Roman street. A heart shape and a footmark point the way of successful traders to the brothel today as clearly as they did 2,000 years ago. As we stood in the amphitheatre, marvelling at its acoustics, a troupe of Turkish girls glided in, right on cue, and performed a charming folk dance.

Almost casually we were told that the Virgin Mary had spent her last years in a house nearby. History and myth blend into one in the blazing Ephesian sunlight, as does our classical and biblical heritage. Great is Diana of the Ephesians ... Some American teenagers brawled among the sacred stones. They didn't seem to be getting much out of the cruise. A Turkish urchin licked his parched lips as he saw them buying the bottles of Coke that were as far out of his reach as the treasures of Tutankhamen are from mine.

Back to the *Atlas*, and a sense of end-of-voyage dereliction. An elderly Californian, with her daughter, prepared gallantly to set off on a seventeen-day coach tour of Europe. We, for our part, looked forward to a quiet few days on a beach in Crete. I had thought we might be glad of some time on solid earth, with no rush, and I was right. The ship threw us off early in the morning at Piraeus, the port of Athens, and prepared to haul on the next shoal of tourists. We drove to the airport and flew south. Days of pleasant recuperation interrupted by just one hectic coach trip. Our tour of the ancient world would not have been complete without seeing Cnossus, the centre of that mysterious Minoan civilization. Wasp-waisted, bare-breasted ladies and bull cults. Monsters in labyrinths ...

Yet Cnossus slightly disappointed us. The proximity of modern Herakleion spoiled the setting of the great palace, and there were simply too many swarms of sightseers. And then, one can take only so many wonders; we were by that time 'mazed' enough – crazy, disturbed, in my Celtic dialect – and couldn't take another labyrinth.

The holiday had given me sketches, rather than large-scale landscapes; but then, I regard myself as an impressionistic writer, for whom three hours in a place is as likely to touch my imagination as three weeks there; and three years would not necessarily bear any creative fruit. Indeed, often I will write first and see later. The joys of discovery are unpredictable. For me, the Pyramids have settled back into books; it is the poor Nefertitis of the squalid streets whom I still see.

CHRISTMAS EVE IN BETHLEHEM

Lucinda Franks

The single guiding star has been shattered by time into a carnival of glittering lights, but the pilgrims still tread the road to Bethlehem in search of the miracle of Christ's birth.

The difference between what is nurtured in our imaginations and what is offered up to us in reality is nowhere more stark than in this biblical town. Christmas in Bethlehem. The ancient dream: a cold clear night made brilliant by a glorious star, the smell of incense, shepherds and wise men falling to their knees in adoration of the sweet baby, the incarnation of perfect love. This simple tableau is so rich with meaning that whether represented on the mantelpiece or in the mind, it seems suspended, complete unto itself, somewhere in eternity.

The modern reality: a teeming rendezvous called Manger Square where carousers trip and break bottles on ancient stone amid strings of coloured lights and shops bearing the signs 'Holyland Souvenirs' and 'Jesus Is Here – Souvenirs, Statuettes.' Flashing lights in the shapes of crosses project from rooftops, an enormous Christmas tree is piled with tinsel, rendering its natural green invisible; radios blare from open cafés; army jeeps and barbed wire welcome visitors to the city. It is a kind of Coney Island of Christianity.

Arriving for Christmas Eve festivities in Bethlehem, one ponders the fact that man has always been man and wonders whether that humble scene described in Matthew and Luke with such flights of poetry was so humble after all. Were the gentle shepherds really an elbowing, shoving crowd eager for a peek into the stable where some curious event was rumoured to have taken place? What were the true motives of the Magi bearing their gifts? Will the chronicles that survive a millennium from now tell of a Bethlehem in the twentieth century AD where Christians from all over the world came to hang lights, imbibe spirits, and fall to their knees in adoration on the anniversary of Christ's birth?

The biblical story of the birth is striking in its absence of information. We never know exactly who the wise men are – philosophers? teachers? astrologers? – nor where in the East they came from, nor why they want to follow the star and pay homage to the King of the Jews. It is as though they are symbols, metaphors created by the writers of the Gospels to represent the enthusiasm that the Nativity created in the land.

So stands Bethlehem today: the symbol of a dream. It has a strange amorphous quality, particularly during this holiday; a place where fact gives way to fable and the present is swallowed by longing for the past. There are probably fewer people in Bethlehem than there are carved representations of people. The tiny shops survive and have survived for centuries – early pilgrims wrote of being offered models in stone and wood of the manger – by selling that which provides tangibility to that which might have been. Their shelves are piled high with mother-of-pearl icons and inexpensive olive wood replicas (both materials are native and carved by local artisans) of every notable, from Mary to the donkey, in the Nativity scene. The imposing Church of the Nativity – laid out in the shape of a cross – is a more grandiose commemorative gesture, and inside, the grotto where Jesus is thought to have been lain, in an animal's feeding trough made of stone (now faced with white marble), is overpowered with candles and brocade and elaborate incense burners.

It is as a cornucopia of symbols that Bethlehem can be enjoyed, and if the symbols are a crazy quilt of tinsel and gold, the raucous and the pristine, the ancient custom and the modern, then that is what makes Christmas Eve at the place of the Saviour's birth almost 2,000 years later so fascinating.

To attest to that, my husband and I have spent two Christmas Eves in Bethlehem. On our last visit, the security at the entrances to the town was formidable. Travelling the short thoroughfare leading from Jerusalem, which is dark and deserted on this particular holiday, one comes suddenly onto a blaze of lights up on the hilltop town. Beneath a banner reading 'Merry Christmas,' soldiers at a checkpoint ask for special permits issued by the Ministry of Tourism which everyone needed to enter the city. 'The whole world is watching Bethlehem tonight,' explained an official. 'If there is any place the terrorists would like to hit, it is here.' After going through several more checkpoints, we park our car outside the centre and climb the slope to Manger Square.

Here, milling around the central Christmas tree, are thousands of people from a myriad of cultures and occupations, some motivated by reverence, others simply by the urge to revel. Dour-faced monks stride with hands tucked in sleeves brushing against women from Iowa in fur-collared coats. Nuns in white stand with heads bowed over rosaries, ignoring the drops of whisky that land on their habits from gaggles of Swedish teenagers happily passing the bottle. Other youths, from Europe and the United States, choose a quieter method of celebration and pass out books of Christmas carols and occupy corners of the square singing 'O Little Town of Bethlehem.' Arab boys, those who are not joining their Western peers in tipsy antics, stroll about selling pretzels and hard-boiled eggs. A group of teen-agers from Yorkshire are trying to push each other into the fountain. Czechoslovak men and women are carrying candles and circling in a dance. In the middle of the square, the international flavour reaches its peak with choirs from Bordeaux, San Antonio, Johannesburg and Stockholm ascending bleachers and singing carols from their native lands. The cold air blows off the Judean Hills, and even Arab Christians in long layered skirts pull tight their burnooses. We warm ourselves with Turkish coffee sold over an open flame and, from another vendor, buy lamb's-wool hats to protect our freezing ears.

We explore the side streets off Manger Square. Some are lighted with neon signs and have flags strung from window to window, full of cafés and cupboard-size shops offering grains, beans, nuts and Tur-kish candies in large barrels. Others are dark and eerie, with passage-ways where donkeys stand motionless and huddles of Arab men crouch smoking water pipes. Bethlehem dates back to ancient times, but it did not come into its own until after the Nativity, when common folk, monks and emperors journeyed here and erected churches commemorating every step of the Holy Family's sojourn. The streets are pungent with aromas of coffee, arrack (grape alcohol flavoured with anise seed) and herb-flavoured lamb roasting on spits. On one of the few streets open to cars we see a limousine parked up on the kerb; a woman with a steeple headdress jangling with coins (it dates back to the Middle Ages, when a married woman carried her dowry in this fashion) squeezes past and disappears, bowing her head, through a low door.

We come upon a promising sign in English and Arabic: Milk Grotto Street. Everywhere you turn in this town there is another sacred site – an historic well, a wall with inscriptions and graffiti written by ancient pilgrims, a cave or grotto that has given rise to monasteries and chapels. The Church of the Milk Grotto is one of the sweetest of edifices, with its mother-of-pearl inlaid staircase and its interior columns, where the birth of Jesus and the flight of Mary and Joseph with the babe to Egypt is carved in stone. The church is built around the grotto where the Holy Family was said to have hidden while Herod's decree for the slaughter of the children of Bethlehem was being carried out. While Mary was nursing the child, a few drops of milk fell on a rock, which was said to have turned from red to white. For centuries, pilgrims chipped stone off the rock and took the chips back home because they were rumoured to have the power to aid lactation. In one corner of the grotto, there is a rare and haunting painting of Mary nursing her son, believed to be an Italian work of the eighteenth century.

The most spectacular of edifices in Bethlehem is, of course, the Church of the Nativity. Its basilica was erected in the fourth century by Constantine the Great, was rebuilt and enlarged by Emperor Justinian in the sixth century, and has since been expanded to include chapels representing the Armenian, Greek Orthodox, Franciscan and Roman Catholic churches, all of which have traditionally squabbled with each other over the control and administration of the historic structure. Fortunately, the Armenian church celebrates Christmas on January 6 and the Greek Orthodox Church on January 7, and the Roman Catholic church has unobstructed dominion on December 24 and 25.

The ecumenical and eclectic nature of the church is actually what has saved it from the whims of fate down through the ages. For instance, the Persians destroyed almost every Christian sanctuary in the Holy Land in AD 614, but when they got to Bethlehem they found, to their surprise, a mosaic on the church walls representing the three Magi in Persian dress, and out of respect for their countrymen, spared the church. The soul of the Church of the Nativity is the Grotto of the Nativity, directly below the altar and divided up into various shrines. Lighted only by candles, the shepherd's cave where Mary and Joseph repaired when 'there was no room for them in the inn' seems to have a mystical hush about it as all humanity – American sailors, Franciscan friars, nuns in robes of blue or white or black, German youths with backpacks, Filipino families in Sunday best – file in and out.

The spot where tradition says the birth took place is marked by a silver star embedded in marble and carrying the inscription *Hic De Virgine Maria Jesus Christus Natus Est*. Visitors kneel down, blank-faced, at the elaborate altar erected above the spot: some kiss the star; a few bring their lips to the myriad silver filigree lamps that hang over the star. Across from this site and down a few steps is the marble-faced manger where Jesus was lain in swaddling clothes after his birth.

Earlier in the day, the Roman Catholic Patriarch, accompanied by church and city officials in full regalia, led a procession from his residence in Jerusalem's old walled city to Bethlehem, where he was met by Girl Scouts and children of the town. Now, the bells of St. Catherine's peal the signal for the climax of celebrations, the midnight mass. Tickets to the service are treasured, and as we present our tickets at the entrance to St. Catherine's (the Roman Catholic church attached to the Church of the Nativity), we are frisked and our satchels searched. We file in line past spotlighted palm trees and statues of the saints in the atrium and into the church proper, where there is standing room only. The shoving, elbowing crowds have now become so still, not even a sneeze is heard, only the low, mystical sounds of the choir singing Gregorian chants.

Amid a profusion of gladioli and flickering candles, the Latin Patriarch, surrounded by Turkish guards with swords and silver staffs, enters the church and leads the procession up the aisle with a doll-like replica of the Christ child in his arms. Following him are prelates and officials, including Mayor Teddy Kollek of Jerusalem, various army officers, an Ethiopian bishop in white robes and a monk in a simple brown robe. The Christ child is lain on a bed of straw at the foot of the altar, and the mass begins. People are pressed together body to body, and the smells of cologne and perfume add to the intoxication of the event. They crane their necks to see the altar, a patchwork of rich colour swimming in and out of view – white, gold and red brocade robes, silver sceptres, red cardinal's hats, a painting of Mary holding up the newborn baby, a blue cross bearing a weary Jesus fashioned in silver.

The television lights (the service is being broadcast all over the world) bounce off the crystal chandeliers, and though they destroy the intimacy of the candlelight, they create an eerie haze that somehow seems appropriate. The scent of incense permeates the church as a choir of children and adults sing the *Kyrie eleison*, their voices echoing against the rough stone walls. Hymn after hymn is sung, the voices of the choir drifting in and out in contrapuntal perfection, and there is a strong feeling growing among the crowd. When the choir sings 'Silent Night,' several people cry or bow their heads. The church bells peal, and strangers from all corners of the world smile at and hug each other. As we leave St. Catherine's and come out into the cold neon-bright night, we feel lightheaded. We have stood at the site of one of the greatest events in history and partaken, on this Christmas Eve, of the belief in miracles.

IF YOU GO

Visitors who wish to attend midnight mass at the Church of St. Catherine's in Bethlehem on Christmas Eve must have tickets. These tickets, which are free, are distributed by the **Franciscan Pilgrims Office**, Jaffa Gate, Post Office Box 186, Jerusalem 91000 Israel. The church holds only about 200 people, and priority is given to pilgrims and diplomats.

Those without tickets may gather in Manger Square outside the church to watch the service, which begins at 11.45 pm, on a huge television screen.

JUST AN OLD-FASHIONED SAFARI

Michael Korda

Only a little more than a decade ago, people who went to Kenya still journeyed into the bush Hemingway-style, with tents, bearers and a 'white hunter,' mostly to shoot the game rather than look at it. Those days have gone forever. The word 'safari' now conjures up pictures of a crowded Nissan minibus full of tourists wearing funny hats and carrying cameras. The game drive, as it is now known, often looks depressingly similar to a sightseeing trip on a Manhattan tour bus.

There's no denying that it's a good way of seeing animals, but it lacks the romance implicit in the idea of a safari. Of course, no journey to see Kenya's wildlife is ever completely free from drama or so plush as to be boring – if nothing else, there are heat, dust, mosquitoes and rough roads (or none at all) to contend with. But the motorized safari, in which the game-watcher travels from lodge to lodge by light plane and views the game from a minibus or Land-Rover, can seem a little tame to those whose idea of Africa has been formed by reading Rider Haggard or *The Short Happy Life of Francis Macomber*.

Personally, I like game drives, though I'm not sure I'd want to go on one with half a dozen strangers. If you can afford it, it's obviously better to have your own vehicle and driver (and to make sure that your driver is knowledgeable and experienced about game), but however you do it, the game drive remains the best way of seeing animals, which is, after all, the whole point of being in Kenya. For those who want an additional spice of adventure, there are at least two ways to get it (a third way would be to get out of your vehicle in the presence of dangerous animals, but this is forbidden and unwise in the extreme).

Staying at a tented camp instead of a modern lodge offers a view of what Kenya was like in the old days, before the game lodges were built. It usually involves living under canvas, without electricity or running water, much the way safaris were done before the jet and the minibus transformed what had been an élitist, romantic adventure in the nineteenth century tradition into just another form of modern tourism.

A hot air balloon safari, on the other hand, though it is hardly traditional, is a more primal experience. From a balloon one senses more easily than in a vehicle that this is the birthplace of life, a kind of Garden of Eden, still preserved. Drifting silently above the plains, it is possible to imagine what it must have looked like in the beginning, when mankind was only just born, a grubby and insignificant mammal scrambling for a toehold among more powerful and impressive species. The awesome landscape in which our race was born cannot have changed much, if at all.

A hot air balloon is a modern invention (if you think the eighteenth century is 'modern'), but it offers a brief, unforgettable grandstand view of Creation, the kind one imagines God might have had on the sixth day, when He'd done the animals and not yet made His big mistake by fooling around with Adam.

In some respects my two visits to the Wilderness Camp at Lewa Downs remain one of my favourite memories of Kenya. The camp is situated in some of the most beautiful country in Kenya, almost 5,000 feet high, and offers a splendid view of snow-covered Mount Kenya. It is, above all, unspoiled country – no minibuses, no roads, no crush of tourists here.

The camp is run by David and Delia Craig, an English couple who, like many of Kenya's white farmers, elected to stay on after the country became independent, and who own a vast ranch (vast even by the standards of Texas) on which they raise every possible kind of farm produce, including wheat, cattle and sheep and – something you can't raise in Texas – rhinos.

The Craigs are genial souls, bronzed, weather-beaten and hardened by a climate that produces boiling, dry heat at noon and freezing cold nights. They and their friends acted as hosts, guides and tour leaders to their guests at the camp, and in the most kindly (but firm) way possible, tried to keep everybody busy and active during every waking hour. People who normally led sedentary lives found themselves getting up before dawn to go on a bird-watching walk, climbing up steep, rocky cliffs, or for a moonlit drive across the countryside, holding on to the seat for dear life, in search of bush babies (curious little animals that seem to be half raccoon and half koala, with eyes as big and round as fisheye camera lenses), rather than disappoint the Craigs.

Even insomniacs found themselves falling into bed at nine o'clock and sleeping soundly for eight or nine hours – not surprisingly, after a day that began while the stars were still visible, ended after dinner with a bush baby ride and a shower of meteors, and which might have included a long hike, horseback riding through the bush in pursuit of giraffes, a visit to the rhino ranch, a swim in an ice-cold pool, a long picnic lunch and a five-mile bird-watching walk!

The first sight of the Wilderness Camp was enough to satisfy anybody who lusts after adventure in the old style: a cluster of twenty or so tents next to a shaded stream, a large, open mess tent, a bar built around the trunk of a tree in the open air – and elephants, zebras, giraffes and monkeys so close to the camp that they sometimes wandered through it casually on their way to water. The tents were comfortable enough, though Spartan, as a tent should be: two cots, a canvas washing space attached behind it, open to the sky, a drop toilet in a thatched hut about twenty yards away.

The food was marvellous, in the British safari tradition: homemade bread and cookies, vast breakfasts of bacon, sausages, eggs and biscuits, dazzling curries and all those nursery foods the English are so fond of – trifle, rice pudding, etc. A huge bonfire smouldered day and night, and when the sun went down, there was nothing to do but sit and drink in silence, listening to the cries of the animals, and waiting until it was time to slip into bed with your hot water bottle, blow out the kerosene lamp and sleep.

Quite apart from the charm of the experience, which was considerable, the chief attraction (for me) is that here you could ride out to see the game on horseback! You could go for early morning game walks and bird walks too (set off at 6.30 am after a blistering cup of tea and fresh biscuits at the campfire, back to camp hot and weary just in time for a pukka sahib's breakfast), but a game ride by horse is better because it gets you right next to the animals, which don't react to horses as they do to people on foot or to cars. On horseback, you can get close enough to a giraffe to touch it, or very nearly so, and actually ride into herds of zebra (both the common zebra and the larger Grevy's zebra, which has narrow pinstripes and round ears like those on a Mickey Mouse hat).

No great riding skill is required, but even if you don't like horses, the experience is worth it. On horseback, you feel that you fit into the landscape, rather than intrude on it, as you do with a bus. The game seems somehow natural, something that's just there for its own sake rather than an object to be searched out, pinned down and photographed.

At some of the bigger reserves, like Amboseli, there sometimes seem to me more buses than animals. In the Wilderness Camp the animals were on their own. That alone makes it worth going, though there's also something pleasantly un-twentieth century about picnics under the trees, in the bush, or shaking your boots out in the morning in case something has crept into them overnight, or most of all the knowledge that you are as far from the beaten track as you are ever likely to get.

If you want a taste of what Kenya was like, this is about the best way to get it, along with a stop on the way at the Outspan Hotel in Nyeri, which looks like a movie set for a novel about Africa in the days of the white hunter and the memsahib, and which seems to have been frozen in time at about 1924. Here is a place to savour the atmosphere of colonial Kenya: English gardens, a billiards room, a pub, photographs of Her Majesty the Queen, a tea that is positively Victorian and includes scones, crumpets, cakes and anchovy toast. If nothing else, it is worth visiting the Outspan Hotel for a Pimm's Cup No. 2 on the veranda, surrounded by a garden that is so English it might almost be in Surrey, except for the occasional monkey or baboon among the trees.

If that isn't adventure enough (or antidote for the spectacle of a bus with eight serious Japanese gentlemen, wearing 'Honda Team' hats and carrying Nikons, in pursuit of a photograph of a cheetah and her cubs, while a busload of Germans with Leicas urges their driver to cut in front of them), there is one further adventure open to you – a hot air balloon trip across the Masai Mara game preserve, within sight of the Tanzania border and the Serengeti Plains, followed by an elaborate champagne picnic in the bush, wherever the balloon lands. My companion on the balloon trip described it as one of the high points of his life, and while I would not go that far, it is nevertheless an extraordinary and in some ways mystical experience.

You set off from the Keekorok Game Lodge at 6.45 in the morning, stand by while your balloon is inflated and the pilot briefs you, step into the wicker gondola and rise into the air. What happens afterward depends largely on the weather. On my first ascent, we skimmed across the plains and gullies for an hour and a half, watching the game from treetop height, then landed on the Tanzanian border, within spitting distance of a pride of lions, to breakfast on champagne, bangers (English sausages), chutney, fresh fruit, cold chicken, three different curries (hot, hotter and one that exceeds description) and Indian pastries.

On the next trip, a thermal carried us to 11,000 feet – not so good for looking at game, but offering instead a breathtakingly dramatic panorama of Africa, as well as the fascination of watching a dozen eagles circle around us curiously, hovering on the same air current. Except for those who suffer from motion sickness or fear of heights, I can't imagine anyone not enjoying it.

Admittedly, everyone in Kenya will tell you – and rightly, alas – that the game has been much reduced, by poaching, by drought, by the pressure of tourism and by Kenya's own population explosion; but when you go up in a balloon, the quantities still stagger the imagination – thousands of zebras, stretching out to the distant horizon, herds of elephants that seem to go on forever, so many wart hogs, wildebeests, impalas and buffalo that it's hard to imagine a lion could ever go hungry.

It is precisely this vastness and richness that makes a balloon safari so worthwhile. Unlike the American plains, the African plains are bursting with life, a landscape that is not so much empty as alarmingly overfilled, like the New York subway at rush hour.

And one senses too the strange feeling that this is a landscape in the process of being created. The vast lava fields, the volcanic mountains, the strange hills in the shape of truncated cones (which Ernest Hemingway compared to a young girl's breasts), the abundance of wildlife, suggest not so much age as raw newness, as if Creation had only taken place yesterday or was still going on, a world without modern man and untouched by him.

Of course, one knows otherwise: somewhere down there are lodges, minibuses full of tourists, landing strips . . . But from a balloon all that seems insignificant, even a figment of the imagination. Only the landscape is real, and the animals on it.

A balloon trip would probably be fun anywhere, but here it is like voyaging in a time machine. One trusts the pilots instinctively – which is just as well, because whereas everywhere else in Kenya one is warned never to get out of the vehicle, here you land in the middle of the game reserve and casually picnic wherever the wind has chosen the site, with elephants walking by and animals watching curiously.

In the end, you know that the Land-Rover will arrive to pick up the balloon and take you back to civilization, but speaking for myself, I wasn't in any hurry. In one morning I was aloft among the eagles, swept over the gullies of the Masai Mara to watch the game, bumped down in the middle of nowhere for a magnificent breakfast, then picked up to ride back to the lodge in the back of a Land-Rover, from which we saw lions, a cheetah with four newborn cubs and some of those incredible birds that, even to one who isn't a bird watcher, suggest a richer, more colourful spirit of creation than that of our hemisphere.

A balloon safari seems an oddity in many ways, but I wouldn't go to Kenya without going on one. Oh, yes, you can see the game closer and better from a bus, but hanging in the still air, silent, sometimes almost motionless, I think you can feel, just for a few moments, what it's all about, get some sense of the immensity of Africa and of what it must have been like, hardly more than a hundred years ago, when man had not yet marked it with roads, hotels or railways.

If that isn't worth one morning and a couple of hundred dollars, I don't know what is.

VENTURING INTO THE WILDERNESS

Almost everyone who goes to Kenya travels on a prearranged safari tour. Bookings for the Wilderness Camp and the balloon safari are therefore normally made through a travel agent or a safari tour operator.

THE WILDERNESS CAMP

The Wilderness Camp is reached by road. The usual way to get there is to fly by chartered light plane from Nairobi to Nyeri, stop for lunch at the Outspan Hotel, then drive to Lewa Downs via Nanyuki (with a stop at the equator). Your driver will deposit you at the camp and will be waiting for you there at the end of your stay.

The Wilderness Camp costs about $200 a person a day (including more activities than you can handle and more food than you can eat). David and Delia Craig, who run it, require a minimum of twelve persons for three days to set up the camp, but they take a limited number of people in their house even when the camp is closed. The cost for staying in the house is something of a bargain by comparison to the tented camp, at about $150 a day for a room for two people. It is wise – indeed essential – to consult a travel agent about the rainy season, since when it rains in Kenya, it really rains. It is also essential to make reservations well in advance. The Craigs' local representative is Bateleur Safaris, P.O. Box 42562, Nairobi, Kenya.

OTHER ACCOMMODATIONS

Other tented camps abound, but not on private ranches or with the same Old World British flavour. The **Fig Tree Camp**, in the Masai Mara, has 25 tents and offers good food and personal service. The **Governor's Camp** in the Musiara section of the Masai Mara has wonderful food but with 47 tents is rather large. Nearby **Little Governor's Camp** has only 10 tents, and is on a lake where animals come to water. The **Island Camp**, in the middle of Lake Baringo, has water skiing and hippos.

Some of the larger game lodges have tents, but they are usually designed to handle an overflow of tourists in the peak safari season and are not tented camps in the full meaning of the word.

GOING ALOFT

The balloon safari begins from the Keekorok Game Lodge and must be booked ahead, usually through a travel agent or a safari tour operator. The full price must be paid at the time of booking, presumably in case people get cold feet at the last moment. The cost is $200 a person, including breakfast, champagne, a game drive afterward, coffee on return to Keekorok Lodge and a certificate suitable for framing, to impress your earthbound friends.

— M.K.

AFRICA'S EDEN IN A DESERT

Joseph Lelyveld

In fantasies for or by children, it is not uncommon to be transported suddenly, as if through a trapdoor, from a place that is forbidding and frightening to a world that is blessedly green and tranquil. The Okavongo Delta is a little like that: a pristine expanse of wetland wilderness surrounded by some of the most arid and difficult terrain in Africa south of the Sahara. Discovering the delta is like unwrapping a piece of fine porcelain that has been packed in straw or wood shavings or rough burlap.

The Okavongo is a mighty river that rises in the highlands of Angola and floods annually in a southeasterly direction as if it meant to force its way to the Indian Ocean. But it never gets remotely close. Instead, it pours into the northern reaches of the Kalahari Desert in Botswana, where it spreads itself thinly over a vast floodplain that is irregularly cut with channels and lagoons.

When the water is at its height, in June or July, the delta is a visual medley of delicate greens and blues stretching across a wide horizon. That horizon – fringed with papyrus and crowned with towering umbrella-shaped trees belonging mostly to the acacia family – is then mirrored in the still surface of the water, broken here and there by water lilies or perhaps a tiny island with a stand of palm trees and tall, tufted grass to sway in the breeze.

The effect is almost pastoral. You would not be surprised to see a shepherd or cowherd, piping or strumming whatever shepherds and cowherds are supposed to pipe or strum. Instead, you hear an abrupt, rhythmic splashing, like the start of an Olympic freestyle race, and glimpse a dozen springbok, lechwe, reedbuck or other subspecies of African antelope flashing through the grass, water glistening from their hooves. If you pursue them on dry land, you may run into giraffes, buffalo or elephants. Chances are you won't see lions and leopards, or pythons, but your guide may well taunt you with the possibility in order to sprinkle an extra pinch of seasoning on an excursion that couldn't possibly be dull.

If you fly over it in a small plane you see that the Okavongo Delta is teeming with wildlife, but you won't come away recalling it as a game park. There are, in fact, great game parks just on its edge, where you can see scores of rare sable antelopes, elephants by the hundreds and buffalo by the thousands; and the landscape everywhere records their passage. But in the delta proper they do not dominate the environment; they are lodgers and boarders who know their place. The bird life, said to number some 400 species, is almost always more conspicuous, but the birds too – ranging from tiny bee-eaters to subtly hued African jacanas and great lumbering saddlebilled storks – are also just inhabitants. It's the delta itself, the whole blooming, humming, chirping ecosystem (to lapse into the seminarspeak of the benign two-legged parasites who study as well as experience it) that is the main attraction, all 5,800 square miles of it.

From the bottom of a *mekoro*, a dugout canoe, skimming along just inches above the sediment the river has deposited over untallied ages, the delta can seem open and illimitable or, when the floodplain narrows to a channel that threatens to disappear in a thicket of reeds and papyrus, close and enveloping. You soon realize that this extensive water system is exhilaratingly unpeopled – astonishing in a drought-prone, cattle-raising country. The explanation lies in two distinct kinds of power: one legally constituted but remote, the other anarchic and noticeably present, especially at dusk.

The first is the Botswana Government, which so far has displayed a rare environmental consciousness, resisting a host of grandiose proposals to exploit the Okavongo. The second, even more relevant in this context, is the tsetse fly. The bite of this notorious insect is seldom troublesome and never fatal to wildlife, but it dooms domestic cattle almost instantly. Thus it keeps at bay the herdsmen who would permit their flocks to devastate the delta in a season or two, whatever the Government said.

The well-informed tourist comes to regard the tsetse, despite its reputation, with gratitude rather than fear. The tsetse can only serve as a carrier of sleeping sickness if it has bitten an already infected human, and cases of the infection have become all but unknown in Botswana. Malaria is a more serious concern, as it is in most subtropical regions of Africa, but nothing to worry about if you come equipped with malaria pills and remember to take your weekly dosage. Beyond this, the entomological risks are no greater than those offered by an excursion into the White Mountains. Take bug spray, jeans and a long-sleeved shirt for early evening – mosquito nets are standard equipment at the delta's campsites.

I'm making it sound as if I really roughed it in the delta when I went there with my wife on a week's trip. The time has come to confess that we did no such thing. In the bush, it is only reasonable to be a little flexible in your standards of cuisine and service, but I would say we went first class. Certainly there have been few other weeks in my life in which I have done, or have had to do, as little for myself as I did in the delta. It was early July, the optimum time, when the water had got as high as it was going to get. The rest of southern Africa seemed a dull, wintry brown, or at least that part of it we could see between the suburban Johannesburg airport and an overgrown African village called Maun, about 530 miles to the northwest. We were flown there in a Cessna six-seater by Mike Myers, our bush pilot and guide, and were stamped into Botswana by the local fireman who, on that sleepy Sunday morning, was doubling as an immigration inspector.

When the delta is flooded, you have a choice of flying in or going by boat. We flew to Xaxaba (the *x*'s get pronounced more or less like *k*'s), a bush camp sufficiently stocked with life's necessities to offer Bloody Marys to those who want them instead of tea. It's one of only four tourist camps in the entire delta; altogether they can accommodate fewer than eighty travellers at any given time. Later in the week we were to spend three nights at Xaxaba, but on that first day we stopped only to pick up a small flotilla of *mekoro* and the team of four Batswana who would pole us across the delta to our first night's camp, at a spot called Jugajugu.

Am I saying we went first class by dugout canoe? Absolutely. It's the only way to go. An outboard motor would work only on the main channels and, besides, the noise pollution should be grounds for ejection from this African Eden. I have ridden in the gondolas of Venice and Kashmir and in a fibreglass canoe through the canyons of the Rio Grande; I even had the luck once, on an excursion almost as exotic as this one, to spend two days exploring Inle Lake in Burma's Shan state, where the boatmen manage the paddles with their feet rather than their hands. But I have never felt quite as complacent and indulged as I did on the Okavongo, where the rippling sound of the dugout skimming over the water, the breeze in the papyrus and a chorus of unfamiliar birdcalls seemed to float on a silence so pure that it was almost a sound in itself – something like the first instant following the final note in a sonata, only infinitely sustained.

At the campsite, the mosquito nets were strung up under a couple of trees that dropped fruit the size and density of bowling pins. Mike Myers said they were African mangosteens. Our only task, while he busied himself with setting up the camp, was to unroll our sleeping bags; then we sat by the fire and watched Mike get our dinner together. The chicken was one of four dishes he had painstakingly taught himself to cook. While a food critic might have encouraged him to lay off the all-purpose monosodium glutamate and be a little more discriminating in his selection of species, we were hungry enough by the time it was served to award him three stars without a quibble.

A Rhodesian expatriate who now spends most of his year in the swamp and the rest in South Africa, Mike seemed to have an easy, joshing relationship with the four Batswana, one that dispensed with such honorifics as 'master' or 'boss,' which most southern African whites regard as a mark of cordial race relations. The boatmen had their dinner of corn porridge ready while Mike was still chopping onions to add to the tomato sauce in which our chicken was stewing. While the conversation of the tourists lagged, theirs got more energetic and, judging from their expressive gestures and convulsive laughter, more amusing.

'That's easy enough for you to say,' grumbled one of three Californians with whom we were travelling, after an especially eloquent but incomprehensible speech in the Tswana language. Perhaps the Californian began to suspect that we ourselves were the object of the boatmen's amusement. In any event, something moved this thrice-wed father of seven to put his manhood on the line and wager that he had more children than the four Batswana combined. A quick census was taken and, although the youngest of the four had no children at all, the Californian lost, 7 to 19. 'Well,' he said, 'I bet I've had more wives.'

The next morning we were back on the water, making our way toward the largest landmass in the delta, Chief's Island, which is eighty miles long and entirely without human habitation. The trip, through water that was seldom deeper than two or three feet, unfolded in a series of sightings and sounds: yellow-billed ducks flying in formation, maribou storks circling overhead in lazy arcs, African jacanas dancing on lily pads, reedbucks splashing through thick reeds so that they were heard long before they were glimpsed, the cry of a fish eagle and the chatter of parrots. Yet it was the moments between these displays that I relished the most, when the silence deepened and the eye was left free to roam across the reflections of the tall trees on the water, or the patterns made by a profusion of delicate violet flowers growing up among the papyrus.

Our second camp, where we stayed two nights, was in a grove of palm, African ebony and knobthorn trees, on a spit of land just across from Chief's Island. (With our campsite close to water on all sides, Mike explained, he would be able to hear animals approaching at night.) On an afternoon's walk, he showed us how to follow a little bird called a honey guide to a beehive in a tree, then identified the grey-crested loerie, which seems to scream 'go away, go away.' One of the Batswana pointed to trampled grass and droppings that showed where a large herd of buffalo had meandered by only hours before. So the next morning we gave chase to the buffaloes on foot. In a quick march we covered about five miles in thick bush before an eruption of snorts and hoofbeats told us we were suddenly upon them. Without stopping to ask why we were doing it, we ran headlong toward the herd, which fortunately stampeded in the opposite direction. I saw an occasional flash of horn or snout through the bush, but never a whole buffalo, let alone the thousand head that were supposed to be there.

The next evening, our fourth in the delta, we saw as many buffalo in herds as I ever hope to see, looking down on them from Mike's Cessna. We had returned in our dugout canoes to the relative luxury of Xaxaba that afternoon. As far as I was concerned, lolling in a *mekoro* and being poled through the shimmering stillness of the delta was enough, but other travellers in Africa seem to feel the need to see wildlife through the viewfinder of a camera. The game flight was the first of several excursions to that end. At Xaxaba there was also a nightly rendezvous with a fish hawk, which came swooping down to the water's surface to grab in its talons a carefully lobbed fish as the shutters clicked. On another cruise, after dark in a motorboat, we were brought in close to a thicket of reeds where a spotlight revealed tiny, gorgeously coloured bee-eaters perched so close together that I thought, at first, they were segments of a multicoloured caterpillar; then thimble-sized frogs that inflated as they croaked till they looked more like bubble gum than living creatures.

This camera safari carried us on our fifth day to Savuthi in the Chobe National Park, beyond the delta's edge in northern Botswana. We lunched at a kind of dude ranch for well-heeled tourists called Game Trekkers, where the tariff, we were told, was about $150 a person a night for accommodation in a well-appointed tent with a flush toilet not too many steps away. Then we jeeped through the bush, to the sites where elephants, hippopotamuses, wildebeests, giraffes and the occasional rhinoceros are known to congregate. For the first time, I saw sable antelopes close up. In an even more memorable moment we came upon some ninety hippos in a pool – it was just possible to count them by their ears and snouts, which peeked above the water – and watched as about fifty of these pachyderms, ranging from babies to overgrown matrons, made their way down a dusty riverbank where a couple of dozen crocodiles were lazily sunning themselves. One by one, the crocs were subjected to the indignity of being ploughed back into the shallows by the stubborn, blunt snout of a hippo. That was pretty good, I had to admit, but I was starting to miss the delta and found that the growl of the jeep engine grated on my nerves.

The next day Mike planned to make another flying trip, this time to a small settlement on the delta's edge where a band of bushmen make a meagre living by selling bows and other artefacts to tourists. I begged off, asking whether my wife and I couldn't simply hire a dugout and go back into the delta for the day. We headed south with a young man named Mongi to do the poling, and as soon as we pushed off from Xaxaba the soothing silence descended again. After a couple of hours on the water, we approached an island and sailed right into a lively reception committee: a troop of disorderly, screeching baboons to our left; a group of tsessebes, a relatively hefty antelope, scampering through the water straight ahead, and, to our right, several dozen springbok leaping over the grass. Heading back to Xaxaba, Mongi prodded what seemed to be a log with his pole and a crocodile went gliding away underwater.

At the end of the week we flew back to Johannesburg. We both felt as if we had escaped from its strained, claustrophobia-inducing absorption with itself for a month or more. By the time we started driving home, we were plotting our next trip to the Okavongo: We will skip the side trips, we agreed, and steep ourselves in the delta for as long as we possibly can.

IF YOU GO
Mike Myers, who has incorporated himself in Johannesburg under the name **Quest Africa** (c/o Safari Plan, P.O. Box 4245, Randburg 2125, Johannesburg, South Africa), charges about $100 a day for the weeklong trip we took. Clive Walker, a well-known southern African naturalist connected with **Educational Wildlife Expeditions** in Johannesburg (P.O. Box 645, Bedfordview 2008), does both five-day and seven-day tours to the Okavongo by aeroplane and canoe. A tour operator in the Botswana capital of Gaborone, **Holiday Safaris**, makes arrangements for excursions into the delta that start in Maun.

For those who are not attracted by the idea of camping, **Game Trekkers**, which also operates out of Johannesburg, maintains two lodges in the delta, the **Khwai River Lodge** and the **San-T-Wani Lodge**, which promise a somewhat higher standard of creature comforts.

The traveller would be well advised to put his arrangements in the hands of one of these specialists. However, it is also possible and cheaper to book in Xaxaba or a similar camp called the **Delta Camp** and hire a *mekoro* and someone to pole it. The disadvantage of freelancing in this manner is that the boatman will almost certainly speak no English, which means he may not be able to impart much information on the surroundings or catch your meaning if you want to change directions.

For travellers on a grand tour of southern Africa, it is possible to make arrangements in advance to fly in or out from Victoria Falls in Zimbabwe, which is actually much closer than Johannesburg. But if you go in for such elaborate arrangements, they need to be made well in advance by someone close to the scene who is in firsthand contact with your pilot and guide.

You can travel farthest in the delta in late June and July, when the water is highest. But other months have their advantages. The bird life is at its best in May. The trees are in flower in September. The tiger fish are biting in October. From December to April most of the camps shut down – there is still game but little water, except in the form of torrential rains, and it is often unpleasantly hot. It is at about that time that the Okavongo starts to rise in Angola, gathering force for its annual flood in the Kalahari.

—J.L.

INDIAN ROAD SHOW

John Russell

Whether high, low, or somewhere in between, the open road is fundamental to Indian life. Much gets done there that in our countries is done indoors – and, quite apart from that, the road in India is in continual and multifarious use. It serves as theatre and nursery, barber shop and botanical garden, menagerie and employment exchange. No one knows India who has not spent time on the open road.

The best way to do it, beyond all doubt, is, as we discovered on a recent trip from Delhi to Gwalior, to be met at the airport by a rented car and a rented driver. You stick with them, and they will stick with you, till the day of your departure. And you will not regret it. First impressions, in this as in many another matter in life, are decisive.

Even at three o'clock in the morning we heard, all over the little forecourt of the New Delhi airport, the words that were to be the leitmotif of our journey. 'No problem, sir! No problem!' was the answer to our every question, spoken or unspoken. Even before our drivers had switched off their engines outside the Taj Mahal Hotel, those same blessed words rang out in chorus from the huge nimble staff members who were massed on the steps. So it began, so it went on, and so it ended. No matter what may be engraved on the hearts of others, 'No problem, sir!' will be engraved on ours.

We had decided to be driven, rather than to take the plane, the train or the packaged bus tour. Our schedule was considerate, with 'nothing in excess' its motto. Not even Diogenes in his bath was more snug than we in our two tiny barrel-bodied, white-painted cars, each with a resourceful driver who doubled as navigator, interpreter and dragoman. Thanks to them, we were free to look, listen, smell and taste.

There were no dead moments in our journey. Some visitors close their eyes to the outskirts of Indian cities, preferring to fantasize about marching through the Hindu Kush in the spring of the year 327 BC, side by side with the Macedonian hoplites who were driven southward by the energizing will of Alexander the Great. Others imagine themselves sitting on silk carpets in a Mogul garden three hundred and some years ago, with cool coloured water flowing down patterned slopes and an all-woman orchestra not far away.

They miss a lot, those dreamers. The outskirts of Indian cities may never take a prize for vernacular architecture, but there is more to be learned about India from its billboards, and from the companionable tumult of its industrial suburbs, than from many an academic study. Stuck in the traffic, we gazed in astonishment at ads that would be unthinkable in calorie-conscious countries. My own all-time favourite came in huge letters and consisted of six words only. 'Pastries, And Suddenly You Feel Irresistible,' it said. How subtle was the placing of that comma, with its digestive implication! How vibrant, the use of 'suddenly'! And how decisive the final 'irresistible'!

It struck this visitor that although Indians are nonstop talkers, their ads might have been written by Tacitus himself. The often seen 'Food, Friends and Thums Up' gave us trouble until someone told us that Thums Up was the name of a much marketed soft drink. Once we know that, what a roomy eloquence resides in those five short syllables! What better way to float a fun-filled evening in front of the homebound teetotal office worker?

The Indian Government doesn't waste words, either. What could be more laconic than 'Be Indian. Buy Indian'? It was left to the opposition in the approaching general elections to ramble in ways that did not serve it well. Here and there on the billboards the candidates of the Congress (I) Party were characterized as a bunch of 'Maharajahs, computer boys, liars, movie stars and thugs.' This sank like a stone with the voters. So did the handwritten call for 'Armed Proletarian Revolution' that in all likelihood emanated from the Indian Communist Party (whose headquarters, by the way, are in one of the prettiest villas in New Delhi).

Traffic in those new suburbs was often halted by pedlars hung with garlands of marigolds, by necessary stops at fruit and vegetable stalls, by itinerant fast-food vendors, by pauses to wonder at glistening seven-foot-high towers of candy or trays of carrots and white radishes shredded and fanned out with an aesthete's hand.

It must also be taken into account that Indians are world champion ablutionists. Give them a can of water and a patch of ground twelve inches square, and they will do a better job of getting themselves clean than most of us can manage in the bathroom. They adore being shaved, too, and particularly if it can be done in the open, with a hand mirror sparkling in the sun to report on progress, a superabundance of very white lather and a razor freshly stropped.

Given that all this may go on somewhere in the middle of the road, that neither buffalo nor camel likes to pull over for the car, and that centuries of immunity from disturbance have bred into the sacred cow an aristocratic nonchalance, it will be clear that progress cannot always be brisk. As for the white ox, with its enormous eyes elongated as if with an eyebrow pencil, it has seen too many a truck overturn to envy us our mode of progression.

The Indian truck has great panache, however. It is large, fast and versatile, though no paragon of stability. Not only is it a travelling art gallery, with every inch of its outer surface covered with painted images, but it is a repository of emblematic wisdom. Not content with our drab little stickers about getting home safe, the Indian truck driver goes all out for poignancy. 'Wait To Love!' we read, if we get too close for safety, and we see for ourselves the grieving beloved, watching all evening long for the driver who lies dead in a ditch.

They are quite right, too. It is nothing uncommon to find the road blocked by one, two or even three trucks overturned, upended, with their guts in the air and their cargoes strewn every which way. As for the broken-down truck, it too is everywhere. Islanded with bricks, big stones and brushwood, it sits there, waiting from the maintenance man, much as the statues on Easter Island waited for centuries for the first explorers to come upon them. Meanwhile, driver and passengers doze the day away in the delicate shade of a eucalyptus tree.

A little farther along on our journey of eight or nine hundred miles, we entered Arcadia. That particular stretch of the road from Delhi had little traffic. Villages were few, migrations pedestrian, the weather flawless from dawn till dusk. The flirtation between desert and watered oasis was a joy to watch. Nowhere was too far from anywhere else. Everybody, without exception, seemed pleased to see us.

It was impossible, though, not to notice the vultures that rode the upper air, with wings spread wide, hooked beak in the locked position, clawed red feet inactive and dreaded eyes ever open. No one ever loved a vulture. At the very best, their manners when on the ground are those of a peremptory housemaid who can't wait for us to get out of the room. And yet, when I nodded off in the noonday shade, I would dream of being visited by a deputation of English-speaking vultures.

How was it, they would say, that despite their millennial record as pro bono sanitation workers, thay had such a bad name? Did they not volunteer for all the nastiest jobs? Why were they not nominated for the Nobel Prize? Very relieved I was, when our drivers set up a discreet honking and it was time to be off.

It is on the road (high or low, whichever we like to call it) that India reveals itself at its own speed. It has its little surprises, as when the flat near-desert landscape of Rajasthan suddenly turns humpy and hairy, as if it had something urgent to tell us, or when a six-lane tollbooth springs up out of nowhere, unmanned, unfinished and apparently no more than notional. The road is a born storyteller, too. Precisely when boredom might strike, it whips out a horse decked out with brilliant feathers behind its ears, a huge dry river bed, brilliant with bone-white sand, or a first glimpse of some celebrated sight – the precipitous bluff of Gwalior, for instance, which E. M. Foster described in a letter home as looking like 'a glorified Orvieto, rising sheer from the plain.'

It is, in fact, in the pursuit of revelation that the low road in India truly pays off. Escorted, regimented, with our time not our own, we should never have come upon the market garden quarter, just across the river from the Taj Mahal, where flowers and vegetables are grown as they were in Mogul times, in strict rectangular beds sweetened and freshened by water pumped from the Jumna.

Nor should we have stumbled upon the idiosyncratic hotel in Gwalior, where not merely keys but even locks were in short supply, and lunch was served on the lawn all afternoon long, in an atmosphere reminiscent of a run-down country house in Chekhov's plays. Nor should we have invited ourselves to the Circuit House in the sacred city of Ajmer, from which there is the view that prompted one of the greatest of French statesmen, Georges Clemenceau, to say that if he had to die, he would prefer to do it in Ajmer.

Otherwise than on the road, and on our own, we should never have been able to linger open-endedly in certain great monuments from the Mogul past, until at last in each place we hit on the precise piece of decoration that answered to our wishes. (Those wishes – eccentric, beyond a doubt – were for tones of sand, biscuit and ginger that looked as if they were laid out on an ivory tray touched with liquorice.)

Otherwise than on the road, and on our own, we should never have got to see the great sequence of palaces that is known as Dig. To stand on the terrace of Dig and hear the slap, slap of laundry being beaten dry on the rocks across the river is one of the perennial Indian experiences. Not that indoors at Dig is to be despised, either, with its general look of a gigantic English country house that has taken on exotic overtones – decanters mounted on elephants' feet, games rooms with orange cushions (now much in decay) and a marble chessboard inlaid in the floor, tiny Chinese trees made with *pietra dura* by Italian craftsmen, and on the roof a huge tank to feed the (by now long dry) water gardens.

These are just a few of the things – great and small, humdrum and ecstatic – that came our way because we took the low road (or was it the high road?) through quite a small part of India. Who can wonder that, when our drivers left us, we grieved? And what did we do? We rushed upstairs and called room service. And what did we order? Pastries. And how did we feel afterward? Despite the promise of that memorable slogan, we felt terrible. So maybe there is such a thing as a cultural divide, after all.

AT ANCHOR IN KASHMIR

Richard Reeves

The last words, the final request of Jahangir, one of the great Mogul rulers of what is now northern India and Pakistan, as he lay dying on a summer day in 1627, were: 'Only Kashmir!' That at least is how the story is told, and I believe it.

I particularly believed it on a summer day centuries later when I was awakened from a sunny nap on the banks of the Sheshnag River by a stream of water thrown from a silver bowl. I was surrounded by maidens, giggling and pointing at my wet expression of wonder. I had never thought of using the word *maidens* before, but I had never been in Kashmir before. And I had never been in the middle of a water fight with laughing young women, saris flying, chasing each other across the greensward of an old British officers' club. A wild toss of the water that runs down from the snowcapped peaks high above the river had brought me into their world – for a moment I would remember long after the maidens' happy ballet began again.

That was in Pahlgam, a hill station, as the British called the small towns where they escaped India's summer heat, at an altitude of 7,200 feet, surrounded by the much higher peaks of the Himalayas at the very top of India. Close to the top of the world, really, with one of the peaks, Nanga Parbat, reaching 26,660 feet into a sky the colour of the Sheshnag, which is saying wonderful things about both of them.

The drive back 'home' from that riverside picnic of wine and the Indian bread called *nan* took us through the floor of the valley – a floor a mile high – through the Vale of Kashmir. The valley is eighty-four miles long – part of it is in Pakistan – and twenty to twenty-five miles wide. We drove on toward Srinagar, fifty-five miles away, through the shimmering green of rice paddies framed by the darker green of the mountains and then the great pickets of the Himalayas. The smoke of thousands of evening fires was beginning to mingle in a sunset haze above the bottom land. That soft light and the smell of burning wood and dried buffalo dung is Kashmir – only Kashmir.

We could not, however, drive all the way. Home was a boat – a houseboat on Lake Dal.

The houseboats on Lake Dal, like much in this part of the world, had their beginnings in the British Raj. Almost 150 years ago, when the British were taking control of India, part of their colonial strategy was to neutralize local populations through treaties or arrangements with traditional rulers – such as the Maharajah of Kashmir. The Maharajah, who governed from a palace overlooking Lake Dal, accepted British money and protection, but one of his conditions was that foreigners would never be allowed to own land near him. So the British, clever devils (including Rudyard Kipling's father), built houseboats on the lake.

We drove through Srinagar, the old capital of Kashmir, now a crowded central Asian city, then went along the canal from the Jhelum River to the lake. Our shikara and our boatman, Mohammad, were waiting, as always, to shuttle us across to our houseboat.

A shikara is like a gondola, only better. The passenger shikara is a variation on the long dugout used by the people of Dal and the attached lakes for transportation and for such work as collecting seaweed to feed their buffalo. Serenely graceful, the boats are paddled by men and women squatting, in the Asian manner, at the very tip of the prow. The paddlers seem suspended above the water as the boat arcs behind and above them. With passengers, the boatman sits in the rear. The passengers arrange themselves on a great couch beneath a canopy, lounging against pillows. This sultanic scene is marred a bit by signs over the canopies of many shikaras with the words 'Full Spring Seats' – springs, as in cushioned coils, to protect what Kashmiris perceive as the vulnerabilities of Occidental backsides.

The *Hermes*, which was the name of our boat, lay on the other side of the lake. It was quite grand; for the price (less than $100 a day with meals for four of us) it was very grand. Our captain, Ashraf, the caretaker of the boat and of us, met our shikara at the back porch, as always, and asked whether we wanted a drink, and at what time dinner should be served.

The back porch of the *Hermes* – a deluxe class boat, the highest of five Government categories – faces the lake and, like any other porch in the world, it's where you sit to take in the sun and watch the passing parade. A water parade – of weed collectors, farmers and the sellers of flowers, vegetables, candy, film, shawls. You name it and it paddles by. The sun, too, seems to float somewhere just behind the mountains at the end of the day; the sunsets, dusk, are lingering magic. Hours, it seems, of the hazy, dreamy effect that film-makers chase for lifetimes.

The layout of the rest of the boat – which, Ashraf bragged, was home for a while to a 'very famous' American, the lawyer Melvin Belli – was typical of the deluxe boats. The porch opened into a wonderfully stodgy Anglo-Indian parlour – overstuffed English-style furniture and heavy Indian rugs. It was only the style that was stuffy; both sides of the room were lined with windows facing the surrounding water. The entertainment, aside from our books, cards and dominoes, was a large battery-run radio that didn't work when the electricity did, and old copies of *Newsweek International, The Economist* and *Der Spiegel*. The best thing about travelling outside the principal cities of Asia is that the reading material is always so old that even if news is your business you begin to understand how it repeats itself. Out there, almost nothing seems new – or urgent.

Next, in this luxurious floating railway carriage, comes the dining room, better than ours in Manhattan. The rugs, a chandelier, good china and passable crystal – all quite acceptable, thank you. And, at the head of table, with wife and two children, I finally got a bit of that paterfamilias image I've wanted to affect all these years.

Unfortunately, the food was terrible. Kashmiri food is not at all like the exciting food of the more southern regions of the subcontinent. Despite the glory of the scenery, the valley is poor. There is not much meat – a little gristly lamb – and the staple fare is starchy rice and vegetables that have the taste stewed out of them. The greens and fruits look a little healthier, but you may not if you indulge yourself with such treats in India. Ashraf would occasionally and hopefully use the dread words 'English dinner?' in the innocent conviction that all Westerners are responsible in some way for what the British can do to perfectly good food. What the Kashmiris do in imitating the British with not very good ingredients was not the reason we or Emperor Jahangir loved Kashmir.

So, if dinner means that much to you, I would advise bringing along some food – if you're travelling from someplace where you can get good sausages and cheese, for example – and taking a strong hand in the kitchen boat tied to your home. Or you might cross the lake to Srinagar once or twice to dine at the Oberoi Palace Hotel. The Palace was once just that, the residence of the Maharajahs of Kashmir. The lawns between the Palace and the lake look as if they have been cut by hand – parts of them have been, almost blade by blade with little scythes – and the cuisine tends toward southern Indian with ingredients imported from outside the valley.

Maybe we were just unlucky, but it didn't matter; you don't go to Kashmir for the food.

The three bedrooms on the *Hermes* are large and comfortable, with the large ceiling fans that are necessary in July and August. The bathrooms, surprisingly, would be fine in any Holiday Inn, except that the view from them is better and you usually have to tell the captain an hour ahead of time if you want hot water.

Once we figured out where all those efficient-looking pipes led – into the lake – we passed up the swimming boats that are moored in the middle of Lake Dal. But other people seemed to be having a great old time splashing into the lake from the sides and roofs of those floating beach clubs.

What I've called Lake Dal is really three attached lakes surrounded by marshes and what they call bayous in Louisiana. Gliding along the watery 'streets' behind the hundreds of houseboats on what appears to be the shoreline of the lake is as close as I've come to another world. Shikaras move silently past wood or clay-brick houses built up to the water. Buffalo, cows and chickens inhabit tiny patches of marshy earth, and gardens of melons, cucumbers and tomatoes literally float beside houses. The floating gardens, islands woven of reeds and stuffed with mud and clay, are anchored by long poles in the water. You can step from a shikara onto what looks like land, but it sinks beneath your feet and then pops up again. Amazing. So are the lotus plants everywhere on the surface, their leaves like giant lily pads but of a texture that repels water as if it were mercury, exploding the liquid into drops like diamonds in the sun.

There are more than enough places and things – from mountains and glaciers to the aphrodisiac sellers who came to me with lotions and potions guaranteed to change my life – to keep the most energetic sightseer busy for a week in Kashmir. The first excursions are usually to the pleasure gardens of the Moguls, terraced formal plantings begun by Jahangir in 1617 – three years before the Pilgrims landed at Plymouth – and bisected by a stepped series of pools and fountains to cool the Emperor's court in summer. The names of the gardens should be temptation enough – Chasma Shahi, Nasim and Shalimar, the last the summer home of Jahangir and his empress, Nur Jahan, 'the light of the world.'

Then there are the villages – I liked Sangram, where acres of willow trees are turned, by hand, into the cricket bats of India. And the temples – I was impressed by Martand, on the way to Pahlgam, a vast eighth century tribute to a pre-Hindu sun god that matches anything built to other gods in Europe.

But, with all of that, I would not think of Lake Dal and Kashmir as a primary destination. It has always been, and is best enjoyed as, a retreat from the almost unbearable heat and chaotic energy of the subcontinent. It is a place to come to from Delhi or Bombay or Calcutta. The best way (if you're not the nervous type) is to just go to the lake, ignoring the Government tourist office and the hustling touts, and hire a shikara for a couple of rupees. Go from houseboat to houseboat, check them out and bargain with the captains. (Arrangements, I should add cautiously, can be safely made with Indian travel companies in New York, any major city in India, or, in Srinagar, at the offices of the Houseboat Owners Association.)

We came from Pakistan. I mentioned that part of Kashmir is in Pakistan. Both India and Pakistan, in fact, claim the entire area and have fought two wars over it. Under international law, the area is not technically part of either country, but India governs most of the valley. That means you can't go from Pakistani Kashmir to Indian Kashmir or vice versa.

Although we began our journey less than a hundred miles from Srinagar, we had to travel many hundreds more, flying first to Lahore, Pakistan, and then walking across the border into India. It took us three hours to go one multinational mile. On the Pakistani side of the border, we dragged our baggage and ourselves from office to office and inspection station to inspection station, filling out forms at every table. Then, with the help of a porter, we walked the half mile to the border, where an Indian porter took the baggage and us to the first of four Indian immigration and customs stations. Each table on that side was manned by rows of tall, turbaned men, each one wearing a plastic tag with the name 'Mr. Singh.' Among sikhs, all men have the same last name, Singh. Finally passed through customs, after being given bottles of orange soda by a sergeant, we walked another half mile to hire a rocking taxi to Amritsar, the holy and troubled city of the Sikhs.

We had time for a visit to the extraordinary Golden Temple of the Sikhs – where each day men lined up to be arrested in religious protest for more Sikh autonomy, and which was later the scene of bloody fighting between the Sikhs and the Indian Army, after which Amritsar was closed to foreigners. We spent the night at Mrs. Bhandari's Guesthouse, which I would call one of the most exclusive hotels in the world. That definition has nothing to do with luxury; it means that you have found the place which will attract anyone of interest who happens to be travelling through. And at Mrs. Bhandari's, even if no one else is staying there that day, there is always a Bhandari or Mr. Singh to share an Eagle beer and pass on the latest gossip about the intense politics of the region or to tell stories about someone you know who was through last week or last year. Then we took the morning Air India flight to Srinagar, the town where Kipling once went to get away from it all, which has since grown into a city of more than 400,000.

Still, you can certainly get away from many things out that way. Leaving our houseboat one morning, we took a short but spectacular winding drive up to a place 8,500 feet high, called Gulmarg – the name means 'meadow of flowers,' which it is – a gigantic high meadow. The cab driver said, 'I'll show you something.' And he did. We went around what seemed to be just another curve on a mountain road and suddenly there it was: the Vale of Kashmir, mile on mile of green lined by the blue and white of rivers, walled in by waves of mountains cresting with Nanga Parbat. I could barely breathe. It was as if I saw the whole world. But it was only Kashmir.

RENTING A HOUSEBOAT
To arrange for renting a houseboat on Lake Dal, write to the Government-approved **Houseboat Owners Association**:

Reshoo Baktoo and Sons
Dalgate
P.O. Box 95
Srinagar, Kashmir
India
Phone: 74547 or 76793

TREKKING IN NEPAL

Steven R. Weisman

At dawn the sun creeps over a high ridge and you can feel the morning chill in your bones. A voice calls from outside the tent, offering hot tea. Shaking off a night's sleep, you groggily splash yourself with warm water from a tin bowl. After a breakfast of oatmeal, dry biscuits and coffee, you are off for another day of trekking up and down the steep foothills of the Himalayas.

In the small mountain kingdom of Nepal, there are only two ways of getting a glimpse of the tallest peaks in the world. One is to fly over them. The other is to walk, because there are virtually no roads in the interior of the country. Some 30,000 people trek in the shadow of the mountains each year, but the enjoyment goes far beyond the thrill of seeing the Himalayas rise up ahead, like jagged snowy monsters cloaked in mist. A trek in Nepal offers the only way to experience the ancient villages, terraced farms, religious shrines, rocky streams and alpine forests of rhododendron trees that are the essence of one of the most romantic and remote regions in the world.

For me, trekking offered another type of opportunity, a challenge to see if I could make it through eight days in fairly rugged mountains and return to tell the tale.

My wife had backpacked through the Smokies and spent many summers hiking in other parts of the United States. But I am definitely an amateur. To save my life, I probably could not pitch a tent and certainly could not start a fire without a match. Because my back still keeps going out, I had to give up running last year. I prefer bathing every day and wasn't at all sure about sleeping bags. So when friends asked us to join them on an eight-day trek, I didn't jump at the chance. But I wanted to see if I could do it, and I wanted to see Nepal.

The country offers a full range of challenges, and mine was actually one of the less difficult. The more adventurous can test their endurance at the higher altitudes, including the regions around Mount Everest and Annapurna. Others can go off into the hills without a guide, live more or less off the land and find lodging in the tiny villages along the route.

My trek was organized by Mountain Travel Nepal, foremost of the many professional agencies based in Katmandu. Mountain Travel supplied the tents, sleeping bags, food and kitchen gear. Its crew pitched the tents and cooked the meals. The 16 trekkers in our group (nine men and seven women) brought their own clothes and camping paraphernalia in duffel bags. But everything was carried up and down the slopes by nimble-footed porters practically half our size. All we had to do was carry day packs and somehow keep going on the trail from 7 in the morning to usually about 3 or 4 in the afternoon, with a break for lunch. When we were ready to leave for the day's outing, the crew had already moved on to the lunch site so that when we arrived, the meal was almost ready. The crew brought some food along, including live chickens, and bought some en route.

Our fellow trekkers ranged from about twenty to fifty in age, but it is not uncommon for children to come along on treks. I have met vigorous people in their sixties and know of people in their seventies who have gone on arduous treks.

With our retinue of 45 Sherpas and porters, we fully realized that we were not about to qualify for the sequel to *Indiana Jones and the Temple of Doom*. In fact, we may have looked ridiculous. But the hiking was strenuous. We started out in blazing heat (in the upper 90s) so punishing that we didn't feel foolish using our umbrellas as parasols. By the end of the week we were up to 12,000 feet, making our way through snow-dappled forests and crisp, thin mountain air. Among our group we experienced all kinds of ailments – altitude sickness, colds, diarrhoea, blisters, muscle aches and nausea. But when it was over, we had seen some of the most breathtaking landscape in the world, and we could say that we had hiked 50 miles up and down the Himalaya Mountains.

Our trek took us through a region northeast of Katmandu called Helambu, also known as Helmu. To the north is a wall of mountains more than 16,000 feet high, but the ridges and valleys in Helambu itself run north and south. Because of its proximity to the capital, the area is ideal for shorter treks. Surprisingly, it is also one of the less spoiled areas because so many trekkers are beckoned by the romance of the Annapurna range or Everest area.

After being dropped off by a bus at a flat, barren and hot outpost east of Katmandu, we made our way along the Indrawati River bed to the site of our first camp at Melemchi Pul. Some of the other, experienced campers came equipped with special trousers and hiking boots, but I trudged along in shorts and a pair of old running shoes that were to serve me quite well. At only 2,000 feet, we sweltered that first day and wondered when we would feel like we were hiking in the mountains. But we were able to cool off at a green bend in the river, where the water rushed by in a refreshing torrent. It was the last time we could bathe in a river until the end of the trek.

I began to see that this trek would give us an extraordinary look at how people live in Nepal. We passed through tiny villages of old stone houses and on the hillsides we saw men ploughing the terraced farms, shouting at their bullocks or water buffalo in the hot sun.

Elsewhere, groups of women stooped to plant seedlings in paddies. On the trail itself, men strained under the weight of bags of rice carried to the market. Farther on the trek, these men could be seen taking enormous sacks of grain on their backs up the rugged mountains to Tibet. There they trade the grain for exquisite jewellery and trinkets that are then sold in the tourist shops of Katmandu.

The nation's commerce thus unfolded before our eyes, and so did its biggest problems. Nepal is one of the world's poorest countries, with a per capita income of $140 in 1983, and its population is growing so rapidly that the country is running out of land to cultivate. The search for a livelihood has led the Nepalese to cut down most of their nation's forests and to carve corrugated terraces into every inch of available hillside. When the monsoons come, they wash the denuded soil into the rivers, a problem that some scientists believe contributes to the silt deposits and devastating floods where the Ganges and Brahmaputra river systems empty into the Bay of Bengal.

The Nepalese Government, with the help of an array of agencies including the United States Peace Corps, has undertaken an ambitious programme of reforestation to halt the erosion. But many experts say it's a losing battle, and what the trekker sees is hill after hill of terraced farms.

On the first day I walked part of the way alongside Lhakpa Norbu, our Sherpa leader, a lean, hawk-faced man with a thin moustache and a friendly manner, ready always to listen to suggestions from the group. During the week, we shifted the planned itinerary somewhat, deciding that one campsite was too windy and drab. So we later walked an extra half day and spent two nights at Tarke Ghyang, where some people took time out from trekking to go shopping for souvenirs. Norbu told me that most groups get along well, but that arguments sometimes develop over the pace and itinerary.

Ours was a congenial collection, and it turned out the hiking was hard for almost everyone, as proved by the second day. It seemed as if we were going straight up, mostly in intense heat, through steep trails carved into the dusty mountainside. Setting the pattern that prevailed for the rest of the week, we awakened at 6 and were on our way an hour later. After a morning of sweating, straining and grunting, we feasted on fried potatoes, fried eggs, bread, honey and marmalade for lunch. The cook also gave us pieces of water buffalo liver that had the consistency of wet string.

By now I was beginning to get over my initial fears that I was going to die of hepatitis or some other disease on this trek. Visitors are warned not to eat uncooked vegetables or to drink the water, even from the most pristine-looking streams. The crew kept water boiling at every stop, and we used it to fill our water containers. Some trekkers like to take the extra precaution of bringing iodine solution or water purification tablets, but I found that drinking thoroughly boiled water worked fine for me.

By the end of the second day, we finally felt we were in the mountains. In the distance to the north we could see the snow-covered peaks of the Himalayas. The hills were still terraced and covered with tiny folds, making them look from a distance like a rich grain of wood.

On the third day I felt that the hard work was paying off in one of the rare privileges offered by a trip like this: the opportunity to see what only those willing to hike through the mountains can see.

A certain magical quality of the mountains began to bewitch us, even though we were exhausted at the end of every day. There was the silence broken only by bleating goats or barking dogs. Occasionally we simply stopped to take in the silent majesty of the vista to the north, where the high and snowy ridges were cloaked with clouds. The spectacular views of the valleys below were all the more satisfying because we knew we had strained up every inch to the top of the ridge in order to look down.

Scattered along the trail were ancient Buddhist stupas, or shrines. We were often invited to stop at Buddhist temples and monasteries, adorned with exquisite, brightly coloured paintings. We took pleasure in the moist, silent air of contemplation that pervaded the temples' interiors. The hillside monasteries had tall flagpoles with prayer flags flapping in the wind, making the buildings seem like silent ships perched in the sky.

Few of the Nepalese we met spoke English. Along the trail, however, small children continually pestered us with shouts of 'chocolate,' for they have learned that trekkers often bring candy to give them. Indeed, one of the bizarre effects of the thousands of trekkers in Nepal in recent years is the higher incidence of tooth decay among Nepalese children.

In the town of Tarke Ghyang, where we pitched our tents for the third and fourth nights, a group of beautiful, willowy women came to our campsite and beseeched us to come to their shops in their homes to look at trinkets and other souvenirs. Each shop was immaculate, with a polished floor and organized displays of bottles, copper pots, pans, jars and Buddhist or Hindu decorations. It was impossible to resist buying a necklace made of yak bone or an intricately embossed and inlaid jewellery box, especially since these elegant women with plaintive almond eyes and dazzling smiles had the persistence of vacuum-cleaner salesmen. Bargaining was intense, but the cost for several pieces did not exceed $10 to $20.

I decided that I had done so well on the trek so far that I could take a day off and loll around Tarke Ghyang on the fourth day while some of the others climbed up and down a nearby ridge. I slept and read in the pale sunlight, enjoying the occasional drizzles but nursing a quiet sense of dread that from now on the climb might be more brutal.

Sure enough, the next day we plunged down into a valley, crossed a rushing stream that was driving an ancient stone mill, and headed back up to a camp in the forest above the village of Melemchi Gaon.

Shortly after lunch, it began to rain. Then it rained harder, making the air fragrant with forest scents. With walking sticks in one hand and umbrellas in the other, we trudged through gullies, spongy under-growth and muck. The splatter of the rain was punctuated by groans from waterlogged trekkers scaling a steep mountainside covered with forest, jagged rocks and slippery mud. It seemed like hours before we arrived at the campsite in a pasture inhabited by yaks. The yaks were not overjoyed to be pushed aside by a collection of bedraggled trekkers and their entourage.

The accumulation of hardships was now taking its toll. I had accomplished a lot, of course. I had learned how to turn over in my snug sleeping bag. I had become used to the dinners of mashed potatoes, thin soup, boiled cabbage and sinewy chicken. I had become practised at squatting over a hole in the privacy of a latrine tent usually erected on a hillside near the camp. And I had recovered from a pounding headache – a symptom of altitude sickness – the previous night.

The rain soon stopped, and when it did we could see through the mist that only a couple of hundred feet above us there was snow on the ground. It was hard to believe that two days earlier, we had been sweltering in shorts and T-shirts. Now we gathered around a bonfire to keep warm, bundled in sweaters and wool hats. I was glad to have an extra pair of dry shoes. Some of the women in the group sang to cheer the rest of us. As they serenaded the campers, the displaced yaks brayed in the background.

The reward for this misery came the next day. Dawn broke cold and crisp, and soon we were climbing through magnificent rhododendron forests with thousands of blossoms of red, pink and white. It was an alpine fairyland.

We kept climbing, this time past fields of purple primroses and beneath canopies of rhododendron trees. In the background were the peaks of the Himalayas, still towering above us like sentinels, even though we had reached 12,000 feet. The air was bracing and dry, as intoxicating as wine. I felt that I was on top of the world, which, in a manner of speaking I nearly was.

The seventh day proved, if I had not realized it already, that trudging down a mountain can be as arduous as climbing up. My running shoes by now had begun to fall apart, and I was relying more and more on my walking stick. I was also increasingly aware that I had not bathed in a week, and the luxuries of Katmandu began to beckon.

The last night of our trek was spent on a wind-buffeted hillside on a ridge not far to the west of the route that we had climbed when we went north. Now we were making our way south, dismayed to discover that we had many steep ridges to scale on the way. We were working hard, and on the morning of the eighth day of our trek, everyone was ready to go home. We made our way quickly down to the village of Sundarijal, and some of us took a last swim in an ice-cold stream just above a green reservoir used by the city of Katmandu.

I had to admit that I was glad to be back but exhilarated with a sense of accomplishment at having trekked through part of the Himalayas and seen rare and spectacular sights. After living in south Asia for five months, however, I have rediscovered the cliché of countless travellers. The adventures here are many. It can be an adventure to go to the local market. But almost every journey becomes a basic exercise in self-discovery.

I have just bought a new pair of hiking boots and am ready to try trekking again.

IF YOU GO

Until 1951, Nepal was virtually closed to outsiders. But since then, it has drawn so many tourists that the Nepalese Government is seriously worried about the environmental degradation they've brought.

Of the 180,000 people who visit Nepal each year, some 30,000 go trekking. Many of them arrange their own trips on the spot in Katmandu, where dozens of organizations offer equipment and guides. But the Government suggests that visitors make arrangements with those organizations registered with the tourist office.

Arranging Your Trek

Mountain Travel Nepal (Narayan Chaur, Naxal, Katmandu; telephone: 12808), is the largest, most experienced agency and probably one of the most expensive. Its prices vary from about $400 for an eight-day trek in the Helambu area to more than $1,300 for a twenty-five-day trek to the Everest region. That's in addition to the cost of getting to Katmandu, which is readily accessible by aeroplane. Other leading trekking companies based in Katmandu include: Himalayan Journeys Pvt. Ltd., Kanti Path, Post Office Box 989, Katmandu, Nepal; Nepal Himal, Post Office Box 3745, Katmandu, Nepal; Treks and Expeditions Services, Corner-house, Kemal Potkari, Katmandu, Nepal and Ongdi Trekking, Durbar Marg, Katmandu, Nepal.

It is best to check with a large travel agency that has had experience with one of the trekking agencies in Nepal.

When to Go

The best time to trek is after the summer monsoon season, starting in October, or in the spring. Trekking in midwinter can mean severe cold and snow at high altitudes. In February, with the coming of spring, the rhododendron trees begin to bloom, and many people prefer this time of year to the late spring, when it can be hot at lower altitudes. April (when we made our trek) and May can be exquisite at high altitudes; the monsoons usually begin in early June.

Getting Into Shape

Anyone planning a trek should be in good physical condition. A regimen of running or swimming before you go can make the difference between pleasure and pain while trekking.

What to Take

Experienced campers know that the weather in the mountains can change abruptly. A warm day can suddenly become chilly when the sun goes behind a cloud or a ridge. So it is essential to bring a range of clothes – swimsuit, sunscreen, sunhat, along with sweaters and wool hat. An umbrella was invaluable. Many trekking organizations supply equipment, and some equipment can be obtained in Katmandu. But I would advise buying yours before you go. Good shoes and day packs are best purchased in the United States. A well-equipped day pack includes such items as a wide-mouthed plastic water bottle, sunglasses, pocket knives, photographic and first-aid equipment. The professional trekking agencies usually supply a list of useful paraphernalia.

Medication

It is advisable to bring medication for diarrhoea and colds. Some treks include a doctor; many can make arrangements for emergency rescues. One should visit a doctor before travelling; most recommend immunizations for polio, typhoid, tetanus-diphtheria and smallpox. Gamma globulin shots are a must. Make sure to have all your shots recorded in a World Health Organization vaccination certificate.

SO YOU WANT TO GET AWAY?

John Vinocur

Islomania: Webster's has not yet legitimized it. The wheels of justice in the big word court seem to grind slowly, its magistrates more intent on recognizing computer talk, glitches and bytes, than yearnings not quite processable with a single keystroke. Islomania comes from Lawrence Durrell, and islomania's problem is probably that not enough people are afflicted to agree entirely on its definition.

Durrell invented a character called Gideon who invented islomania. We islomanes, says Gideon, are the direct descendants of the Atlanteans, and it is toward the lost Atlantis that our subconscious is drawn. This means that we find islands irresistible. Where others tremble at the sight of a well-wrought urn, our hearts pound for little worlds surrounded by the sea.

The isolmane, according to Durrell, fills with indescribable intoxication at the thought of being on an island. Dr. Durrell is documenting a rather advanced case. I admit to buying maps and pictures of islands and framing them – a less severe case than that of the man who secretly tucks them in drawers – but I think islomania is really the pull to be somewhere at sea, yet somewhere still, waveless, and the smaller the better. The appeal is a little bit like having a secret hideout or a tree house as a kid. The island is away from things, and out of grown-ups' control. The farther you get from the sound of the big people's voices, the more water you put between yourself and them, the smaller the turf you have to deal with, then all the more deep the islomanic bliss.

I found out about Île Denis/Dennis Island in a scene reminiscent of the one in an old movie when the young archaeologist comes upon a diagram of an irrigation project that unlocks the mystery of a buried civilization. He thrums with excitement; he holds the document up to the lamp, the yellow light funnelling down on it; he calls his wife, and she rushes into the study, wiping her hands on her apron. 'The riddle of Balumbishi,' he says, all flushed. 'I've solved it.'

'Dennis Island,' I said. 'We're going.'

What I had seen was an aerial photo showing the island as a greenish comma bordered in white sand, in the middle of a gemstone sea. The colours could have been rolled out of a jeweller's pouch: tourmaline blue on aquamarine on purple on indigo. What I liked beyond the picture was the vagueness of the accompanying description. Île Denis was in the Seychelles in the Indian Ocean. If you could get to Mahé, the major island in the chain, then maybe you could find a plane to Dennis. It had two spellings, one *n* or two, depending on whether your atlas was in French or English. A Frenchman owned it, it seemed. There was a copra plantation on the island, and the owner took in guests.

It sounded perfect, an islomane's almost unspeakable fantasy: The Seychelles are near nowhere, and Dennis, with a population of thirty-five for 350 acres, lies on their outer edge, almost beyond reach and, I hoped, beyond care.

A strange coincidence followed. I mentioned Dennis Island to a friend, no islomane but a constant voyager, and he got untypically sheepish. He hemmed and hawed, and finally it all came out in a rush. He had been to Dennis Island, and he was never, ever supposed to tell anyone about it. It was almost a covenant: *omerta*; I didn't see nuttin'. The truth was, he said, it was such a marvellous place that no one should ever talk about it. Didn't I once demand total secrecy about a village inn in Normandy where they served oysters, lobster and dessert for 132 francs, he asked. Well, Dennis Island was the same. It needed protection.

Months later, after visiting Dennis, I finally worked out the ethics of the situation. Pierre Burkhardt, who owns the island, says he'll never have more than fifty people there at once. There's no way to enlarge it, and, he says, there's no way for him to make money out of it. He calls it 'the island at the end of the world' and says it makes no difference who knows about it because not many are going to try to come.

We did. It was eleven hours in the air from Paris to Mahé, with a stop in Djibouti, on the east coast of Africa, a place so bare of plant life that the major tourist attraction is a bar with a zinc palm tree. In Mahé, we waited around for six or seven hours for a little plane to take us to Dennis. I sat up next to the pilot, a slight man with a very strong resemblance to Nguyen Cao Ky. The thought of how we were going to land never really occurred to me until Dennis rose out of the sea at the horizon. Getting closer, I understood: from the air the island appeared covered in vegetation, through which somebody had shaved a strip, rather like a parting in a very thick head of hair. The cut turned out to be grass running from one side of the island to the other. The pilot's job was to put the plane down on the strip with the Indian Ocean behind us and then to stop it with the Indian Ocean still in front of us. He did so while my four-year-old son giggled and his mother drowned in sweat. Finally, Dennis Island. Pierre Burkhardt was there waiting under the roof of a shed.

He tells everybody that Dennis isn't a hotel, that he's not a hotelkeeper, but basically a lover of islands who, as an entrepreneurial islomane, decided to buy one. Pierre is over sixty, blue-eyed, and blessed with the kind of lank, silvering hair that PR outfits love for photos of their board-chairman clients. He was, in fact, president of a French-Belgian paper-pulp consortium, the largest in the Common Market, and therefore somebody who actually knew how to purchase an island. In 1975, the Seychelles sold him Dennis, discovered in 1773 by Denis de Trobriand in the service of the King of France and not much thought about since. The Government insisted on the right to operate a lighthouse and extracted a promise from Pierre that he would keep five cows 'to maintain the agricultural character of the island.'

My great concern in coming to Dennis was the chi-chi factor, the island's potential for polished blazer buttons – mainland hobbles on my sense of islomania. But it was pointless. Bless the French, who know tropical climates through centuries of colonialism and long ago realized that it's impossible to keep buildings at the edge of the ocean and the equator looking like designer showrooms. And so bless the very un-designerlike print curtains in our little bungalow, the mosquito nets over our beds, the lights too low-powered for shaving well at night, the generator that coughed out every once in a while, taking Dennis's electricity with it, the green lizards whipping through the eaves of every building, the chickens scratching at the edge of our veranda and the general mood of gracious underachievement.

Strive not, Dennis says.

While we were there, a German couple, a building contractor and his wife, nice people really, pulled out a bit early, a case, we suspected, of them being uncomfortable without some kind of tally sheet, a point-system of accomplishment. 'What did you do today?' the contractor asked me at one point. We were at the big open lodge Pierre Burkhardt built for eating meals, for leaning against a bar, and for playing pool. I was kind of hard pressed to tell him. I had waded a lot, chased crabs with my son, and then, well, I wasn't sure. It's hard to quantify wandering around, following the shoreline, knowing that if you keep the water on your left, you wind up back where you started, feeling pretty close to joy with the idea of having circumscribed all the existence at hand.

Actually, I poked at things. I went across the airstrip to look at what was grandiosely described as the copra plantation. The truth is, Pierre has a couple of men who gather up fallen coconuts and put them into a machine, modelled on the engine of the *African Queen*, that grinds and shreds them and turns out coconut oil. The men are watched by very large tortoises whose cousins occasionally turn up elsewhere on the island. Since Dennis is not a locus of the work ethic, there is not much on the product end.

The idea of walking around with a map of Dennis is silly – it's that small – but I had one anyway from the Seychelles geodetic survey, and there were a few mysterious place names on it that I inspected but never really figured out: Muraille Bon Dieu, Madame Guichard, La Mère Boeuf. The nicest name, I thought, was Sans Tache (spotless) and it turned out to be the beach near our bungalow. It was a totally accurate description.

Burkhardt's spread is on the side of the island where the beaches are soft and creamy and the wind breaks. On the other side, the reef is closer to shore, and things look rougher, and wilder. The palms bend, the water gets roiled on the coral and splashes iridescent in the sun. I spent a lot of time there. When the wind picks up and the sounds are of the tide and the trees moving, when there is nothing at the horizon but blue meeting blue, the islomania in you just whoops and leaps. Nobody around! Nobody coming! Gone!

Milder cases of islomania, and people who take Dennis Island simply as a lovely, isolated place to spend a week or two, actually do other things than follow my itinerary. They can go deep-sea fishing, windsurf, lie in the sun, paddle around looking at the underwater landscape, read books, sleep, eat, and never see a newspaper. A couple of times a week, the little plane comes in and a few people get off or on – an event at which you can strike the pose of an old-timer or an eccentric who prowls the beaches and coconut groves. The food is good, especially the fish and the curries, and sometimes a couple of the Seychellois who work in the kitchen or at Pierre's farm will play music that sounds a bit Cajun.

The conversation is reasonable too, although my discussions with Pierre Burkhardt brought me a sad realization. Island-buying is very much out of my reach. I will remain a renter, taking a tiny share a couple of weeks at a time and pretending that all of it belongs to me. It's a harmless fib, and Dennis Island co-operates better than any place I know.

TINY ISLANDS
From France
Three tour operators can make arrangements to visit Île Denis, departing from and returning to Paris: **Maine Montparnasse Voyages** (widely known by its initials, MVM), 16 Rue Littré, 75014 Paris (45 44 69 60), offer stays of one to two weeks or more (count three additional days for travel time). From March to October, the prices, which can vary because

of exchange-rate fluctuations, range from about $1,500 to $1,700 a person for the first seven nights. The rates, which include meals on the island, change weekly, in accordance with seasonal air fares. An additional week costs about $550 or $600 a person; for stays of 9 or 12 days, the price is prorated, based on the prevailing weekly rate.

Both **Africa Tours**, 9-11 Avenue Franklin D. Roosevelt, 75008 Paris (47 23 78 59), and **Jet Tours Prestige**, 19 Avenue de Tourville, 75007 Paris (47 05 01 95), offer trips of 10 days and 9 nights, with additional stays of one or two weeks. Again the prices vary, beginning at about $1,500 a person a week, with air fare and meals. An additional week costs about $550 or $600.

From Almost Anywhere

If you wish to make your own arrangements, it is advisable to make reservations by letter (write to Dennis Island Lodge, Post Office Box 404, Victoria, Mahé, Seychelles) or by Telex (2319 DENIS, Seychelles); the telephone link to Île Denis is highly unreliable. Include all arrival details, and the hotel will arrange your round-trip flight between Mahé and Île Denis; the fare, about $150, will be added to your hotel bill. Rates are about $160 a day for two, with meals; single occupancy with meals is about $100 a day, and a third person in a bungalow pays about $60 a day for meals. Children between 2 and 12 are charged about $40 a day, with meals. (Children under 2 stay free, but parents should bring food for them.)

You can fly to Mahé from Paris (Air France), Bombay (Air India), London, Frankfurt, Amsterdam or Rome (Air Seychelles), Johannesburg or Colombo (British Airways), Nairobi (Kenya Airways) and Hong Kong (British Airways).

FROM THE SOUTH PACIFIC TO THE CARIBBEAN

WHERE BIRDS AND BEASTS BEWITCH

William F. Buckley, Jr

Upfrontwise, be advised that the Galápagos Islands lie on the equator, about 600 miles west of Guayaquil, which is a coastal city – the coastal city – in Ecuador, which is what happens between Peru and Colombia.

Using round numbers, it takes three hours to fly to Miami (from New York); four hours to fly to Guayaquil from Miami, and an hour and a half to fly to the islands. But when you count in the usual attritions – the one-hour stopover in Miami; overnight in Guayaquil; three hours the next morning at the airport at Guayaquil (they routinely warn you that the flights are oversold, so that if you want to be certain to be on that flight, be there three hours ahead of time); two hours at the airport at Baltra, waiting for your bags (they tend to come in on the auxiliary prop-plane flight); a half-hour bus ride to the ferry; a fifteen-minute ferry ride; and then a second bus and an hour-and-a-half ride (if you are lucky, you will find a seat) to Academy Bay – you have consumed most of two days.

There is a sense in which it is fitting that it should be a little bit difficult to reach the Galápagos Islands. One day, one supposes, a cartridge at the neighbourhood airport will transport a passenger to the snows of Kilimanjaro nonstop, no fuss. I hope the day is far off, because when one reaches the Galápagos one should feel that a certain amount of labour went into the voyage: necessary way stations, before reaching the shrine.

Because the islands are nothing less than a shrine for naturalists and for historians. They are appropriately remote, and it is because they are remote and because they are situated exactly where they are that the confluence of natural forces over the course of a few million years made possible the phenomena one finds there. The word unique is loosely used. Not when applied to the Galápagos Islands. Nowhere on earth is there what is to be found there. It is first exhilarating to consider this; after that, one is entitled to ask whether the exhilaration wears off. More quickly for some, obviously, than for others.

We left Newark at about noon, got to the yacht *Sealestial*, at anchor in the Galápagos, at about five o'clock on the afternoon of the following day. You may, not inexplicably, be asking yourself, toward the end of the second day: Was this trip necessary?

That is the moment when, if you want to shore up your self-confidence, you do well to pick up a book. Rather than look outside at the bay? – At Academy Bay? – On the equator? – Where Charles Darwin, well, sort of . . . discovered evolution?

Yes. Academy Bay is commonplace. It harbours a resident fleet of a dozen or two middle-sized, middle-aged power boats, thirty-five to fifty-five feet long; a couple of biggish passenger liners; hilly surroundings of dull green; a nothing village (population: 4,000), and a little hotel. Turn, instead, to page 22 of *Galápagos: Islands Lost in Time* by Tui De Roy Moore, and you will read this kind of thing:

> One of [the] sections of the earth's surface is the Nazea Plate, which, through continental drift, carries the Galápagos cluster slowly toward the coast of South America, where the continent overrides the oceanic plate. Thus the Nazea Plate is forced down to be reabsorbed into the earth's mantle. At the present rate of movement it will take about 14 million years for the Galápagos Islands to be inexorably engulfed by the interior of the planet.

So you learn that 14 million years from now the Galápagos will be integrated into the mainland of Ecuador, a datum you may wish to dwell on, congratulating yourself that, having come to the Galápagos now, you are clearly not a procrastinator. It is your descendants who will face the problem of wondering what the Galápagos Islands were like, back when they were entities of their own.

You are indeed visiting the islands because they are unique. Certainly not because they are beautiful – though there are differences of opinion. It makes a great deal of difference if you are a naturalist, even if you are a naturalist manqué. Zoo nuts should go to the Galápagos even before Paris, Rome or Venice. Listen to what it does to you, if zoology is your aphrodisiac. The same elegant writer previously quoted goes on to describe the marine iguanas, which are huge attractions to the tourist interested in seeing marine iguanas, which you will see in the Galápagos or not at all: 'They have long scaly tails, short legs with sharp claws, and thin spiny crests running down their backs. They have been described as utterly hideous, yet in this natural setting they [are] starkly beautiful.'

Even men of great imagination are arrested by the islands' ugliness. Herman Melville was there shortly after Darwin, and wrote rudely about the 'blighted Encantadas' – that is the name the Spaniards had given them. 'Little but reptile life is here found, the chief sound of life is a hiss.' And went on, 'Take five and twenty heaps of cinders dumped here and there in an outsize city lot; imagine some of these magnified into mountains and the vacant lot the sea; and you will have a fit idea of the general aspect of the Encantadas.'

But then again there is that other eye in the mind's curiosity, and it sees Galápagos as Darwin did. 'Considering the small size of these islands, we feel the more astonished at the number of their aboriginal beings, and at their confined range.'

It is ironic that the islands were called the Islas Encantadas, because the facile translation of the Spanish words yields you 'Enchanted Islands,' and conventional understanding is that enchanted islands will be enchanting. But *encantada* also means 'bewitched,' and bewitched islands are by no means necessarily enchanting, even as the Galápagos most emphatically are not enchanting, except in the sense that cadavers are enchanting to medical students, or beetles to coleopterists. The visitor will do well to ask himself how he is likely to respond to the enticements of zoology before committing himself to spend much time at the Galápagos. Notice I said 'much time,' because a (very) few days there are at worst endurable, at most, distracting and engrossing even to non-naturalists. Still, even as one would not recommend a week at the Bayreuth Festival to people maturely indifferent to music, so one should never lightly sign on for eight or ten days at the Galápagos unless one is prepared to believe that a marine iguana can be starkly beautiful.

It happened that a familiar seventy-one-foot ketch (familiar because I have crossed the Atlantic on it) was to pause, westbound to Tahiti, at the Galápagos, and its owner suggested I coincide my movements with its. A permit for the *Sealestial* to visit the islands, difficult to obtain, was arranged. The permit did not, however, relieve us of the requirement that we travel with a guide. Charles Darwin would be required to use a guide in the Galápagos today.

Ours was the total enthusiast. Darrel Schoenling was born in Chicago not very long ago, and graduated in 1981 from Brown, where he specialized in evolutionary biology before going on to teach at the Collegiate School in New York. The American Museum of Natural History helps Ecuador to recruit English-speaking guides who, in order to qualify to spend the ritual one year in the Galápagos, need to present themselves as preliminarily qualified by having done previous work in zoology, and then to submit to a rigorous course of specialized learning lasting a half year. They are expected to know everything about the islands and their myriad and arcane inhabitants, and certainly Darrel does, blending profound knowledge with a nice sense of the appropriate level of interest of his audience.

Approximately 18,000 tourists visited the Galápagos in 1984, up

from 12,000 the year before owing to a relaxation of the rules by
Ecuador, which simultaneously raised the visitors' (foreign visitors –
Ecuadorians pay minimal fees to visit Galápagos) fees, from $5 to $30,
the proceeds going toward the maintenance of the islands. Maintenance involves, among other things, killing alien species imported
there during the anarchical nineteenth century, even after the publication of *Origin of Species*, when people visiting Galápagos knew that it
was something special but evidently did not feel that there was any
point to be served in keeping it that way. It wasn't until the 1930s that
it was regulated as something of a natural monument. And so they
would bring in predatory animals that threatened the delicate balance
that, in 1835, caused Darwin, after spending five weeks there on his
five-year cruise aboard the *Beagle*, to draw his breath and write
excitedly in his journal, 'Here, both in space and time, we seem to be
brought somewhere near to that great fact – that mystery of mysteries
– the first appearance of new beings on this earth.'

The principal servant of the tourists is a 250-foot passenger boat of
10,000 tons or so called the *Bucanero*, which we visited one festive
evening. It was built in 1951 in Scotland and used in the northern
British islands and in Nova Scotia before being converted to its present
mission. It has more staterooms than are used by its ninety passengers,
because no vessel is permitted a greater number of passengers; some of
the islands can be visited by no more than a half-dozen people at one
time, and none of them by more than ninety people at one time. (All
these fine judgements are made by the Intendencia del Parque
Nacional Galápagos, and are geared to the amount of traffic the
animal and bird population can endure.) It isn't that there is any
apparent danger of frightening the iguanas or the sea lions or the
hawks or the frigate birds, because these do not frighten in the least.
No one ever told the animal world of the Galápagos that human beings
are capable of inflicting damage. Indeed seamen aboard the *Beagle*
reported that in order to shoot a bird on the Galápagos it was first
necessary to situate him at the correct end of the rifle.

The other major vessel is the *Santa Cruz*, and is said to be more
luxurious than the *Bucanero*, which is good news; though the *Bucanero*'s
quarters are habitable, its public rooms roomy. All manner of people
travel to the Galápagos, though more young than older people,
inasmuch as one needs to be moderately spry to make one's way across
the lava beds, up the hills, over the rocks along the shore: though, of
course, any passenger who wishes to do so can eschew any part of the
day's outing. The *Bucanero* sails out of Guayaquil every eighteen days,
taking two and a half days to reach its destination. Once there, the
island cruises are for three, four or five days. If one books passage for
longer than five days, one will be revisiting islands already seen. That

is for addicts, or students.

The last of the four legs of the *Bucanero*'s hegira brings the passengers back by sea to Guayaquil. Other tourist detachments will have returned by air. And most of these, one notes, will travel on to Quito, the capital of Ecuador, a half hour's flight from Guayaquil but 10,000 feet higher than the coastal city. Quito is beautiful to look at, its baroque churches spectacular. Guayaquil has only a renowned cemetery to which, having lived a lifetime in Guayaquil, it cannot be presumed that its inhabitants repair with any great sense of loss.

The routine, then, is to sail from island to island, distances that vary from a mile to fifty miles, skipping some, but touching down on ten or twelve. Each has something of special interest – a particular species of bird, for instance; or of reptile; unusual lava formations. There is, as far as I could discover, no animal in the Galápagos in any way dangerous, though I did spot, coming in on the dinghy to the *Sealestial* from the *Bucanero*, what was identified as a sea snake. It looked like a wriggling little eel, dirty-white. Darrel told us reassuringly that its jaw is so small it would have a difficult time biting you except where human tissue is very thin, as between, say, thumb and forefinger. 'However, if it does bite you, you will die,' he remarked, moving on to other subjects, like the hawks we saw that afternoon. Four of them, feasting on a young sea lion. We had moved within a foot or two of them, disturbing them not in the least, and causing Darrel to shout out that it was nothing short of miraculous that birds of prey should, even while feeding, permit human beings to come so close to them. We saw blue-footed boobies, which characteristically give birth two days apart to four offspring. Generally one the oldest survives, since there is not enough food about for the mother to bring in to keep all four fed, and the oldest, stronger than his siblings by a couple of days, has the strength to wrest the food from his juniors. I don't know whether Darwin called this an early expression of the law of primogeniture.

The Galápagos are, of course, interesting not only to naturalists but also to historians of romantic, even legendary haunts. It is recorded that no one lived there permanently until almost 300 years after the islands were discovered, in 1546, by the Bishop of Panama. The first person credited as a genuine resident was called Patrick Watkins, an Irishman who lived on Floreana Island between 1807 and 1809. It is not known whether he was marooned there or asked to be put ashore, and the guidebook (*Galápagos Guide*, written and photographed by three former Peace Corpsmen, Alan White, Bruce Epler and Charles Gilbert, under the sponsorship of the Charles Darwin Research Station in the Galápagos Islands, is a fine and readable guide) gives no third alternative. He evidently got on by giving visiting whalers vegetables in return for rum. But then one day, while the whalers were on an island looking for water to drink and tortoises to eat, Patrick Watkins stole one of their whaleboats and, along with it, five of their slaves, and set sail for Guayaquil. He arrived there alone. The guidebook's final words on Patrick Watkins might have been written by Evelyn Waugh: 'Whether he ate them or pushed them overboard to conserve water, is not known.'

Succeeding settlers tended to meet violent ends. It wasn't until 1832 that it occurred to Ecuador to send out a military detachment to declare the islands a part of Ecuador. But the ensuing settlement became a penal colony. Several subsequent governors were assassinated, two in slave rebellions.

In 1926, a small settlement of Norwegians settled on Santa Cruz Island at Academy Bay, raising vegetables for the tuna fleet. The airstrip on the north of the island was built in 1942 by the United States military-industrial complex, back when it was called the arsenal of democracy, and it is there that the tourists, and anyone else flying to the Galápagos, land. If they have planned carefully, they will pick up their vessel, whether the *Bucanero* or one of the small, Chris-Craft-style power boats, at the adjacent harbour, sparing themselves the arduous bus rides down to Academy Bay.

The reading public – forget the touring public – should have a look at the book by Tui De Roy Moore. She is all but a native of the islands, her Belgian parents having taken her there, at four years old, to avoid a world war. She grew up there, with her younger brother, in the style of Swiss Family Robinson, and one of those recondite genes Charles Darwin occasionally had to wrestle with gave her remarkable powers to express what it is to grow in perfect harmony with the creatures of Galápagos. Reading that book, and then seeing the islands – or, better, seeing the islands while reading that book – gives one a window on the excitement of the world of the naturalist, much as one supposes a deaf man, reading Tovey, can actually sense what music can do to you. The strayest page will give you words and phrases like opuntia trees and epiphytic lichens and liverworts. You come upon tender clumps of ferns, and explore rain-filled ponds and sphagnum bogs. You are excited by the sight of shady spots of yellow-crowned night herons sleeping away the daylight. You marvel, when the weather is hot and calm, at myriad microscopic organisms that glow at night.

Before you sleep, you might gaze at the tranquil mangrove-surrounded cove with the flashing blue phosphorescence, the lightest movement in the water provoking showers of light. Perhaps, coming home, you will have rowed your small skiff quietly on moonless nights, every darting fish, every small shark, leaving a sparkling trail, like so many shooting stars in a black water sky; and the green sea turtles are there, outlined in a blue glow, dozens of feet away.

The islands, enchanting here, never bewitching, did this to that girl, who serves now as guide, photographer and naturalist in the Galápagos: and one shouldn't, if one can avoid it, deny exposing oneself to anything that had that effect on her.

If your experience is like my own, you will return with a sense of having approached a phenomenon, had a searching look at it, and tiptoed back, to a world in which hawks keep their distance, marine iguanas vanish with the coming of the glacial age, and that which engrosses one most is, for better or worse, the doings of men and women, the words they write, the songs they sing, the tempers they exhibit.

The enchanted isles are properly cordoned off. There shouldn't be regular, licentious traffic to those islands, not only because such traffic would rob them soon of their allure, but also because they would lose that singular glamour that gives them what enchantment they have. There should always be moats, and gates, and portcullises to surround distinctive oases, whether natural or cultivated; whether we speak of the Galápagos, or the Winter Palace. The islands are comfortably remote, safe, inviolable, and so tend to remain in the memory.

A SUMMER SEA THAT TEEMS WITH LIFE

Peter Benchley

At night, we would haul our mattresses and pillows out onto the deck, in faint (and usually futile) hope of intercepting a whisper of breeze that sometimes rippled the silent sea. But though darkness did lower the temperature a bit – from the mid-90s to the high 80s – it did nothing to relieve the stultifying humidity. It was like trying to fall asleep inside a sponge.

Still, after a while the gentle motion of the boat and the crystal clarity of the air and the swarms of sentinel stars would lull us to the edge of the abyss. And then – BAM! A report like a distant cannon shot would echo across the still water, followed by a trickle of splashes and another thunderous boom.

We would spring upright, those first nights, and search the blackness for the pirates who were coming to board us, or the boat whose engine had exploded. But by the third or fourth night the sounds had become as familiar – and as curiously comforting – as the clatter of garbage cans being hurled to the street by sanitation men outside the apartment window in the city.

Giant Pacific manta rays were leaping into the air, flying clear of the water – in glee or agitation or, as some scientists insist, to rid themselves of parasites – and then slamming their tons of weight down on the surface of the sea. To us they were reminders that only a few dozen metres beneath our restless frames there teemed societies of infinite variety and stunning complexity, that while we sought sleep, countless creatures below were feeding and breeding, dying and giving birth.

We were in the Sea of Cortez in the summer, and the combination of location and season had produced the most bountiful underwater environment I had ever seen. We had come to film an ABC *American Sportsman* segment on hammerhead sharks, and sharks we found in profusion. Our trip amounted to a private charter through the southern Sea of Cortez, but our ship, the *Don José*, and other vessels take groups and individuals on a variety of different kinds of journey. There are trips to see the whales and wander the desolate landscape, trips for snorkellers and divers and those who just enjoy riding on boats. And, spectacular as the sharks and manta rays were, they were only ensemble players in the repertory company that thrills divers and snorkellers and swimmers in the Sea of Cortez.

The more formal name for this sea is the Gulf of California, but that denies the romance and colour in the history of this 750-mile-long pocket of water that separates Baja California from the Mexican mainland. Aeons ago, the Baja peninsula didn't exist; it was part of the mainland, down at the southern end of the San Andreas Fault. And then, in what must have been one of the planet's more sensational earthquakes, the fault went into spasm. Baja was heaved into the Pacific Ocean, and the Pacific flowed into the newly created canyons. At its north end, where the Colorado River feeds it, the sea is, as seas go, relatively shallow: no more than 600 feet. But down south, where we were, it drops as deep as 10,000 feet, an unusual depth for a body of water that is, on average, no more than 95 miles wide.

The eponymous Hernando Cortez is said to have come upon the sea in the mid-1530s and to have been the first to detect that Baja California was a peninsula instead of an island. (Incidentally, Cortez is also credited with creating the word *California*. Supposedly, as he was cruising up the Pacific coast of the North American continent, he complained to an aide, in Latin, that the place was stinking hot – as hot [*calidus*], in fact, as a furnace [*fornax*].

We came upon the sea from the north, via Los Angeles, San Diego, Tijuana and a short jet flight to La Paz, at the southern end of Baja. The plane was all-economy class, full to the gunwales, staffed by surly flight attendants whose only (or, at least, preferred) English-language phrase was 'Sit down!' – and several hours late.

In La Paz, we boarded the *Don José*, an eighty-foot motor vessel with accommodations for up to twenty people. It was no accident that we had come to this steaming part of the world in the hottest of all months (August). As I learned from the underwater photographers Howard Hall and Stan Waterman, the appearance of the abundant wildlife in the Sea of Cortez is cyclical and definitely seasonal.

While the temperature of the water in the summer can go as high as 90 degrees Fahrenheit, in the winter it can drop to the mid-50s. Different critters like different climes. To photograph the whale sharks off Cabo San Lucas, for example, one should come in the late spring. For the migrating grey whales off the Pacific coast of Baja, winter is the best time. For billfish and tuna, sharks and rays – all of which come up from the south – mid- to late summer is prime time.

But there is more to photographing in the Sea of Cortez than just picking the season; you have to pick your spot as well. Our spot was to be a sea mount called Mar Isla, a couple of days north of La Paz. Sea mounts are volcanoes that died in the sea millennia ago; extinct though they themselves may be, they are cynosures for vast aggregations of marine life.

Mar Isla sticks up 4,000 feet from the bottom of the sea, and tops off 65 feet below the surface, well within the reach of scuba divers. Nutrient-rich deep-water currents strike the sea mount and well upward, bringing with them the animals that feed in them. Those animals lure larger predators, which in turn attract still larger predators, until finally, the entire food chain is concentrated on one small area at the top of the sea mount.

Because the water is so rich in plankton and other microscopic organisms, visibility is often poor: The sea mount is invisible from the surface. So it was hard to believe, descending down the anchor line into the gloom, that anything of interest lived nearby.

But within seconds of arriving on the rocky, weed-covered plateau, we thought we have been transported into an underwater circus. Vast schools of jacks blanked out the sunlight from above; moray eels poked their heads from crevices and eyed us curiously; sea turtles flapped lazily away; an octopus, furious at being discovered, scampered across the rocks, changing colours every few steps; groupers hovered patiently, as if assuming we had brought them something to eat; a solitary hammerhead cruised by on patrol, ignoring us completely; and, in the deep water over the edge of the sea mount, a pair of manta rays flew with wondrous grace, rolling over and over again, like children on a sand dune.

The profusion of life on our first dives deceived me into concluding that it would be only a matter of time before the huge schools of hammerheads – seldom seen in other parts of the world – would swim into the range of our lenses.

As it turned out, it took exhausting days of dangerous diving to find the schools. Hammerhead sharks are pelagic (open-ocean) animals, and they are forever on the move, so it was coincidence when they passed over the sea mount: We had to spend hour after endless hour swimming in water nearly 1,000 fathoms deep, peering down, hoping to spot them. When we did find them, they were never in water shallower then seventy or eighty feet, and most often they were more than a hundred feet down.

Air had to be conserved fanatically: To run out of air in deep water in the open sea is a poor idea. Time down had to be monitored strictly: To stay too long in water too deep was to invite a crippling (and perhaps fatal) case of the bends. And one's companions had to be kept constantly in sight: A two- to four-knot current ran everywhere around the sea mount, so it would be an easy thing to be swept away.

Always when we went into the water, we were stuck by the delight of entering the unknown, for every day brought something that one or more of us had never experienced. Once, we were confronted by a cranky sailfish, who swam up to us and waved his bill and raised and lowered his sail like a bull hunching its shoulders before a charge. Again, we were surrounded by herds of porpoises and pilot whales, who clicked and chirped and whistled at one another, commenting (we imagined) on the clumsiness of the aliens floating in their midst. And then, a few miles from the sea mount, we swam with a colony of sea lions, who barked at us underwater and swam nose-to-nose with us and challenged us to chase them.

One day, we were rewarded with one of nature's rare gifts. A young girl in our crew had gone swimming beneath the *Don José* and had seen an enormous manta ray – eighteen to twenty feet from wingtip to wingtip – resting in the shadow of the boat. She put on a scuba tank and swam down to the ray, expecting it to fly shyly away, as most mantas will do when approached by divers.

But the manta did not leave, and the girl saw that it had been injured. Apparently, it had run into a fisherman's nets, for the flesh on one side of its head had been torn and tattered, and shreds of rope trailed behind in the current. She drifted down on top of the manta. It allowed her to sit on its broad back, and when she plucked the ropes from its gaping wound, all it did was shudder.

When the wound was clean, the manta did begin to fly. The girl held on, and the manta made no effort to shake her off. As we returned to the sea mount, we saw a mythic sight: a giant creature of the deep banking and rolling and soaring and diving, with the slim figure of the young girl flowing along.

When the girl ran out of air, the manta returned to the spot beneath the boat, and I swam down to it and floated aboard and was taken on a tour of the sea mount. And when I was out of air, someone else took my place.

For three days, the manta conducted guided tours of its neighbour-hood. Every morning, he would be hovering motionless under the boat. In deference to his gargantuan size – which we equated, rightly or wrongly, with advanced age – we called him Grandad. (In fact, when our film was developed, it proved that he was a she.)

Since none of us had ever before been able to ride a manta, we wondered why now we had been afforded the privilege. A cold, scientific analysis suggested that this particular giant regarded humans as only a new form of parasite, nothing to fear or even to bother avoiding. I preferred a more anthropomorphic, Androclean explanation: A human had been kind to the animal, and the animal was responding in kind.

Both my children dive, and when they are somewhat more accomplished – for scuba diving in the Sea of Cortez is not for freshman divers – I hope to return with them to the Mar Isla sea mount, to **see** the hammerheads and the turtles and the groupers and, maybe, **a** friendly manta ray named (evidence to the contrary notwithstanding) Grandad.

UNDER FULL SAIL
ON THE BARK *SEA CLOUD*

Noel Perrin

Clipper ships are 'the noblest of all sailing vessels and the most beautiful creations of man in America,' Admiral Samuel Eliot Morison wrote. Once I would have taken that for the typical hyperbole of a sailor. Now I wonder why he limited himself to America. If there are man-made objects on other continents as beautiful as a square-rigger under sail, I haven't seen them – and I spent a good part of my youth travelling from one great cathedral to another, with ample time for side trips to the Parthenon, the Alte Pinakothek in Munich and the Vatican Museum – not to mention the Great Buddha of Japan. The difference is that all these things are objects, though glorious ones, while a square-rigger under sail is a living creature. Objects stay the same, but living creatures change, and hence are beautiful in many ways.

My experience with clippers began on a Sunday afternoon in March. I was in the eastern Caribbean. Two days earlier, sixty of us had flown down from New York and Miami to the island of Antigua, where we had been getting to know both each other and the Caribbean. Now the ship's tender of *Sea Cloud* was taking us on board for a week's cruise through the Lesser Antilles.

A long, slender white-hulled ship lay quietly at anchor in St. John's Harbour. But it wasn't the 247-foot hull that caught your eye. It was the four masts soaring up from it, going up 190 feet, the height of the tallest white pines. And the slanting lines of ropes that climbed those masts, the slender spars, the furled sails.

As I now know, I was looking at a four-masted bark. There is a similar four-masted bark docked at New York's South Street Seaport, the *Peking*. Even stripped as she is, she's a beauty. But *Peking* is a carthorse to *Sea Cloud*'s thoroughbred. *Peking* was designed to carry heavy freight, and she shows it. *Sea Cloud* was designed for speed and grace, and never mind the cargo capacity. Even sitting quietly in the harbour, *Sea Cloud* looks alive.

At 5 pm, the voyage began. Rather to my disappointment, we left Antigua under power (there are four big engines below deck) en route for the Îles des Saintes, off Guadeloupe. There was a distinct odour of diesel fuel as we headed out into the Caribbean. Not until Monday afternoon, when we left the Îles des Saintes, did the sails go up.

When they did, it was worth the wait. Almost all of us passengers were up on deck, getting in the way, jumping over coils of rope, watching six or eight young sailors swarm up each mast and begin to unfurl the sails. We not only watched, we listened. *Sea Cloud* is a German ship with a thoroughly international crew. The officers and the mast captain gave their orders half in nautical German and half in nautical English. They did not use loudspeakers or portable transmitters or any electronics at all. They shouted their orders, just as sailors did in Melville's day.

Soon eighteen of the twenty-nine sails were set, and we were bowling along toward Bequia. As the crew came down from aloft, I noticed that two of them were women.

Now came a frustrating hour for me. I was not a regular passenger on the ship, but part of the entertainment. Ordinary cruises usually keep the passengers amused between meals with swimming pools and shuffleboard and endless films, but *Sea Cloud* offers education. A colleague from Dartmouth and I were along on this trip to talk about nautical books: *Moby Dick, Two Years Before the Mast*, a C.S. Forester. It was my fate to give the first lecture, and while I did my best with Forester, I noticed that the passengers' eyes kept stealing up to those billowing sails. I could hardly keep my eyes off them myself.

When I finally finished, I went below to change for dinner. Do not imagine me tumbling down into the bilge, or even going into some cramped little corridor. The interior of *Sea Cloud* is almost as fancy as her rigging.

Sea Cloud was built in 1931 by a woman with a taste for luxury, Marjorie Merriwether Post was enormously rich, she had just taken a course in marine engineering, and she personally did all the interior design. She did not skimp. Some of the cabins resemble what I imagine rooms at Versailles to have been like; the ship's lounge has the kind of wood panelling you see at Oxford and Cambridge. It's a small lounge, and now that sixty passengers are using it, it tends to get crowded. There is still room for the ample bar facilities one sees on any passenger ship.

My fellow passengers were mostly middle-aged and prosperous. This is a luxury trip. For nine days in the Caribbean, people have paid up to $5,700 for one of the thirteen original Post staterooms with panelled walls, antique furniture, fireplaces and bathrooms with gold-plated fixtures. There are also twenty-eight ordinary cabins that were added to the ship just a few years ago. These run about half the size of the originals, and I found mine perfectly comfortable, if not at all thrilling.

On this particular voyage, everybody was connected with either Dartmouth or the College of William and Mary. The youngest passenger was a thirty-seven-year-old former naval officer who spent most of his time in cut-off jeans, hobnobbing with the crew (though he blossomed into three-piece-suit elegance at dinner time); the oldest must have been near eighty. But most of us were people in their fifties and sixties, romantically drawn to life under sail but not necessarily knowing much about it. I fell into this category myself.

The crew were nearly all young. Ten or eleven nationalities were represented; six of the crew, including two officers, were American. One older-looking sailor was said to be a wealthy European business-man who had taken a year's leave to serve before the mast. All, in this warm climate, wore blue T-shirts and shorts; nearly all sported a good-sized knife, worn in a sheath on the belt and secured with a length of rope. This was so that if they should get caught in the rigging, a hundred feet above the rolling deck, they could cut themselves free. Interaction between passengers and crew was frequent and easy. There was even a morning when passengers were invited to haul on the ropes as we raised the sails – maybe a third of us did so. Passengers were not allowed in the rigging, though there was a rumour that our naval officer got up there anyway. Rumours spread fast on a ship this size.

As for the meals on board, they were good, but with one exception not spectacular. Breakfast was a buffet: everything Germans like in the morning, such as wurst and cheese, and everything Americans like, such as scrambled eggs and bacon. Lunch was also a buffet, usually served on deck. Lots more wurst; a hot dish or two – maybe the giant grilled crayfish that I almost came to prefer to lobster; soup; fruit; pitchers of tropical juices; wine for those who wanted it.

Dinner was four courses, served formally, and accompanied by an unlimited supply of German white wine. High-quality stuff. This is a ship that takes wine seriously. The French reds were outstanding, too. And there was one dinner, with tournedos and snails, that would get a star from anybody.

The one serious complaint I heard was from two or three passengers who dote on desserts. This ship is not a heaven for chocolate-lovers. Except for some nicely baked cake at afternoon tea (also on deck), sweets tended to be neglected. I didn't miss them, if only because I was so busy stuffing myself with fresh fruits, but there were those who did.

By no means all our time was spent at sea. In the course of the week we landed on six islands, including three of the Grenadines that are too small for regular cruise ships to approach. In port, we got not only the usual shopping, luxury meals (with luxury desserts), and well-planned tours (all included in the cruise price), but a new kind of perspective on *Sea Cloud*. Except on Martinique, where she docked at a pier in Fort de France, *Sea Cloud* always anchored in a bay and sent us ashore by tender. Then, as soon as it was dark, the crew would light up her rigging – and some master of *son et lumière* had planned that lighting system. *Sea Cloud*'s masts form a spire, and 185 feet or so of ropes, spars, mastheads, and loosely furled sails glowed with white light. The top of each mast shone red. 'Magical' is a word to use with extreme caution. But there's no avoiding it here. The effect of that bright rigging on the water was magical. And because their ships lacked electricity, it's one sight Melville and Dana never got to see.

On the other hand, Melville and Dana participated in all kinds of manoeuvres that we did not. There is a built-in conflict, on a luxury sailing cruise, between the wish to sail as much as possible and the need to keep to a schedule and to avoid making the passengers seasick. Which way it tips is apt to depend on the captain.

Our captain was a new one, with lots of experience on conventional cruise ships and very little with square-riggers. He also had a passion for promptness exceeded only by his passion for predictability. Consequently, he chose to sail only by daylight – and even then not during dinner, lest we heel over and send that beautiful wine sliding across the table. From before dinner to the next morning we used the diesels. He seldom tacked. He never came about – that process that sounds so thrilling when Lord Horatio Hornblower does it on H.M.S. *Clorinda*. We never came out of harbour under sail, but always tamely motored out to sea, found our course, and then shifted to canvas. We never, when the ship was 'ghosting' along at a couple of knots, had the chance to board the tender, run out in front, and see the ship sail toward us under full sail, as Ishmael could see the *Pequod* – 'bearing down upon her boats with outstretched sails, like a wild hen after her screaming brood.'

'All this was thrilling,' Melville says, and it's a thrill I'd have liked to have had. On the other hand, previous captains of *Sea Cloud* did all these things – one of them was replaced for doing them to excess, caring too much for sailing the ship and too little for the comfort of his passengers – and there is every reason to think that future captains will tip the balance back a little. (Gossip at sea travels so fast that I heard the rumour of the new American captain exactly one day after the owners in far-off Hamburg had appointed him. He is Edward D. Cassidy, former captain of the United States Coast Guard training bark *Eagle*.)

There were two moments on the cruise that stand out especially. One was on the second day at sea, as we sailed under a fair breeze through the Grenadines, bound for Admiralty Bay. Jim Cox, my colleague from Dartmouth, was lecturing on deck. We had all just found our sea legs. The ship was rolling gently, the tops of the masts making small, slow arcs across the sky. The sails seemed to be trying to lift the ship out of the water – but not aggressively; it was the mildest of upward thrusts. Even as I listened, my eyes aloft, my ears on what Jim was saying (he's an exceptional teacher), I could feel myself fall in love with the ship. It all happened in about two minutes, and it's the nearest thing to pure platonic love I am ever likely to know.

The other moment, curiously enough, was in the crowded, dirty harbour in Martinique. Martinique is a microcosm of the modern world: full of beauty, desperately overcrowded (360,000 people on a 431-square-mile island, despite constant emigration), bustling with ugly growth. Fort de France is its New York. And in the harbour there, as we came in on Friday morning, we saw almost every other kind of ship there is. Container ships from France, Germany and England squatted at commercial piers. A Russian cruise ship with a stern like a waffle iron (it lets down – I suppose for driving vehicles aboard) was docked in front of a big, graceless Homeric Line cruise ship. Even the United States Navy was there: The homely little launch of the commander-in-chief of the Atlantic Fleet was bustling about the bay all morning; his ship stood farther out. You couldn't have asked for a more dramatic setting for *Sea Cloud*. If you imagine Katharine Hepburn, age twenty-two, against a backdrop of Gulliver's Yahoos, you will have a fairly accurate sense of how she looked.

In my life, I have cared hardly at all about sailing, let alone the pretentions of yachting. My idea of real dreariness is to be trapped all day aboard someone's wretched little sailboat on Long Island Sound. Too much sun, too little space. And you're not even going anywhere.

But to sail on a tall ship is quite another matter. Right now *Sea Cloud* is the only one available. Some day I hope there'll be fifty.

UNDER SAIL ON *SEA CLOUD*
BOOKING PASSAGE

Sea Cloud generally sails out of Nice into the western Mediterranean until early July. From then until the end of August, she cruises the Adriatic and Tyrrhenian seas (Rome-Sicily-Dubrovnik). After that she moves to the Greek islands, returning to the Caribbean in the winter. The trips range from 11 to 13 days; each includes a week on board. Prices start at about $4,500 a person and go up to almost $7,000. This includes round-trip air fare from New York.

Each cruise is a separate venture under the auspices of a different organization, among them the History Book Club, the Smithsonian Institution and the University of Virginia Alumni Association. In most cases, joining the appropriate organization is easy. The simplest way to start is to get in touch wth **Travel Dynamics**, 132 East 70th Street, New York, NY 10021 (212 517 7555), the agency that charters the ship from its German owners roughly nine months of each year, and which organizes the trips. One or two lecturers go along on each cruise (attendance at their lectures is far from compulsory), as well as a tour director and a cruise director supplied by Travel Dynamics.

Sea Cloud is owned by Windjammer Segeltouristik GMBH of Hamburg, whose American representative is Joseph H. Conlin, 516 Fifth Avenue, New York, NY 10036 (212 575 1234). The whole ship may occasionally be chartered for from $20,000 to $24,000 a day.

SIGNING ON AS CREW

If you're young and adventurous and want to join the crew, a representative of the German owners periodically interviews candidates at the Travel Dynamics office in New York. You needn't have sea experience. In fact, as Tim Maguire, the second officer, told me, they almost prefer people without it – no habits to unlearn. You will have to go up a mast your first day on board. The pay is 500 marks – about $215 – a month. In the past you had to sign on for six months; this will probably soon change to a year. Competition for places is keen.

— N.P.

FROM THE ATLANTIC TO THE PACIFIC

A SALEM SAMPLER

P. D. James

For an Englishwoman, a first visit to New England can be a disorientating as well as a fascinating experience. Perhaps because I had been told so often by friends how similar the Eastern Seaboard is to England, it was the differences that at first struck me most forcefully: the vast scale of the countryside, the very different architecture, the elegant white painted clapboard churches, the unfamiliar birds with familiar names, the glory of the autumn foliage unmatched by even the richest autumnal colours back home. But then I would only have to turn a corner and the countryside would be startlingly familiar, bringing with it a keen and particular memory and a sense of being completely at home. And then the disorientating process would begin again as the names evoked their own strong nostalgic images. I found myself half expecting and missing Salisbury's soaring spire, Framlingham's majestic ruined castle or the Cam, green and narrow, sliding under the humped bridges of Cambridge.

But Salem is a different matter. It takes its name from no English county or cathedral town, and one comes to it without the weight of nostalgic associations. The name is, in fact, derived from the Hebrew *shalom*, meaning 'peace' – an inappropriate choice for a city founded on religious and social conflict and with so stormy a history of dissent. And the image the name evokes is both sinister and tragic, founded upon the witchcraft trials of 1692 and the hysteria that led up to them.

I came to Salem half expecting a city still darkened by the memory of old cruelties, old terror, and that atavistic memory is, indeed, still potent. But what I discovered was one of the most interesting and attractive cities in America. It has everything I look for in a town. It is small enough to be manageable in imagination as well as on foot. Like most exciting cities it is on the sea, and the air one breathes has the salty tang of the ocean. It is a city both practical and romantic. Like an old lady who knows that her best days are over it wears its beauty proudly and is careful of its past. The old part offers at every turn something of interest or beauty to delight the eye.

Salem's domestic architecture is superb. To walk from Washington

Square via Hawthorne Boulevard to Chestnut Street is to experience a visual education in the history and architecture of New England surely unsurpassed by any other city on the Eastern Seaboard. There can be few cities in the United States in which the history of a community is so clearly visible in its buildings or in which the spirit of a splendid long-dead past is still so keenly felt. This is particularly true of the city's maritime history. It was settled in 1626 by Roger Conant and a party of emigrants from Cape Ann; the community was at first mainly employed in fishing and farming and, of course, in religious discussion and dissent. But the city's glory began in the seventeenth century with the growth of commerce and trade, particularly the increasingly lucrative trade with European ports and the West Indies. The city took as its motto 'The wealth of the Indies to the uttermost gulf,' and it was to prove wealth indeed.

Then, following an era of privation after the Revolutionary War, when ports controlled by the British were closed to the Salem fleet, the great Chinese market was discovered, opening fresh routes to trade, commerce, cultural and artistic development and spectacular wealth. I stood before the balustraded portico of the **Custom House** on Derby Street, built in 1819, and pictured those tall ships, the *Grand Turk* and a fleet of thirty-four vessels putting out from Salem harbour to dare the great seas of the Horn.

It was in this same Custom House that Nathaniel Hawthorne toiled and dreamed, and I wondered how often he lifted his eyes from the hated ledgers and looked out over the ocean. All is quiet now, but I could close my eyes and hear the raucous shouts of the sailors, the rush of wind billowing the rising sails, the creaking of timbers and the thud of the barrels of salted cod; and there still comes on the breeze the waft of faraway spice islands.

The sea captains rarely sailed direct to China. They would call in at ports on the Pacific Coast for furs, at the Hawaiian Islands for their fresh supplies, then sail on to Cathay, returning with their rich cargoes of tea, spices, coffee, chinaware, embroidered shawls, silks, delicate fans and feathers for the ladies' bonnets. They made huge fortunes and made them young. Many were able to retire by the age of thirty, and it is this youthful, confident prosperity and the exotic cargoes on which it was founded that gives Salem its atmosphere, felt as strongly in the cobbled streets as it is on the waterside, an atmosphere that is strongly Yankee, commercial and maritime and, at the same time, mysterious, glamorous and Oriental. And the wealth of those young sea captains is still visible in the houses they built for their womenfolk: courage, daring and, perhaps, not a little human greed dignified in Palladian columns and windows, in refined cornices, in carved ornamental urns.

One of my interests – indeed, it amounts to an enthusiasm – is for domestic architecture, and for this reason alone Salem would be a delight to me. I wondered why the city hadn't raised a monument to its chief architect, Samuel McIntire; and then I realized that it doesn't need to. One can say of him as one can of Sir Christopher Wren in St. Paul's Cathedral, 'If you seek his monument, look around you.' The McIntire houses that grace Washington Square, Federal Street and Chestnut Street seem to me unique in their dignity, their elegance, their symmetry and in the precision and absolute rightness of their detail; and, happily, they are wonderfully preserved.

McIntire is Salem's own son, born in the city in 1757. He learned his trade of carpenter and joiner from his father, and one can see in the quality of the woodcarving how skilled he was in the basics of his art. These are houses for his time and for all time; livable in, gracious, unpretentious, American in spirit yet universal in appeal. Two of the finest are the property of the Essex Institute: the **Gardner-Pingree House** (1804) at 128 Essex Street and the **Peirce-Nichols House** at 80 Federal Street.

The former, one of McIntire's last works, is conceded to be one of the finest neoclassical buildings in America. It is a square brick-built house of three storeys, the third capped by a cornice and balustraded parapet. The façade is lightened and softened by bands of white marble at each floor level and graced with an elliptical porch and by beautifully proportioned windows. The interior work is a fitting memorial to the architect and to the craftsmen and cabinetmakers who worked for him.

The Peirce-Nichols House was designed by McIntire in 1782 and remodelled by him in 1801 for the wedding of Sally Peirce and George Nichols. It is a magnificent mansion, for me the most attractive of all the McIntire dwellings. It, too, is three storeyed with a balustraded parapet and belvedere. The house has a classical simplicity that is enhanced by the porch with its Doric pediments and the fluted Doric pilasters at the four corners. Neither of these fine mansions should be missed.

There are, of course, earlier houses, and perhaps the most celebrated is the **House of the Seven Gables** at 54 Turner Street, reputed to be the setting of Hawthorne's novel of that name. The original house was probably built about 1668 but was considerably restored in 1910; as is not uncommon with celebrated national monuments, there is even some doubt whether this is the actual house described by Hawthorne. But these doubts are unlikely to spoil the pleasure of thousands of lovers of one of America's great masters of English prose who find the romance and spirit of his novel admirably expressed in this dark, weather-beaten and rambling old house. Hawthorne himself was born in 1804 at 27 Union Street, a house built before 1692, the witchcraft year, and still standing. It was beneath this gambrel roof that the shy, oversensitive boy spent his lonely childhood, and it was Salem, its sights, its sounds, its history, that helped to shape his genius.

But one cannot come to Salem and remain untouched by those terrible and turbulent events of 1692. From the first accusations in March to the last execution in September of that year, more than four hundred people suffered the terror of being suspected of witchcraft; hundreds were imprisoned in appallingly overcrowded unhealthy jails or were forced to flee their homes; nineteen were hanged, and one old man, Giles Corey, who resolutely refused to plead, was pressed to death under planks weighted with stones.

One of the most common misapprehensions about these horrors, and one to which foreigners are particularly prone, is that the phenomenon was peculiar to Salem, that the witchcraft trials and the epidemic of hysteria, bigotry and fear that led up to them were the result of an intolerant Puritanism that the place – the people themselves – generated almost as if there were an infection in the New England air. Nothing could be further from the truth. The Colonists believed implicitly in the existence and the malevolent power of witches because the England from which they had come believed in it implicitly, as did the whole of Christendom.

It was this burden of fear, superstition and intolerance that the Pilgrims carried with them to the New World. Salem may have been the final flare-up, but the infection had been in the blood of Christendom for generations. And the deeds that were done in Salem, horrible as they were, were not worse than in any other place. No witch was burned alive in Salem, nor was any use made of the dreaded water test whereby the suspects were bound and half drowned to demonstrate their guilt. Before we are too ready to condemn the credulity and intolerance of the Colonists, we might consider some of the practices of our own time when torture and oppression are still rampant and only the methods have become more scientific and ingenious – at least Judge Sewall, one of the most fanatical of the Salem judges, later had the grace and humility publicly to confess and repent, an act not typical of twentieth-century torturers.

I felt little of the sinister power of that dreadful year in the Witch Museum. Interesting as it is, it is too much the usual tourist attraction to provide more than a frisson of fascinated distaste. Nor did I feel it when I stood before the two oil paintings by the New York artist T.H. Matteson in the Essex Institute Museum, *The Trial of George Jacobs* (1855) and *Examination of a Witch* (1853). These are vivid and dramatic examples of nineteenth century historical painting but, for me, too Victorian in style and feeling to evoke the spirit of Colonial Massachusetts. But I did feel the atavistic power of that witchcraft year when I contemplated one of the documents on display: the contemporary record of part of the evidence, fading paper on which a long dead hand had meticulously recorded, no doubt as a Christian duty, the words that could be twisted to send a follow Christian to a shameful and horrible death. What I felt at that moment was not only pity for those tormented and martyred souls but a sense of our kinship with their judges.

No visitor should leave Salem without finding time for the city's museums, particularly the **Maritime National Historic Site** at the old wharfside, the modern **Peabody Museum** on East India Square and the **Essex Institute Museum** at 132 Essex Street. Apart from its administration of the historic houses and gallery of period rooms, the Essex Institute displays in its five spacious galleries an enthralling collection of the art and artefacts of Essex County: glass, ceramics, portraits, furniture, a military collection and children's dolls. The Peabody Museum is notable for its maritime exhibits. I was particularly interested in the relics of the whaling fleets, the objects fashioned by the sailors from whalebone, the old oil paintings of dramatic kills and the primitive panorama of the dangers and excitements of a whaling voyage made in 1854 by Thomas Davidson of Salem and still looking as fresh and vigorous as the day he painted it.

But it was to Chestnut Street that I finally returned. It is surely one of the most beautiful streets in America, one in which every house is a delight. To walk down Chestnut Street in the peace of an early evening, particularly when it is free of cars, is to step back in time. One can smell again the spice-laden air of the wharf and picture those nineteenth century ladies in their silk-embroidered shawls, sipping tea in their drawing rooms behind the columned porticoes and listening spellbound while some gallant sea captain regales them with tales of his hazardous voyage round the Horn and the splendours and mysteries of far Cathay.

A DAY OR TWO IN SALEM
SUSTENANCE

The Lyceum, 43 Church Street (617 745 7665), was once the town lecture hall; Thoreau, Emerson, Webster and Holmes all spoke there, and Alexander Graham Bell placed his first long-distance telephone call – to Boston – from it. Specialities include such fare as veal Oscar, a preparation of veal, crab meat and asparagus with béarnaise sauce, and shrimp Rockefeller, baked with spinach, shallots and cheese and served with white sauce. About $40 for two with wine.

Chase House (617 744 0000), Pickering Wharf, has views over the water from three sides (Pickering Wharf itself is a shop- and restaurant-lined replica of a commercial wharf of earlier times). Specialities are lobster – boiled, baked or stuffed – and an old-fashioned seafood dinner that includes clams, scallops, shrimp, whitefish and lobster. Dinner for two with wine about $40.

Bull and Finch/Topside's (617 744 8588) are both at 98 Wharf Street, on Pickering Wharf (Bull and Finch is the street-level pub, Topside's is the upstairs dining room). Specialities include veal Marsala and baked shrimp stuffed with crab meat; dinner for two with wine about $40.

Roosevelt's, housed in an old commercial building at 300 Derby Street (617 745 9608), has such specialities as steak Diane and sole stuffed with crab meat, topped with cream sauce and cheese. Dinner for two with wine about $35.

OVERNIGHT

Hawthorne Inn, overlooking Salem Common at 18 Washington Square West (617 744 4080), is decorated in traditional New England style. The **Main Brace** restaurant specializes in New England fare, and the **Tavern on the Green** bar overlooks Salem Common. There are 89 rooms; doubles are about $65, suites, $110.

Salem Inn, 7 Summer Street (617 741 0680), is a Federal house built in 1834 and restored and opened as an inn in 1983. There are 20 rooms; doubles with private bath: about $70, including Continental breakfast.

Suzannah Flint House, 98 Essex Street (617 744 5281), is a late-eighteenth century house with two guest rooms, each with a fireplace. Doubles are about $65, including breakfast.

Stephen Daniels House, 1 Daniels Street (617 744 5709), is a largely eighteenth century house with four guest rooms furnished with canopied beds and antiques. Doubles are about $55.

WHERE SHAKER SIMPLICITY ENDURES

Wilma Dykeman

Travellers seeking Pleasant Hill, Kentucky, find it necessary to leave the broad Interstate highway system south of Lexington and follow, for a brief interval, more leisurely state roads that meander through tranquil bluegrass countryside.

Such a turning aside is entirely appropriate. The utopian founders of the Shaker Village at Pleasant Hill, also known as Shakertown, believed it was necessary for travellers-through-life to separate from main thoroughfares of custom and commerce and seek a unique spiritual experience. That experience was to be sought through celibacy and confession of sin, withdrawal from the world and communal ownership of property, but also through dedication to excellence in labour, whether the task was ploughing a field, shaping a delicate yet sturdy chair or lifting a hymn of praise and thanksgiving. The religious celebrations of the Shakers – or the Believers, as they called themselves – might have puzzled nineteenth century America, but their ingenuity and integrity in all matters practical won wide approval. Pleasant Hill is a legacy of that Shaker experiment.

A visitor to Pleasant Hill first encounters the legacy of excellence in the sturdy fieldstone fences that line the roads leading to the village and divide its more than 2,000 acres of farmland in neat patterns of cross-stitching. Grazing on the rolling grasslands are herds of plump beef cattle and Leicester sheep, the breed the Shakers originally imported from England for their fine wool.

To enter the village, atop a gently sloping hill, is to enter another century, where time might be measured by seasons rather than by stop-watches. Simplicity was the key to the Shaker way of life, as evidenced by the 27 brick, limestone and clapboard buildings; they are all that remain of the 266 built here following establishment of Pleasant Hill in 1805. White plank fences edge the tree-shaded main road through the village. Cars are forbidden, and there are no guided tours. A handbook helps visitors find their way through the exhibits. At each site, women in blue Shaker costumes and white caps describe the people who sawed the timbers for these worn floors, formed these clay bricks, cut these stones from cliffs of the nearby Kentucky River gorge, squeezed apples through this juice-stained cider press, filled barrels and crocks with carefully preserved foods in spacious basement storage rooms, wove these blue and red rag rugs and plumped up mattresses on these trundle beds.

The **Center Family Dwelling House** is a good introduction to the community, which at its height had 500 members, making it the third largest of all eighteen Shaker villages in the United States. Today Pleasant Hill and Hancock Shaker village, with its twenty buildings on more than 1,000 acres of land near Pittsfield, Massachusetts, are the only restored Shaker villages open to the public, although just under a dozen surviving Shakers remain in communities that are open to visitors at Canterbury, New Hampshire, and Sabbathday Lake, Maine. Each of the original communities of Shakers – the official name was the United Society of Believers in Christ's Second Appearing – was gathered into families of a hundred or more adults.

The two doors of the Center Family House provided separate entrances for men and women; in the large family dwellings such as this men and women lived on opposite sides of the house. The dual doors lead to forty rooms exhibiting the furnishings, inventions, industry – yes, the character – of the Believers. A long broad hall immediately imparts a sense of light, air, austerity. Hanging from peg-boards along both walls are the distinctive Shaker chairs, stored thus to keep floors clear of clutter and clean in every corner. Altogether, there are 2,996 such pegs in the village, which held everything from brooms to cloaks to wooden sconces.

Bedrooms, dining rooms, kitchen – even basement and attic of the Center Family House are spacious and light. One room displays the long desks, benches and slates that equipped the schoolroom for children of ever-welcome converts or orphans adopted by the society. Upstairs there is a small infirmary, complete with improvised walker and crutches, a crude wheelchair with a shawl rail (on which hung a shawl to protect the patient from draughts) and mementos of various medicines. Seeking remedies for common ailments of the day, Shaker sisters, as they were called, turned to the nearby woods and fields, and some of the wild plants they used – lobelia, liverwort, snakeroot – still flourish along roads in the vicinity. They cultivated other medicinals in their gardens, and dried and sold many herbs, one year up to 3,000 pounds. It has been noted that the Believers were remarkably healthy. They recorded few epidemics or accidents, and their average life span ran to seventy-one years, almost twice the average of the time.

Throughout the Center Family House, furnishings are utilitarian and often of pleasing design. A small example: The graceful oval boxes for storage called finger-lap boxes, which were created in thirteen sizes, remain popular today because of their efficiency and attractiveness.

As ingenious as they were industrious, Shakers are credited with inventing the wooden clothes peg, the circular saw and the washing machine. They also proved that a new broom may indeed sweep clean. One of their celebrated innovations was the flat-sided broom, which swept a larger area more efficiently than its predecessor, the hitherto familiar bunched rush or straw broom. For housekeepers of the day, it proved a great boon. For the Shakers, it proved an impressive commercial success: By 1850 they were marketing up to 50,000 handmade brooms a year.

Examples of their inventiveness abound, ranging from the mechanical fruit peeler to the important double-chamber iron stove. Long before their neighbours gave up the wasteful practice of warming their homes by fireplaces, the Shakers devised a small stove, similar to many current models, the upper portion of which functioned as a radiator. Its efficiency kept the large high-ceilinged rooms of the village at a constant 60 to 65 degrees, even in the coldest months.

Atop the Center Family House is the tower containing the village bell, whose sweet tones once awakened the Believers at four o'clock on summer mornings, at five in winter.

Atop the nearby **Trustees' Office** building is a structure of another use – an overhung window that functioned as something of a watch-tower. From such lookouts, spies could make certain no 'private unions' took place. Though celibacy was the rule, it was not always easy to practice. Occasionally a Believer departed the society; such action brought strong comment in the 'Journal,' the daily account of village life: 'A puff of trash has blown away,' it would note. Or, 'Mary returned to the World today. Silly girl, the wolves will get her.' A visitor poised at one of the lookouts today might wonder how often a Pleasant Hill resident such as Mahalia Polly must have been spied along the village paths, in the shadow of those imposing buildings, since it was recorded that she was frustrated in 'private unions' five times but 'finally eloped with a village miller.'

Today, as in the past, the Trustees' Office building is used for the administration of Pleasant Hill and for entertaining visitors. This may be the handsomest village structure, thanks to the famous twin spiral stairway which graces its interior. The superb craftsmanship of this stairway is a monument to the young Kentucky convert Micajah Burnett, who is credited with having begun, at age twenty-three, to lay out plans for Pleasant Hill and spending the rest of his life fulfilling that dream.

This stairway leads to the rooms for overnight guests at the Trustees' Office. Altogether, the **Inn at Pleasant Hill** provides a total of seventy-two rooms for guests – all with heat, air conditioning and private bath – scattered among fourteen buildings; visitors who have trouble with stairs should request special consideration in room assignments. Pleasant Hill is the country's only historic village where all overnight lodgings are in the original buildings.

In the dining room of the Inn, in the Trustees' Office, visitors share another pleasure from the Shaker past: good food in generous portions. Pleasant Hill has always been famous for its fare and its sharing. During the dark Civil War era, an entry in the 'Journal' noted: 'Oct. 12, 1862. Colonel Gano of General Morgan's command came and ordered breakfast for 200 troops, which was produced with alacrity, and they came in from the Lexington road where they had encamped. During this time the Sisters were cooking and baking with all the means at their command to keep a supply till about 400 had eaten.' A later visitor recalled 'a most bountiful meal taken with the Shakers. In 1886 I happened to be one of a party of about a dozen wheel men. After climbing the long hill we were in a receptive mood for a square meal, and the hour being high noon we decided to try our luck with the Shakers. Never shall I forget the meal we sat down to on that occasion. Like Oliver Twist we "asked for more," but unlike him we were not denied.'

Nor is there any denial today at the hearty country breakfast, served buffet style, or at lunch and dinner, where fresh vegetables and fruits, homemade breads, meats and salads are served family style, with relishes and jellies such as once helped support the society. Lunch, or 'midday daily fare,' as it is called, offers choices of fruit, garden salads and soup, along with entrées of fish, country ham or a small tenderloin steak. Dinner includes appetizer (especially seasonal fruits and soups), entrées of fish, chicken and steak, vegetables, hot breads and beverage. For both lunch and dinner there will be the Shaker dish of the day, a regional entrée characteristic of the era when Pleasant Hill flourished – such as pork tenderloin or chicken livers or ham prepared in special ways. There are also delectable desserts, such as Shaker lemon pie, Southern chess pie, fruit tarts and sorbets. County law prohibits the serving of any alcoholic beverages.

Those seated at a cherrywood table beside one of the dining room's tall windows may look out to the vegetable garden beyond, with its neat rows of tender lettuce, blue-green onions and cabbages and broccoli, potato and tomato and squash vines and other vegetables soon to be passed and repassed for second helpings from plain oval serving dishes.

Glimpses of the garden lend a sense of immediacy to Pleasant Hill, as do demonstrations of the society's everyday work. In buildings scattered along the gravel paths, women and men spin (from flax and from the wool of those Leicester sheep), weave and quilt; others work at coopering, broomcraft and cabinetry. The whine of saws and the smell of wood shavings are reminders that Shaker furniture, especially the strong, simple and graceful chairs, shaped largely with foot-propelled lathes and hand-operated drills, captured the hearts of Americana collectors everywhere.

But Pleasant Hill was basically a farming community. Little wonder that thrifty dwellers on these productive acres should devise a more efficient grist mill, invent a mechanical corn shucker and sheller, and import improved strains of beef and milch cows, pigs and sheep. The community's gravity water supply from an immense cypress cistern was Kentucky's first municipal water system. Neighbours might have laughed at some of the Believers' gyrations and fervent religious shouts, but they respected Shaker ingenuity and integrity.

Nowhere was the integrity more sustained and influential than in the seed business, which became an important source of income. One of the most interesting displays in the Center Family House includes the great wooden storage chests, well-labelled cabinets and handmade wooden scoops and measures necessary to this industry. Seeds were culled from a sixteen-acre sauce garden (so-called to differentiate it from the medicinal garden), dried, graded and packaged in envelopes, which sold for three to seven cents each. Their reliability became so widely known that the community sometimes grossed up to $4,500 a year on sale of seeds, an impressive sum for that time and place.

Pleasant Hill's paths lead from one phase of Believers' lives to another, each inviting consideration of the careful construction, the sense of balance and permanence that influenced each building and product. The **Ministry's Work Shop**, between the Trustees' Office and the Meeting House, is a plain two-storey frame building, but it contained the offices of the ruling ministry. The two elders and eldresses who led the community, which practiced 'perfect equality' of men and women, engaged in 'useful hand labour' in this shop. Today it serves as one of the guest houses for overnight visitors.

A more elaborate building is the **East Family Dwelling House**, a twenty-two-room structure of richly coloured brick. Just behind is the yellow frame **East Family Sisters' Shop**, where carding, spinning, weaving and needlework are demonstrated today.

At the opposite end of the village is the **West Family** complex. Near the **West Family Sisters' Shop** is the small building once used as a **Preserve Shop**, where sisters stirred great kettles of preserves, herbs and even peach leaves in concoctions for the outside world's market. There is also the sturdy little **Drying House**, where fruits from three orchards were dried for winter use; its single room suits its purpose as well as the sisters' round-bottomed egg baskets suited their purpose.

The building at the centre of Shaker life was, of course, the **Meeting House**, which, at Pleasant Hill, stands next to the Trustees' Office and was the single frame structure that could be painted white. At first, it looks like the most ordinary of the main buildings, but its construction posed extraordinary problems.

A community of 500 Shakers needed a large auditorium. But because of their vigorous dance form of worship, an expression of their religious fervour, they also needed a great hall free of any ceiling supports which would dangerously obstruct their dances. Entering the sixty-by-forty-four-foot auditorium of the Meeting House, which is free of pillars or partitions, a visitor realizes the challenge was well met. Wrote one historian of the structure: 'In a century and a half, the Shaker Meeting House has stood the vicissitudes of weather, insects, instability of central Kentucky soils and the hard usages of Shakers and the subsequent tenants who have worshipped here ... The woodwork in this building is comparable, if not superior, to that in any of the standing ancient English manor houses.'

The quiet of the room today, with its rows of empty benches and ubiquitous peg-boards, contrasts sharply with the excitement that once flourished there. A guest who observed a Shaker service in 1825 wrote that it began with a step-and-shuffle kind of dance, which increased to a 'vertical commotion' of leaping, yelling, shrieks and shouts. The furious whirling continued until the exhausted dancers 'sank on the floor, whilst others were scarcely able to get to their seats.' In the Meeting House, the Believers said, they were visited by angels. Gabriel was said to have come, attended by 10,000 little angels who beat their swords against shields as they sang with the faithful. More sceptical visitors from the world that the Shakers had rejected also came, often to laugh, and to marvel that men and women who expended so much energy in religious rites could still pursue the hard work essential to their survival.

The Believers had first arrived in this country on August 6, 1774, when a storm-battered vessel three months out of Liverpool put in at New York harbour. Aboard were nine members of the religious sect, which was long familiar with persecution and flight. The roots of the sect extended back to the early eighteenth century, when a small group of French Protestants, called the Camisards, fled their native country to escape arrest, torture and death. In England, their number multiplied under the leadership of an enthusiastic Quaker couple named James and Jane Wardley, but purposeful unification of the group fell to an unlikely leader: an illiterate twenty-three-year-old named Ann Lee.

Ann Lee, born in the grime of industrial Manchester, had as a child worked in the textile mills, and the four babies born to her by her blacksmith husband had all died. She saw in the sordid world around her the 'depravity of human nature and the odiousness of sin.' Dissident Quaker friends introduced her to their group, whose spirit often moved them to dance, leap and whirl, but whose concerns filled a need in the hard workaday world. Ann Lee had found her spiritual home.

The new convert, described as a short, charismatic woman with fair complexion, 'penetrating' blue eyes and 'a certain dignity,' preached a unique blend of mysticism and practicality: 'Lift your hands to work and your hearts to God.' For nine years, Ann Lee sought understanding of human motives and emotions, and she concluded that confession of sin and celibacy were fundamental to salvation. She said Christ had appeared to her in a vision and shown her that 'His second coming would be in a woman.' The United Society of Believers in Christ's Second Appearing was born, with Mother Ann, as she was then called, as its mentor. Society members, who referred to themselves as Believers, were known to the world as Shakers.

Mother Ann's effectiveness earned her the tribute of persecution. Mobs broke up Shaker meetings, and Believers were publicly stoned. Mother Ann was once imprisoned for fourteen days without food, and a demand was made that her tongue 'be bored through with a hot iron.'

After the persecution abated, she told her followers of a vision directing her to go to America, where ideas of freedom were in ferment. But arrival in New York was followed by a desperate struggle for survival.

The Shakers formed their first settlement in the wilderness just outside of Albany. By 1779, their fame had spread to New Lebanon, New York, where a spirit of revivalism had kindled interest in the strange new little colony. A Shaker 'gathering' was established in New Lebanon, one that eventually became the mother colony governing all Shaker communities. In 1781 Mother Ann and two associates began a journey across New England. For two years a familiar pattern of conversion persecution unfolded in Connecticut, Massachusetts (mobs at Harvard were especially ferocious), New Hampshire and Maine. Mother Ann never recovered from this trip – she died in 1784 at age forty-eight – but her followers established communities in the states she had visited.

Shortly before her death, Mother Ann prophesied the opening of the Gospel in Kentucky, Tennessee and Ohio, then known as the Southwest. The spread of religious revivalism in the early nineteenth century brought Shaker communities to Kentucky and Ohio, and eventually eighteen Shaker villages were founded, extending from Maine to Indiana. The three largest were in New Lebanon; Union

Village, Ohio, and Pleasant Hill, Kentucky.

Wherever they lived and worked, Believers followed rules of simplicity, utility, careful craftsmanship, conservation of natural resources and equality of races and sexes which, if understood or adopted by the outside society, would surely have shaken it more than all the whirling and dancing that earned the sect its name of Shakers.

The problem of survival – always critical to the society because of the rule of celibacy – gradually grew more acute, at Pleasant Hill and at the Believers' other communities. The Industrial Revolution made Shaker goods less competitive in the marketplace. The Civil War took a heavy toll on all the colony's resources. Finally, the society failed to gather enough converts and orphans to compensate for the lack of natural growth. By 1881 most of the Shakers still at Pleasant Hill were either too young or too old to work. In 1910, Pleasant Hill was officially dissolved as a community. The dozen remaining Shakers deeded their last 1,800 acres of land to a nearby merchant, who agreed to care for the survivors during their lifetime. Not until 1968 did Pleasant Hill reopen as a non-profit educational corporation. The village, which receives no Government funding, became the first historic site to be entirely designated as a national landmark.

Whether strolling before bedtime under a golden willow or a mulberry tree, savouring wholesome fare in the dining room, shopping for crafts at the Carpenters' Shop or floating down the Kentucky River in a paddle-wheel boat that leaves from Shaker Landing, a short drive from the village – whatever mood a visitor follows here, its theme will be simplicity.

Much of the Shaker legacy is embodied in their most famous song, incoporated by composer Aaron Copland as a theme in his *Appalachian Spring*:

> *'Tis the gift to be simple,*
> *'Tis the gift to be free;*
> *'Tis the gift to come down where we ought to be.*

For a short but significant interval, the Believers turned aside from the world and made Pleasant Hill a place where those gifts may be found even now.

EXPLORING PLEASANT HILL

Pleasant Hill is just off U.S. Route 68, 25 miles southwest of Lexington and 7 miles northeast of Harrodsburg.

HOURS AND PRICES

Pleasant Hill is open from 9 am to 5 pm daily except on December 24 and December 25, when the village is closed. From Thanksgiving to March, however, hours may vary. Admission to the village is $4.50; $2 for students 12 through 18; $1 for children 6 through 11 and free for children under 6. A trip on a paddle-wheel boat up the nearby Kentucky River, daily from late April through October, costs $4 (reduced rates for young people). The combined price for admission to the village and the boat trip is $7.

Meals are served in the dining room at the Trustees' Office. Lunch is about $5 to $8; dinner about $10 to $14 and breakfast is about $5. The **Inn at Pleasant Hill** offers 72 rooms in 14 buildings. A double room is about $40 to $70; a single is $30 to $55. Reservations are recommended for lodging and meals. There is a no-tipping policy.

VILLAGE ACTIVITIES

From April through October demonstations of Shaker crafts are held and programmes of Shaker music are presented on weekends. Shaker-style items and reproductions may be purchased at the Craft Sales Shops in the Carpenters' Shop and in the Post Office. On sale are reproductions of Shaker chairs (a painted ladderback is about $130), Shaker flat brooms ($10) and finger-lap boxes ($18 to $80). The village does not ship items and takes no mail orders.

Shaker Heritage Weekends, held each September, offer programmes of music, ballet and crafts. Special one-price weekend rates are effective from the end of December through February; the rate is about $100 per adult for two nights and five meals, from dinner Friday night to breakfast Sunday morning. The cost includes admission to the village and all special programmes. For details, write: Shakertown at Pleasant Hill, Inc., 3500 Lexington Road, Harrodsburg, KY 40330. Phone: 606 734 5411.

– W. D.

SAMPLING SHAKER LIFE, FROM MAINE TO OHIO

In addition to the Shaker village at Pleasant Hill, Kentucky, there are other restored villages and museums devoted to preserving Shaker heritage, several of which are described here. Specific information about special events at each location is available by writing to the sponsoring organization. Hours and admission prices are subject to change.

SABBATHDAY LAKE SHAKER COMMUNITY, MAINE

This community is one of two that remains a functioning Shaker settlement. Guided walking tours include visits to the Meeting House, the Central Dwelling House, the Ministry Shop and the Boys' Shop, where young boys were housed. A museum contains Shaker furnishings, still painted in bold colours, and such household items as clothes pegs, cushions, brooms and aprons. The herb garden remains productive, and visitors may buy seeds and traditional herbs the Shakers used. Special events and workshops focus on Shaker culture, and a large collection of materials on Shaker heritage is available for study.

Hours: 10 am to 4.30 pm Monday through Saturday, May 31 through Columbus Day, closed Sunday. Library open year-round by appointment. Admission is $2.50; $1.25 for children 6 to 12, free for children under 6. The most extensive walking tour is $3.75. Further information: United Society of Shakers, Sabbathday Lake, ME 04274; 207 926 4597.

HANCOCK SHAKER VILLAGE, MASSACHUSETTS

This nineteenth century village serves as a living example of Shaker culture. Visitors may take guided tours, participate in workshops and see demonstrations of typical Shaker crafts and pastimes. Buildings to visit include the brick Family Dwelling, furnished with original pieces, the Ministry Office, the round stone barn, the Meeting House and the Schoolhouse.

An antiques show is held in October, along with a special weekend featuring demonstrations of seasonal Shaker activities. A permanent exhibit focuses on Shaker agricultural life. There is a luncheon restaurant and picnic facilities. Shaker reproductions, herbs, books and food are sold in the gift shops.

Hours: 9.30 am to 5 pm, May 26 through October 31. Special events are held later in the autumn and in the winter. Admission: $6; $2 for children 6 to 12, free for children under 6; $5.50 for students and senior citizens. Further information: Hancock Shaker Village, P.O. Box 898, Pittsfield, MA 01202; 413 443 0188.

CANTERBURY SHAKER VILLAGE, NEW HAMPSHIRE

A guided tour includes visits to 7 of the 22 buildings: the Meeting House, the Ministry, the Sisters' Shop, the Laundry, the Schoolhouse, the Creamery and the Carriage House. Along with the original Shaker furnishings, items of interest include the herb garden and special exhibits in the Carriage House. Simple lunches and traditional Shaker meals are served in the Creamery between 11 am and 3 pm. On Friday evenings a candlelight dinner (reservations are necessary) and tour begin at 6.30.

Hours: 10 am to 5 pm. Tuesday through Saturday and holiday Mondays, from May through October 20. The day's final tour begins at 4.30 pm. Admission is $4.50, $1.75 for children 6 to 12, free for children under 6. Further information: Shaker Village Inc., Canterbury, NH 03224; 603 783 9977.

SHAKER MUSEUM, OLD CHATHAM, NEW YORK

This museum's collection is considered the outstanding study collection of Shaker culture; a wide range of exhibits present a comprehensive view of Shaker life. Of note are the model blacksmith's shop, a cabinetmaker's shop and a small chair manufacturing shop. The museum also offers special programmes. Events include an annual antiques and art festival and a craft show held the third Saturday in September. Reproductions and publications are sold at the gift shop, and the reference library is open year-round. Picnic facilities are available.

Hours: 10 am to 5 pm, daily, May 1 to October 31. The library is open Tuesday through Thursday year-round. Admission: $3.50; for students 15 to 21, $2.50; $1.50 for children 6 to 15, free for children under 6. $3 for senior citizens. Further information: The Shaker Museum, Chatham, NY 12136; 518 794 9100.

SHAKER HEIGHTS, OHIO

This town is situated on land once occupied by the North Union colony of Shakers. Visitors may see historic Shaker sites and the Shaker Historical Museum, which contains artefacts from the North Union community and other Shaker settlements.

Hours: The museum is open from 2 to 4 pm. Tuesday through Friday; 2 to 5 pm. Sunday; other times by appointment for groups. Admission: Museum is free during regular hours; special fees are charged at other times. Further information: Shaker Historical Society, 16740 South Park Boulevard, Shaker Heights, OH 44120; 216 921 1201.

– Carol Plum

TRACING WILLA CATHER'S NEBRASKA

A. L. Rowse

Few Americans seem to realize what a treasure they have in Red Cloud, a veritable little *ville musée*. How many people know where it is, or have ever been there?

And yet, as Mildred R. Bennett tells us in her excellent book *The World of Willa Cather*: 'Red Cloud, Nebraska, has probably been described more often in literature than any other village its size.' I think we should say 'small town' rather. The marvellous thing about it is that it has preserved itself utterly unspoiled, hardly changed since the early days of about a hundred years ago. For that we must be grateful to the public spirit, the local pride of its townspeople in their great writer – and, yes, to their artistic conscience, in a world that sees all too much destruction going on around us.

Here is a place with the charm unbroken, the spell still upon it that first drew me to it more than twenty years ago. Several people have asked me, slightly puzzled, why I am so keen on Nebraska; and I remember even Johnny Carson at Burbank being taken aback by an Englishman knowing who a 'Cornhusker' is. (He was one himself – and anyway I love these relics of old American folklore in almost tribal names, a Georgia 'Nutcracker,' North Carolina 'Tarheel,' Indiana 'Whosier,' if that is how it is spelt.)

Red Cloud appears, under different names, in several of Willa Cather's novels – in *My Antonia*, *A Lost Lady*, *Lucy Gayheart* and *The Song of the Lark* – and in various short stories. It should not need saying that she was one of the finest of American writers, and that most of her books are to be regarded as classics. But it does need saying that, in my view, Willa Cather gives a truer picture of Americans and American life than all the muck-rakers of modern fiction. A picture of the true-hearted, old and rooted country life of America – where you can still leave your house door unlocked and rely on your neighbours. This is the America the outside world knows little of – and would have a better appreciation and under-standing of, if it did: for one thing the sheer generosity of American life, and the decency you wouldn't suspect from the sensation-mongers and many best sellers, and even intellectuals, today.

Willa Cather was an intellectual herself, with the highest standards; but she knew the raw facts of life as well as any. Her books have poetic sentiment, but no sentimentality; there is even a vein of iron beneath the poetry. She knew the harshness and hardness of pioneering life on the unlicked prairie, the poverty and almost unbearable strain; but also the bravery and stoicism in that first generation of pioneers who lived in the hutments – the shelters they constructed out of the sod – as the first menfolk of her family there did.

Red Cloud is named for an Indian chief in what was Pawnee country. It began as a pioneering settlement alongside the Republican River, about 120 miles southwest from Lincoln, capital of the state, right down on the border with Kansas. The border here is made by the Great Divide one looks up to from the little town, between the streams on their way to the River Platte, famous route of the Oregon Trail.

Willa Cather's work always had a devoted following in England, though her cultural sympathies were markedly French. (These inspired her historical novel about Quebec, *Shadows on the Rock*.) So when an invitation came my way to lecture at the University of Nebraska at Lincoln, I accepted with alacrity, with the hope of getting to Red Cloud. I mean no disrespect to Lincoln, which is a well-designed, well-laid-out capital city – it is wonderful what the two generations since Willa's early years at the university there have accomplished on the bare prairie, parks and waters, avenues of trees planted and grown up.

But Red Cloud was my mecca – nearly a quarter of a century ago, on my first visit – and I was not disappointed. I saw it all in the light of that writer's imagination, the spell this girl of genius who had grown up there laid upon it – just as Thomas Hardy laid his spell upon Dorchester, or Nathaniel Hawthorne upon Salem.

I stood on the Indian mound above the Republican River, and looked across at a house isolated among its trees, rather grander than the usual, built on the same foundation as the now-vanished house which used to excite Willa's curiosity as a girl and ultimately was the inspiration for the home of Captain Forrester and his wife in *A Lost Lady*, one of her most perfect works, a novella. Most of her books, by the way, are not long: They are beautifully proportioned, unlike the ungainly, thousand-page-long best sellers of today, unmanageable to read.

Alas, the original house of *A Lost Lady*, a biggish frame house with its own drive to it, is one of the spots marked out by Willa's genius to have been lost; I missed it sorely; with my passion for seeing places that have been written about, that are alive in literature, brought alive by genius, I should love to have penetrated it, savoured its atmosphere.

In those days, one could not enter what had been the Cather home from 1884 to 1904. It was still a private house, visitors not welcome. It was, and is, a pretty house on the corner of Third and Cedar streets; I viewed it hopefully in vain, recalling its memories a little sadly. Willa herself describes it in an early novel, *The Song of the Lark*: 'They turned into another street and saw before them lighted windows, a low storey-and-a-half house, with a wing built on at the right and a kitchen addition at the back, everything a little on the slant – roofs, windows, and doors.' And somewhere in a story she describes how the snow would sift in between the chinks of the roof of her attic bedroom in those long Nebraska winters.

Frustrated as I was on my first visit, I was yet lucky in meeting Mildred R. Bennett, the woman who has made it her life's mission to transform all this and to preserve Red Cloud as the *ville musée* it is. I will confess that I then did not believe that it was possible to achieve what she has subsequently accomplished. Wait till I tell you what her devotion and drive, her scholarship and imagination, have brought about. All she could show me those years ago were a few stray objects and trinkets of Willa Cather's which she had collected, and one could not even enter the Cather home. Those household articles were the beginning of a museum, and today it is housed in the old home, furnished as it was in Willa's girlhood days a century ago.

On subsequent visits to Lincoln I made the acquaintance of Willa's youngest sister, Elsie, who showed me many of the family treasures, portraits, albums of photographs, china, the tea service we drank tea out of. (She gave me my copy of *A Lost Lady*.) Much of all this had now come to Red Cloud, and the Cather home looks today as Willa knew it: the family furniture in the front parlour, dining room and kitchen – where their maidservant lived, whom they brought with them from Virginia.

For we must remember that Willa was Virginia-born, of good old stock that had been in Virginia for five or six generations. She came to Nebraska with the family at the age of nine: It was those impressionable years of growing up that entered into the lifeblood of her imagination. Only one of her novels, her last, *Sapphira and the Slave Girl* (1940), is about Virginia.

All her life she was in love with Nebraska, and today we can see the house and home, the unchanged townscape and unspoiled country-side, where her dreams took shape and have become an abiding bequest of the grown woman to our literature.

Her little attic bedroom, where she dreamed her dreams – to be so richly fulfilled – still has the wallpaper of small red and brown roses she put up. And the veranda is where she read and read, pulling the shade to, for she always had an instinct for privacy, would never allow her books to be filmed, and had all her letters destroyed. Another contrast with writers today, too much of whose private affairs are washed in public. It was the Duke of Wellington who complained that he had been 'much exposed to authors'; well, Willa wasn't one for exposing her personal life. All the same, for myself I should like to see her novels and stories on television or film, or on the stage, now that I expect the time limit has expired.

The coming of the Burlington Railroad was the making of Red Cloud, and on the southern edge of the town is a replica of the 1897 depot, delicately reconstructed on the other side of the line, a little mecca in itself for railroad buffs. Though I am not expert enough to be one of them, I love the romantic names of the old railroads, the Chesapeake & Ohio, the Lackawanna, the Atchison, Topeka & Santa Fe.

Everything is as it should be in that delicious little depot, just the kind of station that would have been familiar to Abraham Lincoln: the signals and timetables, the ticket office and benches, even the oil lamps. The Burlington Railroad put Red Cloud on the map, and it plays a great part in Cather's books as in her life.

A Lost Lady begins with the railroad: 'In those days it was enough to say of a man that he was "connected with the Burlington." There were the directors, the general managers, vice presidents, superintendents, whose names we all knew; and their younger brothers or nephews were auditors, freight agents, departmental assistants. Everyone connected with the Road, even the large cattle- and grain-shippers, had annual passes; they and their families rode about over the line a great deal.'

And so did Willa herself. Her brother Douglass worked on the railroad in Colorado. Willa several times visited him out there – unmarried, like herself, he was her favourite. And thus there came about the most popular of her books, *Death Comes for the Archbishop* – about the missionary Bishop Lamy of Santa Fe – which became a best seller in Britain as well as in the United States.

Come with me back to the centre of the town, where memories and associations are thickest. Pivot of the place is the very vertical, highly decorative red brick and sandstone Willa Cather Historical Centre. This was the former Farmers' and Merchants' Bank Building, erected in 1889 by Governor Garber, prototype of Captain Forrester in *A Lost Lady*. He had rather grand ideas (and I think overspent himself); certainly the most, or the only, grandiose building in the town – though one dares hardly to venture a word against Victorian architecture nowadays.

Inside I recall a touch of Art Nouveau in the tesselated pavement – which reminded me of Mark Twain's very grand Art Nouveau house at Hartford, Connecticut. More important are the collections within – the library, first editions, books, portraits, photographs of things and people as they were.

But what is wonderful about Red Cloud is how little changed it is: Some Guardian Angel – in the shape of Mildred Bennett and her faithful flock – have stood on guard against the Devil of Destruction.

Stand on the front steps, look around and see for yourself. Across the street is the State Bank building of 1883, the year before the Cather family arrived from Virginia – one of the first brick buildings in the town and made of native brick. Among the things I specially noticed were the pretty decorative brick cornices those early buildings have just under the eaves. Next to this on the north is the Opera House built two years later, exactly a century ago, where William Jennings Bryan spoke at the height of his fame and oratory. The gist of his message was put more succinctly by a lady than by himself: 'Raise less corn, and more hell!' In this building Willa graduated from high school in 1890. Actually she wrote the most perceptive account of Bryan ever written, for on top of everything else she was a brilliant journalist. You will find it in the excellent anthology of Nebraska writing, published by the discriminating university press there: *Roundup: A Nebraska Reader*, edited by Virginia Faulkner.

All round in this old heart of the town are still the houses of the people she knew, still inhabited for me by her characters of them in her books, just as they were in life. At the back of the Royal Hotel is the site of the Boys' Home Hotel, since demolished, of *My Antonia* – Willa's own favourite, as was the original of Antonia, the spirited Czech girl with whom Willa was more than half in love. (She always thought of herself as a boy – and, for a writer, had the advantage of ambivalence, a doubled sensibility.)

In Franklin Street was the earlier brothel – the House of the Soiled Doves, built by Fannie Fernleigh, prototype of Nell Emerald in *A Lost Lady*. Willa certainly knew the facts of life all right, and from both sides, without making a song and dance about them. I suppose if she were writing today she might be a bit more outspoken about her tastes.

Turning down Seward Street is the little Catholic church in which Antonia was married; on the south side the Baptist church – now the Church of Christ – the Cather family attended. At the corner of Cedar and Sixth is the Episcopal church Willa joined in 1922, after her full career in Pittsburgh and New York. She had noticed as a girl how children longed for colour in the blank church windows; here she put up stained-glass windows in memory of her parents – the Good Shepherd for her father, for she remembered how in Virginia he kept sheep.

The country around Red Cloud speaks no less eloquently of Willa and the Cathers, though one hasn't space to do it justice. Nineteenth century America, perhaps the most creative period of the United States, is brought home to one by the little churches of the different religious sects, many of them immigrants; and no less by the small country schools, to which the people owed so much. So many of those early primary school teachers were so dedicated to their work – several of the family were teachers, my friend Elsie Cather all her life.

Up toward the Divide is the big frame house of Uncle George, a wealthier member of the family; it appears in *One of Ours*. When I was there it was standing empty, fast going derelict, echoing and ghostly in its isolated position, trees growing round the gully by its side, the tulips someone had planted still growing for nobody at all.

Not far is the Catherton cemetery, the first grave that of Aunt Aloerna (Aunt Vernie), who died a young woman of thirty-three on December 30, 1883, that first hard winter when they had to break the ground with an axe – as for Shimerda's funeral in *My Antonia*. But in Maytime all in Nebraska is beautiful: a gentle breeze in the cedars planted around the little wayside graveyard, open furrows beyond, meadowlarks singing sweet over the vast fields. I could wish that Willa were buried among her people here. But never mind, her memory is all round.

And every Maytime people from all over the United States make their pilgrimage to Red Cloud – brought together by the devotion and organizing energy of Mildred Bennett and her helpers, among them Professor Robert Knoll of the University of Nebraska, the faithful townspeople, properly supported by the capital of the state to which Willa brought worldwide fame.

For further reading I recommend: *The World of Willa Cather*, by Mildred R. Bennett (University of Nebraska Press); *Willa Cather: A Critical Biography*, by E.K. Brown, completed by Leon Edel (Knopf); *Willa Cather Living: A Personal Record*, by Edith Lewis (Knopf); *Roundup: A Nebraska Reader*, edited by Virginia Faulkner (University of Nebraska Press). And, of course, all the writings of Willa Cather.

GUIDE TO THE RED CLOUD AREA

No visitor to Red Cloud should miss the experience of being alone on the tawny Willa Cather Memorial Prairie, five miles south of Red Cloud on Route 281. This is a 610-acre tract of rough, hilly and virtually treeless pasture, never broken by a plough. Wild flowers in season mix with the native grasses, which hosts prairie birds such as the lark, plover and blackbird. The southern boundary line is the Kansas-Nebraska border. On the north end a natural spring has begun flowing again. Through a break, the treeline of the Rupublican River Valley opens up.

A historical marker at the prairie's entrance has Cather's words, recalling her arrival in Red Cloud in 1883 as a nine-year-old:

'This country was mostly wild pasture and as naked as the back of your hand. I was little and homesick and lonely and my mother was homesick and nobody was paying any attention to us. So the country and I had it out together and by the end of the first autumn that shaggy grass country had gripped me with a passion I have never been able to shake.'

GETTING THERE

Red Cloud, population 1,300, is on the north side of the Republican River at the junctions of highways 136 and 281. The agricultural area has seen a population decline for several decades.

The best way to get to Red Cloud from Lincoln, 139 miles away, is to take Interstate 80 west to Exit 312, then south on Route 281.

ACCOMMODATIONS

Basic motel service at Red Cloud is provided by the **Green Acres Motel** (402 746 2201) on Highway 281 on the north side of town. Rooms range from about $20 to $30.

In Hastings, about 38 miles north of Red Cloud, the **Holiday Inn** (402 463 6721) $35 to $45, is at the north entrance to the city on Route 281.

Grand Island, population 37,781, has a greater number of motel rooms, including two **Holiday Inns: Interstate 80** (308 384 7770) and **Midtown** (308 384 1330); **Ramada Inn** (308 384 5150); **Island Inn** (308 382 1815), and **TraveLodge** (308 384 1000).

Dreisbac's at Grand Island, South Locust Street and Fonner Park Road (308 382 5450) is considered by many to be the best steakhouse in Nebraska. Complete steak dinners are $9.95, $10.95 and $11.95.

– Dick Herman

DISCOVERING THE LAND OF LIGHT

N. Scott Momaday

It is indeed the land of light. But as I think of it now, the country is less than easy, less than wholly hospitable. There is an ancient resistance in it, something of itself withheld. From the plain, at a distance, you look at the mountains, and they are grand and sharply defined on the blue sky; they are beautiful as in a photograph. On postcards they are glossy and imminent. But in the round they are formidable, even forbidding. You approach them and they recede; their far summits ride across the pure, cold light, and even the deer do not attain them. This landscape has always been remote, in some sense inaccessible, and it is an anachronism. Northern New Mexico lags a bit behind the times; it persists in the spirit of the frontier, and in its high fastnesses it is still a wilderness.

One autumn morning in 1946 I awoke at Jemez Pueblo. I had arrived there in the middle of the night and gone to sleep. I had no idea of where in the world I was. Now, in the very bright New Mexican morning, I began to look around and settle in.

When my parents and I moved to Jemez I was twelve years old. I could not have imagined a more beautiful or exotic place. The village and the valley, the canyons and the mountains had been there from the beginning of time, waiting for me, so it seemed; they were my discovery. Marco Polo in the court of Kublai Khan had nothing on me. I was embarked upon the greatest adventure of all; I had come to the place of my growing up.

The landscape was full of mystery and of life. The autumn was in full bloom. The sun cast a golden light upon the adobe walls and the cornfields; it set fire to the leaves of willows and cottonwoods along the river; and a fresh, cold wind ran down from the canyons and carried the good scents of pine and cedar smoke, of bread baking in the beehive ovens and of rain in the mountains. There were horses in the plain and angles of geese in the sky.

Gradually and without effort I entered into the motion of life there. In the winter dusk I heard coyotes barking by the river, the sound of drums in the kiva and the voice of the village crier, ringing at the rooftops. And on summer nights of the full moon I saw old men in their ceremonial dress, running after witches.

I had a horse named Pecos, a fleet-footed roan gelding, which was my great glory for a time. I did a lot of riding in those days, and I got to be very good at it; my Kiowa ancestors, who were centaurs, would have been proud of me. I came to know the land by going out upon it in all seasons, getting into it until it became the very element in which I lived my daily life.

This was discovery, crucial, once and for all. And it was, I see now, a matter of some moment and intricacy. For not only did I discover an incomparable landscape in all of its colours and moods, but I discovered myself within it. From that time I have known that the sense of place is a dominant factor in my blood. It happens that I have travelled far and wide, and I have made my home elsewhere. But some elemental part of me remains in the hold of northern New Mexico. And when I sojourn there I am ever mindful of a line in Isak Dinesen, 'In the highlands you woke up in the morning and thought: Here I am, where I ought to be.'

Above Jemez Pueblo, San Diego Canyon ascends from the plain to the mountains. On Saturdays and Sundays, when the good people of Albuquerque and Corrales and Bernalillo drive up to take the mountain air, the women of Jemez Pueblo sell fresh bread at the side of the road at Canyon. The bread is baked in outdoor ovens, or *hornos*, and it is heavy and sweet and delicious, especially good for dipping into the very hot chili that is served in the pueblo on feast days. The rock formations at Canyon are of a red that cannot easily be imagined.

The village of **Jemez Springs** is huddled in this canyon at an elevation of 6,200 feet. The upper end of the village is dominated by the magnificent ruin of the church of San José de Jemez, built in the early seventeenth century and destroyed in the Indian rebellions that followed. In places the walls are eight feet thick. The little rooms of the old Indian town of Guisewa lie adjacent to the church, and they are like a maze. Prehistoric cave dwellings are numerous in this region, and there are ancient rock paintings about.

When I was a boy I climbed into the great octagonal bell tower of the church – the view commands the whole of the village of Jemez Springs and indeed the whole of the canyon to its mouth. It is a breathtaking sight. The walls of the canyon rise hundreds of feet directly above the village, and the hours of daylight are relatively few, but the consequent early morning and later afternoon light is extraordinary. It exists for a time as a diaphanous aura on the high skyline, then it touches fire to the western vertical face of the cliff; and in the afternoon the shadow of the west wall rises slowly on the east wall until the great rock face, above timber, half red and half white, blazes above the dark canyon floor. Snow comes down from the north with the big logging trucks, hauling their tons of pine. In summer the canyon is lime green with aspens and willows and cottonwoods, and yellow with paintbrush and chamisa.

Jemez Springs is named for the hot waters that rise out of the earth in this vicinity and which are said to be as rich in their mineral content as any springs in the country. In the centre of the village is a bathhouse where an attendant will wrap you up after your bath and you can melt yourself down through your pores – and Los Ojos Bar, where you can build yourself up again.

A few miles north and east toward the summit of the range, there is one of the most beautiful valleys in the world. **Valle Grande** is a huge caldera, formed a million years ago when there was great volcanic activity here. The magma chambers under the volcanoes collapsed and whole mountains were engulfed and formed the valley below. Cattle graze far below eye level; they appear to be dark pin-points of colour on the immense field of bright grass. This is an enchanted place, kept by eagles. Once I drove along this road in winter. The snow reached almost to the tops of the fenceposts, and on the other side and close by were working cowboys. I thrilled to see them in their sheepskins and chaps, their horses steaming and lunging in the deep snow. And on another occasion, years later, I counted seventeen elk, as they emerged one by one from the woods on the valley's rim.

Across the summit the Rio Grande Valley lies out in the blur of distance, the Sangre de Cristos, southern horn of the Rockies, looming beyond. The ancient city of Santa Fe glints in the south, but the way of this journey is north, against the current of the great river. Espanola, once the capital of the territory, touches upon a circle that describes the heart of northern New Mexico.

The village of **Abiquiu** is situated on a hill overlooking the long, undulant depression of the Rio Chama. It is a various landscape – grassy banks, rolling plains, bluffs of red and rose and purple and blue. Abiquiu is an old Penitente village (the Penitentes were a religious society composed of men who scourged themselves to blood and carried heavy wooden crosses on the Fridays of Lent and especially during Holy Week), and the birthplace of one of New Mexico's great and enigmatic men of history, Padre Martinez, of whom more later. It is also the home of the artist Georgia O'Keeffe. One day in the early '70s I called upon this venerable lady – she was already in her eighties – for the first time. She met me at the door in a black suit and a white shirt. Her hair was swept severely back, and she seemed quite handsome and impressive in her formality. We sat in the front room among objects rare and beautiful – paintings, skulls and skeletons, boxes filled with smooth, coloured stones.

We talked for a time, and she told me of how she had made the fireplace before which we sat, quite a lovely earthen sculpture, with her own hands. I saw that her hands were large and expressive, and I could easily imagine them shaping the delicate arch of the firebox. Then it occurred to Miss O'Keeffe that she had neglected to offer me refreshment, and she became slightly flustered. 'Oh, I am sorry,' she said. 'Wouldn't you like a drink?' I replied that I was quite comfortable, but she pressed the point and I said that I would have a scotch, please.

She excused herself and went out of the room. Long minutes passed, and she did not return. I grew uneasy, then concerned. There was a din, a rattling of metal objects, which I took to come from the kitchen. I got up, sat down again, wrung my hands; I wondered whether or not I should investigate. Then, to my great relief, she reappeared. But she was empty-handed, and there was a consternation in her face. 'It's my maid's day off, and I do not know what she did with the key to the liquor pantry,' she explained. 'Oh, please, don't give it a thought,' I blurted. 'Really, I'm fine.'

But Georgia O'Keeffe had got it into her head that I was going to have my drink, and to my deep distress she excused herself again. Another long time elapsed, again the banging of pots and pans, more wringing of my hands. And then, with pronounced dignity and not a hair out of place, she entered the room with my drink on a small silver tray. Later she confided to me with a twinkle in her eye, did this octogenarian, that she had taken the pantry door off at the hinges with a screwdriver.

> And then, in those days, too,
> I made you the gift of a small, brown stone,
> And you described it with the tips of your fingers
> And knew at once that it was beautiful –
> At once, accordingly you knew,
> As you knew the forms of the earth at Abiquiu:
> That time involves them and they bear away,
> Beautiful, various, remote,
> In failing light, and the coming of cold.

So ends a poem I dedicated to her.

On another occasion, over wine and goat cheese, she said to me, 'This is simply the place that I like best in the world.'

Farther north the village of Tierra Amarilla lies in the plain of the Rio Arriba. It is indeed a yellow land, shining with pale winter grass or gleaming with fawn lilies and mariposa tulips. To the north is Chama and the narrow-gauge railroad that runs over Cumbres Pass into Colorado, and to the west the wilds of the Jicarilla Apache reservation. There I used to drive out upon the dirt roads to corrals far away in the mountains where slim Apache boys and girls, their boots taped about the insteps, broke their sleek horses. And in the early sunlit mornings herds of elk ventured out upon the snowfields. But the circle turns to the east. The road runs just south of the Rio Brazos for a time, then across the west branch of the Carson National Forest to Tres Piedras, then southeastward across the Rio Grande Gorge to Taos.

Taos is definitive. There is something quintessential in its character. Of all places, Taos seems to me to represent best the soul of the Southwest in general and that of northern New Mexico in particular. It is Santa Fe, Gallup, Scottsdale and Tombstone concentrated into a single point of remarkable density and energy. Certainly it is not everyone's cup of tea. The cold can be bitter, the locals exclusive, the streets muddy and the conveniences of the modern world elsewhere. And Taoseños complain of Taos in the very way that New Yorkers complain of New York. But in the March dusk, say, sitting before a piñon fire and looking through the swirls of snow to the last light on the mountain peaks, *la sangre de Cristo*, you know that you inhabit the real world and that here, just here, the real world is ineffably beautiful.

There are many ghosts in Taos; in a very little while you are aware of their presence. Charles Bent and Kit Carson lived here, and their homes are museums. The stark and simple beauty of the Hacienda Martinez is like that of the church of San Francisco de Asis at Ranchos de Taos. It remains in the mind's eye for its own sake. The hacienda was the home of Severino Martinez, then of his famous son, Don Antonio José Martinez (1793–1867), the 'dark priest' of whom Willa Cather wrote in *Death Comes for the Archbishop*. From obscure beginnings in his birthplace of Abiquiu he rose up to become a revolutionary force at Taos and in the territory. So controversial was he that at last Bishop Lamy was moved to pronounce upon him the most grave sentence of excommunication.

But Padre Martinez served his people well. Concerned that they be literate, he introduced the first printing press into New Mexico, and he published the first newspaper. He made of his home a kind of monastery to which the best young men of his time and place came to study and to formulate ideas. He made of Taos a centre of learning in the nineteenth century.

One cannot be long in Taos without coming upon the ghost of D.H. Lawrence. His books, and books about him, are plentiful in the bookshops. Some of his paintings are on display at La Fonda, on the Taos plaza. Half a century after his death, his name is dropped about, especially by non-residents. Lawrence lived here less than two years, all told, between 1922 and 1925, but he seems to have done a remarkable lot of work in that time, including the writing of *St. Mawr* and *The Woman Who Rode Away*, in which he evokes the landscape of northern New Mexico. Actually, he lived on a ranch some twenty miles north of Taos, near the village of San Cristobal. The Lawrence Ranch, at an elevation of 8,600 feet, is a magnificent 160-acre expanse of timbered mountainside overlooking the vast plain of the Rio Grande. The log cabin in which he lived remains intact, and there is a small chapel in which Lawrence's ashes are interred.

D.H. Lawrence, too, made a profound discovery of this landscape. 'In the magnificent fierce morning of New Mexico,' he wrote, 'one sprang awake, a new part of the soul woke up suddenly, and the old world gave way to the new.' And again, 'What splendour! Only the tawny eagle could really sail out into the splendour of it all.'

The sojourner in this land, this *tierra de la luz y el encanto*, would do well to close the circle by going the old mountain way through the Penitente villages of Penasco, Las Trampas and Truchas to Chimayo and Espanola. On the east is the jagged spine of the Sangre de Cristos, on the west the sandstone cliffs, the long, low peneplain that descends to the great river. Horses and cattle graze in the mountain meadows. Bright strings of chilies gleam. There is everywhere the smell of pine and cedar. Here are the weavers and woodcarvers whose antecedents came from Spain, then Mexico, bearing the old santos and reredos, the trappings of that aged, hard-bitten Christianity to an even more ancient world.

And in this place of discovery, that at last is what is discovered: the New World, ancient, as the poet has it, as light.

NEW MEXICO HOSPITALITY

The following is a short list of inns, kitchens and restaurants in northern New Mexico. In my view these establishments are exceptional.

SANTA FE

The Shed (505 982 9030) is open for lunch only, and the queues are often long. The wait is worth it. Specialities include *posole*, a stew of hominy, pork and chilies, and red chili enchiladas. The blue cornmeal tortillas are superb. So are the desserts, among them the mocha cake. Main dishes run about $4 to $5.

The Periscope (505 988 2355) is also a luncheon establishment, but dinner is served on Saturday. The shopping is done daily; the menu – which may feature anything from Sudanese to Indonesian dishes – is imaginative and trustworthy. A four-course lunch is about $15, and the six-course Saturday dinner is about $40 a person, including wine.

La Tertulia (505 988 2769), once a monastery, has atmosphere to spare. The food is distinctly New Mexican: *chilies rellenos*, green chili enchiladas, *carne adobada* – pork marinated and simmered in chili sauce. Steaks and chops also available. Dinner for two with wine about $30 to $40.

La Posada (330 East Palace Avenue, Santa Fe, NM 87501; 505 983 6351), is a converted mansion from the late nineteenth century, decorated in a traditional Southwestern style. Double rooms about $40 to $60 a night; suites: $60 to $120, and *casitas*, consisting of a living room, bedroom and kitchenette: $75 to $200. Some rooms have fireplaces. The **Staab House** restaurant (named for the mansion's original owner) specializes in fresh seafood; $40 to $50 for two with wine.

TAOS

Michael's Kitchen (505 758 4178) is a bakery and coffee shop. It is where, on a given morning, the diverse cultural elements of Taos come together. The menu is appropriately hodgepodge, including both enchiladas and hamburgers. Lunch about $3 to $5, dinner less than $10. No alcohol is served.

Whitey's (505 776 8545) is elegance, Taos style. This fine restaurant is a conversion of the home of Dorothy Brett, artist and close friend of D.H. Lawrence. It is small, cosy, tasteful and rightly run. Try the rack of lamb or the Provimi veal; dinner for two with wine about $40 to $50.

Casa Cordova (505 776 2200) in Arroyo Seco, just north of Taos, is heroic. Try the game dishes if they are available. Open for dinner only; about $50 to $60 for two with wine.

La Fonda, on the plaza (P.O. Box 1447, Taos, NM 87571; 505 758 2211), is quiet and traditional. Double rooms about $55, suites $65. No restaurant, but mildly erotic paintings by D.H. Lawrence may be seen on request.

ESPANOLA

El Paragua (505 753 3211) is a place on which a food critic can stake his reputation. There is no more authentic New Mexican kitchen than this; specialities include *chilies rellenos* and *enchiladas supremas*. Dinner for two with drinks about $30 to $40.

CHIMAYO

Rancho de Chimayo (505 3551 4111) is a charming restaurant near Espanola and within easy reach of Santa Fe. The *carne adobada* and the *enchilada colorada* are special; dinner for two with drinks about $30 to $40.

JEMEZ PUEBLO

If ever you should have the chance, sample one of the chili stews on a day of celebration at the pueblo. The best I ever had was a *posole* prepared by Sefora Tosa on a cold day in 1948. As far as I know, it remains available, on occasion, to the truly, truly blessed.

— N.S.M.

RITES OF SPRING IN NOME

Barry Lopez

As well as John Andrews can recall, it was a group of Japanese lawyers and doctors. In June of 1980 they came to Nome to search for butterflies and eighty miles north of here, on the Kougarok Road, they found a butterfly so rare (they told him that night in the bar at the Nugget Inn) it meant the whole trip to them. Mr. Andrews says he can't remember the name or the colour of the butterfly, but that's not the only time. Once a man got off the jet from Anchorage and asked, right off, 'Where's the bird?' Mr. Andrews knew he meant the one nesting eleven and a half miles out on the Teller Road, and told him how to get there. He knew about it because there had been such a hullabaloo the week before when someone first saw it out there. Mr. Andrews – he's been a tour guide here for twenty-three years – apologized, again, for not knowing precisely what sort of bird it was. He thinks it might have been a sparrow.

Mr. Andrews's vagueness and perplexity are understandable. Nome's notoriety lies more with its gold-rush past, exuberant and heart-breaking days at the turn of the century, when 20,000 people camped in tents on the beach and sporting men organized sled dog races – the first in Alaska – to break the boredom of winter. Today it is northwest Alaska's major commercial port, a village of 2,300 people, mostly Eskimo, living in the Bering Time Zone, an hour ahead of Hawaii, six hours behind New York. The buildings along Front Street have their clapboard shoulders turned to the Bering Sea, which lies frozen seven months of the year.

Visitors from the south come up here each summer to stare at the faded remnants of the gold rush – a dancer's high-buttoned boot, a miner's stout tools; to view a cultural presentation by Eskimo dancers and story tellers from nearby King Island, and to buy carvings of walrus ivory and other native handiwork. And, one must note, though many local residents shake their heads in grim disapproval to hear it, not a few come to visit Nome's fabled bars. Once in a while someone will come who knows, or asks about, the coming of the animals.

The Bering Sea is like a Serengeti of the oceans. The shallow waters of its broad coastal shelf support probably the largest clam fishery in the world; it, in turn, feeds some 275,000 Pacific walrus. With the first warm weather in April the solid ice front starts to break up and millions of birds begin to feed in the open water. Fifty-foot bowheads and smaller, white beluga whales push north through the ice remnants, followed by migrating walrus and by hundreds – not tens – of thousands of seals – ringed, spotted, ribbon, and the much larger bearded seal. In their wake come vast aggregations of herring and prodigious runs of salmon, feeding on incalculable tons of shrimp and other small creatures. With the arrival in May and June of nesting populations of birds – alcids, waterfowl and shorebirds – the spring migration comes to some sort of formal close.

The biological richness of these waters accounted, more than a thousand years ago, for the swift development of a sophisticated culture called Thule. Anthropologists believe these people, precursors of modern Eskimos, may have expanded as far east as northern Greenland with their efficient, marine-mammal hunting technology in as few as three or four generations. Today on the streets of Nome it is not uncommon to be offered tangible evidence of their nearly fabulous existence – a toggling harpoon head of fossilized ivory, a seal-bone drill – by an Eskimo in need of cash.

Because the Bering Sea teems so with life (in the summer, grey, minke, and killer whales will arrive) and is also a focus of imminent oil explorations, a government-sponsored inventory of its wild creatures is in progress. Don Ljungblad, of the Naval Ocean Systems Center in San Diego, has been following bowhead whales on their spring and autumn migrations through here for four years. Of all the aggregations of life he has seen – 200 or 300 female walruses resting on an ice floe with 50 or more of their dark-skinned calves; 600 startled oldsquaw ducks hurtling in broken skeins at fifty miles per hour over open water – the one he recalls most vividly is of whales. On April 17, 1981, in a lead – broad crack – in the ice a half mile wide, a hundred miles west of Nome, Mr. Ljungblad counted 320 bowhead whales in a ten-mile stretch – as awesome a sight to him, he said, as the sight of the buffalo in Nebraska must have been to mountain men in the 1820s. Also in that lead, almost incidentally, Mr. Ljungblad counted 79 beluga whales, 415 walruses and a bearded seal before breaking off the contact at the International Dateline, the Russian border at sea.

On a flight out of Nome with Mr. Ljungblad one recent spring, just south of the Bering Strait, I stared in silent disbelief at the sudden appearance of two other whales, rare enough to be thought mythic in these waters – narwhal. Darker, spotted and marble relative of the beluga, the males have ivory tusks six to eight feet long spiralling forward out of their upper jaw.

Such sights of marine mammals, particularly of walrus and whales, afford people flying in and out of Nome occasional pleasure; to sight birds – in such numbers and in such variety as to make the imagination stumble – is more certain.

In May 1981, I was told, you could have stood on Front Street and watched sandhill cranes pass overhead in a nearly unbroken stream for two and a half hours. At Safety Lagoon, twenty miles to the east, flocks of brant and Steller's eider cover the water; Aleutian terns nest on the shorelines; knots, turnstones and sandpipers scurry wildly over the tidal flats. Moving with more hesitant steps are larger relatives of these latter three – the whimbrels. Gliding serenely among the geese, impeccably white, are whistling swans. Fifteen species of plover raise their young nearby.

Because of the closeness of the Asian mainland, birds rare in North America are found here rather commonly, in small numbers. Add to this simple profusion the spectacle of so many different breeding displays, subtle and baroque, by birds in bright nuptial plumages and it becomes clear why this area (and nearby St. Lawrence Island) is internationally popular with bird watchers.

According to Henry Springer, an authority on the birds of the region, Woolley Lagoon to the west of Nome is an even better place to watch geese than Safety Lagoon. For variety he suggests an afternoon at Cape Nome, between town and Safety Lagoon, to watch 'a most impressive migration of sea birds' – murres, tufted and horned puffins, guillemots, auklets, and pelagic cormorants.

Or one might drive inland on the Kougarok Road and watch peregrine falcon hunt. Or lie on one's back on a tundra slope and watch the passage high overhead of snow geese, their bright whites like starched linen, on their way to Siberia.

According to Mr. Springer, the best time to see these migrations and aggregations is from about May 20 to June 10 – a bit earlier or later, depending on when the ice goes out.

By June, Alaska king crabs, who have spent the winter near shore, are migrating back to deeper water. King salmon have come into the rivers to spawn. (They will be followed by runs of chum salmon, who will be followed a week or so later by pink salmon.) Walrus will have passed through the Bering Strait to summer in the Chukchi Sea. Bowhead whales will be far to the north and east, in Canadian waters. Beluga whales will be feeding in river estuaries with their newborn calves. You might look up from your lunch in the Nugget Café to see a grey whale rolling to seaward, beyond the window. Or find spotted seals hauled out on the beach near Safety Lagoon.

The surrounding tundra is nearly preternaturally quiet, the call of a redpoll like the voice of a nuncio in a medieval courtyard.

Nome is an unpretentious town of weather-battered streets of bright, dusty summers and dark, hard, wind-blown winters. It is characterized like most northern coastal villages by the gutted trappings of a sudden-cash economy, by the seemingly endless detritus of the military, and by incongruous Government structures in an aboriginal landscape. With the arrival of migrating animals in the spring comes a reprieve, the opportunity, for a few weeks, to draw nearer another, much older order.

It is remarkable that one who does not live here can take advantage of this. There are flights twice a day from the south, by small jet. It is possible to rent a car. Or just walk out east of town to the bridge over the Nome River, to watch the birds and salmon. On a drive inland one might see moose and caribou or red fox.

If one were fortunate to an extreme one might see musk ox – but probably not. And probably not those other exotic creatures of the region, arctic hares half as tall as a man, moving in studied silence across the tundra, wary as Bedouins. It is the suggestion they are there, however, and the certain knowledge that they have been seen – like the narwhal or a Ross's gull – that puts such a keen edge on an evening's walk along the beach or a morning's determined trip to Woolley Lagoon.

Mr. Andrews, whose business it is to know such things, says a room and meals here for two cost about $250 a day, and that the rooms are hard to come by from May to September. I would have to offer a further caution: but for the birds, which are so accessible, one might see other animals only fortuitously. As much as Nome is a place from which to witness one of the great animal migrations on earth, the earth is vast and the animals are other cultures with rhyme and reason of their own.

The town itself may seem tattered and subdued, a victim of bleak weather and isolated life. Some may find nothing here. But the passion of a group of Japanese lawyers for a rare butterfly, or of someone who would chance upon 1,000 sandhill cranes, or touch the back of a struggling salmon in the Nome River, this passion, these incidents, can revitalize a life gone stiff with a vague despair over what men have done, and threaten to do, to the planet they live on.

You can touch something here amid the wreckage of mineral schemes to keep Nome alive, beyond the reach of the white radar domes on the distant hills, that is like a genetic memory. Lying in your hotel room at night it is possible to imagine Thule whale hunters camped on the beach below; or a bowhead offshore breaking ice with its head to blow and draw breath; or musk ox moving slowly in their long, wind-blown skirts across the land. One takes such memories and goes home. One makes a slight bow to the hills and the sea and takes such memories home.

AFTERWORD: ENCHANTMENTS
AT FIRST ENCOUNTER

Cynthia Ozick

One morning in Stockholm, after rain and just before November, a mysteriously translucent shadow began to paint itself across the top of the city. It skimmed high over people's heads, a gauzy brass net, keeping well above the streets, skirting everything fabricated by human arts – though one or two steeples were allowed to dip up into it, like pens filling their nibs with palest ink. It made a sort of watermark over Stockholm, as if a faintly luminous river ran overhead; yet with no more weight or gravity than a vapour.

This glorious strangeness – a kind of crystalline wash – was the sunlight of a Swedish autumn. The sun looked new: It had a lucidity, a texture, a tincture, a position across the sky that my New York gape had never before taken in. The horizontal ladder of light hung high up, higher than any sunlight I had ever seen, and the quality of its glow seemed thinner, wanner, more tentatively morning-brushed; or else like gold leaf beaten gossamer as tissue – a lambent skin laid over the spired marrow of the town.

'Ah yes, the sun does look a bit different this time of year,' say the Stockholmers in their perfect English (English as a second first language), but with a touch of ennui. Whereas I, under the electrified rays of my whitening hair, stand drawn upward to the startling sky, restored to the clarity of childhood. The Swedes have known a Swedish autumn before; I have not.

Travel returns us in just this way to sharpness of notice; and to be saturated in the sight of what is entirely new – the sun at an unaccustomed tilt, stretched across the northland, separate from the infiltrating dusk that always seems about to fall through clear grey Stockholm – is to revisit the enigmatically lit puppet-stage outlines of childhood: those mental photographs and dreaming woodcuts or engravings that we retain from our earliest years. What we remember from childhood we remember forever – permanent ghosts, stamped, imprinted, eternally seen. Travellers regain this ghost-seizing brightness, eeriness, firstness.

They regain it because they have cut themselves loose from their

own society, from every society; they are, for a while, floating vaga-
bonds, like astronauts out for a space walk on a long free line. They are
subject to preternatural exhilarations, absurd horizons, unexpected
forms and trasmutations: The matter-of-fact (a battered old veranda,
say, or the shape of a door) appears beautiful; or a stone that at home
would not merit the blink of your eye here arrests you with its absolute
particularity – just because it is what your hand already intimately
knows. You think: a stone, a stone! They have stones here too! And you
think: How uncannily the planet is girdled, as stone-speckled in
Sweden as in New York. For the vagabond-voyeur (and for travellers
voyeurism is irresistible), nothing is not for notice, nothing is banal,
nothing is ordinary: not a rock, not the shoulder of a passer-by, not a
teapot.

Plenitude assaults; replication invades. Everything known has its
spooky shadow and Doppelganger. On my first trip anywhere – it was
1957 and I landed in Edinburgh with the roaring of the plane's four
mammoth propellers for days afterward embedded in my ears – I rode
in a red airport bus to the middle of the city, out of which ascended its
great castle. It is a fairy-book castle, dream-like, Arthurian, secured in
the long ago. But the shuddery red bus – hadn't I been bounced along
in an old bus before, perhaps not so terrifically red as this one? – the red
bus was not within reach of plain sense. Every inch of its interior
streamed with unearthliness, with an undivulged and consummate
witchery. It put me in the grip of a wild Elsewhere. This unexceptional
vehicle, with its bright forward snout, was all at once eclipsed by a rush
of the abnormal, the unfathomably Martian. It was the bus, not the
phantasmagorical castle, that clouded over and bewildered our
reasoned humanity. The red bus was what I intimately knew: only I
had never seen it before. A reflected flicker of the actual. A looking-
glass bus. A Scottish ghost.

This is what travellers discover: that when you sever the links of
normality and its claims, when you break off from the quotidian, it is
the teapots that truly shock. Nothing is so awesomely unfamiliar as the
familiar that discloses itself at the end of a journey. Nothing shakes the
heart so much as meeting – far, far away – what you last met at home.
Some say that travellers are informal anthropologists. But it is
ontology – the investigation of the nature of being – that travellers do.
Call it the flooding-in of the real.

There is, besides, the flooding-in of character. Here one enters not
landscapes or street-lit night scenes, but fragments of drama: splinters
of euphoria that catch you up when you are least deserving. Sometimes it is a jump into a pop-up book, as when a cockney cab driver, of
whom you have asked directions while leaning out from the kerb, gives
his native wink of blithe good will. Sometimes it is a mazy stroll into a

toy theatre, as when, in a museum, you suddenly come on the intense little band following the lecturer on Mesopotamia, or the lecturer on genre painting, and the muse of civilization alights on these rapt few. What you are struck with then – one of those mental photographs that go on sticking to the retina – is not what lies somnolently in the glass case or hangs romantically on the wall, but the enchantment of a minutely idiosyncratic face shot into your vision with indelible singularity, delivered over forever by you own fertile gaze. When travellers stare at heads and ears and necks and beards and moustaches, they are – in the encapsuled force of the selection – making art: portraits, voice sonatinas, the quick haiku of a strictly triangular nostril.

Travelling is seeing; it is the implicit that we travel by. Travellers are fantasists, conjurers, seers – and what they finally discover is that every round object everywhere is a crystal ball: stone, teapot, the marvellous globe of the human eye.

NOTES ON THE CONTRIBUTORS

WILLIAM HOWARD ADAMS teaches at the Graduate School of Architecture, Columbia University. He is the author of *A Proust Souvenir*.

A. ALVAREZ is the author most recently of *The Biggest Game in Town* and *Offshore – a North Sea Journey*.

MARGARET ATWOOD writes novels, poetry and criticism. Her most recent novel is *The Handmaid's Tale*.

PETER BENCHLEY is the author of *Jaws* and *The Deep*. His most recent novel is *Q Clearance*.

OLIVIER BERNIER is the author of *Louis the Beloved, the Life of Louis XV* and *Secrets of Marie Antoinette*.

WILLIAM F. BUCKLEY, JR, is the editor of *National Review*, host of Public Television's *Firing Line*, and author most recently of *Right Reason*, a collection of his writings.

JOHN CHANCELLOR is senior commentator at NBC News.

WILMA DYKEMAN is a novelist and historian whose books include *The Tall Woman*.

LUCINDA FRANKS, winner of a Pulitzer Prize for national reporting, writes frequently about the Middle East.

BARBARA GELB is a biographer and a frequent contributor to *The New York Times*.

SONDRA GOTLIEB, a novelist married to the Canadian Ambassador to the United States, is the author of *Wife of . . . An Irreverent Account of Life in Powertown*.

MACDONALD HARRIS is the author of twelve novels, among them *The Treasure of Sainte Foy*. The most recent is *The Little People*.

JOSEPH HELLER's most recent novel is *God Knows*.

HAMMOND INNES is the author most recently of *The Black Tide*.

P.D. JAMES is the author of *The Skull Beneath the Skin*.

HENRY KAMM is chief of the Athens bureau of *The New York Times*.

MICHAEL KORDA, editor in chief of Simon & Schuster, is the author, most recently, of the novel *Queenie*.

ANTHONY J. LAMBERT, a London editor, writes frequently about railroads.

JOSEPH LELYVELD, chief of the London bureau of *The New York Times*, is the author of *Move Your Shadow: South Africa, Black and White*.

PHYLLIS LEE LEVIN is a writer who lives in New York.

BARRY LOPEZ is the author most recently of *Arctic Dreams: Imagination and Desire in a Northern Landscape*.

N. SCOTT MOMADAY's next novel, *Set*, is about a boy who turns into a bear.

CYNTHIA OZICK is the author of *The Cannibal Galaxy*, a novel, and *Art & Ardor*, collected essays.

NOEL PERRIN is a professor of English at Dartmouth College; his most recent book is *Second Person Rural*.

CAROL PLUM is an American journalist living in Rome.

FREDERIC RAPHAEL is a screenwriter and novelist. His most recent novel is *Heaven and Earth*.

RICHARD REEVES is a syndicated columnist and author of eight books, including *The Reagan Detour*.

A.L. ROWSE is emeritus fellow of All Souls College, Oxford, a Fellow of the British Academy, and the author of many books on Shakespeare.

JOHN RUSSELL is chief art critic for *The New York Times*. His most recent book is *Paris*.

HAROLD C. SCHONBERG is the retired cultural correspondent and former senior music critic of *The Times*.

ISRAEL SHENKER, a former reporter for *The Times*, lives in Scotland. His most recent book is *Coat of Many Colours: Pages from Jewish Life*.

D.M. THOMAS's most recent novel is *Swallow*.

JOHN VINOCUR, assistant to the executive editor of *The New York Times*, has been chief of the Paris and Bonn bureaux.

JOHN WAIN is an English novelist, poet, and critic.

WILLIAM WEAVER, who lives much of the year in Italy, is a writer, translator, and music critic. He is the author of *Duse*, a biography.

STEVEN R. WEISMAN is the New Delhi bureau chief of *The New York Times*.

PATRICIA WELLS, restaurant critic of *The International Herald Tribune*, is the author of *The Food Lover's Guide to Paris*.

INDEX

ABOUT THE EDITORS

A. M. ROSENTHAL is the executive editor of *The New York Times* and has been in charge of its news operations for the past fifteen years. He is the recipient of a Pulitzer Prize for his work as a foreign correspondent for *The New York Times*. Mr. Rosenthal is the author of *38 Witnesses* and co-author with Arthur Gelb of *One More Victim*.

ARTHUR GELB is deputy managing editor of *The New York Times* and supervisory editor of the new Sophisticated Traveller magazine. He was formerly chief cultural correspondent of *The Times*. He is co-author with his wife, Barbara, of the Eugene O'Neill biography, *O'Neill*.

MICHAEL J. LEAHY is the editor of *The New York Times* Travel section. He has been a *Times* editor since attending Columbia University's Graduate School of Journalism, where he won a Pulitzer Travelling Fellowship that took him around the world. NORA KERR, deputy editor of the Travel section, was formerly an assistant metropolitan editor of *The Times*.